Harmful Eloquence

HARMFUL ELOQUENCE

Ovid's *Amores*
from Antiquity
to Shakespeare

———

M.L. Stapleton

Ann Arbor

THE UNIVERSITY OF MICHIGAN PRESS

Copyright © by the University of Michigan 1996
All rights reserved
Published in the United States of America by
The University of Michigan Press
Manufactured in the United States of America
⊗ Printed on acid-free paper

1999   1998   1997   1996   4   3   2   1

A CIP catalog record for this book is available from the British Library.

Library of Congress Cataloging-in-Publication Data

Stapleton, M. L. (Michael L.) 1958–
    Harmful eloquence : Ovid's Amores from antiquity to Shakespeare /
    M.L. Stapleton.
        p.   cm.
    Includes bibliographical references (p.   ) and index.
    ISBN 0-472-10707-0 (alk. paper)
    1. Ovid, 43 B.C.–17 or 18 A.D. Amores. 2. Elegiac poetry, Latin—
Appreciation—Europe. 3. Love poetry, Latin—Appreciation—Europe.
4. Shakespeare, William, 1564–1616. Sonnets. 5. Ovid, 43 B.C.–17
or 18 A.D.—Influence. 6. Poetry, Medieval—Roman influences.
7. European poetry—Roman influences.   I. Title.
✓ PA6519.A73S73   1996
    871'.01—dc20   95-26354
                                                            CIP

In memory of my father, Leo J. Stapleton, 1926–90

pater atque hominum rex
—*Aen.* 1.65

Preface

haec sibi proposuit thalamos temerare pudicos;
nec tamen eloquio lingua nocente caret.

(Ovid *Am.* 1.8.19–20)

She drawes chast women to incontinence,
Nor doth her tongue want harmefull eloquence.

(Marlowe *All Ovids Elegies* 1.8.19–20)

Ovid's persona in the *Amores,* the young man who assures us that he is no circus-rider of Love ("non sum desultor Amoris" [1.3.15]), warns us against the verbal dubiety of Dipsas, the aged attendant of the married woman named Corinna whom he is attempting to seduce. As the story of the love affair progresses, the speaker's admonitions become ironic as they redound on him. First, *Amores* 1.8 proves that the young man actually aspires to be *desultor Amoris,* one who wishes to draw any number of chaste women to incontinence, with an eloquence that their husbands would certainly find harmful. Second, his own eloquence is often harmful to him. Third, he is sometimes not "eloquent" at all. He undercuts himself and destroys his credibility, which the foregoing passage illustrates. Even as he warns us about the immoral Dipsas, we discover that he is eavesdropping on her conversation with Corinna in a plot against them both. So *eloquium* ("eloquence") becomes somewhat indeterminate in the *Amores,* especially when paired with the adjective *nocens* ("harmefull").

As philologists have remarked over the past century, Publius Ovidius Naso was the giant on whose tenuous shoulders the love poets of the Middle Ages and Renaissance loved to stand. However, our philologists have devoted comparatively little of their scholarship to medieval appropriations of the *Amores,* focusing instead on the twin legacies of the *Meta-morphoses* and *Ars amatoria.* Recent and very impressive studies are Leonard Barkan's *The Gods Made Flesh: Metamorphosis and the Pursuit of Paganism* (New Haven: Yale University Press, 1986); Ralph Hexter's *Ovid and Medieval Schooling: Studies in Medieval School Commentaries on Ovid's "Ars amatoria," "Epistulae ex Ponto," and "Epistulae heroidum"* (Munich: Arbeo-Gesellschaft, 1986); and Jonathan Bate's *Shakespeare and Ovid* (Oxford: Clarendon Press, 1993).[1] Yet just as Ovid taught the West that love can have rules and that mythology is more palatable and easily remembered if rendered into erotic narrative form, he also bequeathed the *desultor Amoris* as the classical paradigm of the lover who narrates a sequence of poems. He taught Dante, Petrarch, and Shake-speare to build new versions of the old model, the man who reveals, and thereby undoes, himself. I attempt to fulfill a need by analyzing this inher-itance and by tracing its transmission, dissemination, and reworking.

I began with my eventual ending. My project started four years ago as an essay that noted the similarities between Christopher Marlowe's trans-lation of the *Amores, All Ovids Elegies* (c. 1595–1600), and Shakespeare's Sonnets (c. 1593–1609), particularly in the cultivation of the literary per-sona and the anti-Petrarchism one finds in Sonnets 127–54. In the course of making the connections between antiquity and the early seventeenth century, I discovered that Shakespeare was not the first to use the *Amores* as a model for the subversion of conventional love poetry and that no one had really explored the impact of this Ovidian text on the literature of the West. So I have attempted to finish by writing the beginning.

Chapter 1 draws together recent scholarship on the *Amores* and the relationship of this text to the erotica in general. The chapter establishes that Ovid knew what a persona was, and it distinguishes between the speaker in the *Ars amatoria,* often referred to in criticism as *magister Amoris,* and the narrator of the *Amores,* whom I name *desultor Amoris* (despite the narrator's protestations). It provides a fairly close reading of

---

1. Bate's prose style is a model for all academics: clear, concise, conversational, engaging. Besides the excellent books mentioned, several articles in scholarly journals were invaluable. See Leslie Cahoon, "The Anxieties of Influence: Ovid's Reception by the Early Trouba-dours," *Mediaevalia* 13 (1989 [1987]): 119–56; Gerald Bond, "*Iocus amoris:* The Poetry of Baudri of Bourgueil and the Problem of Persona," *Traditio* 42 (1986): 143–93; "Composing Yourself: Ovid's *Heroides,* Baudri of Bourgueil, and the Formation of the Ovidian Subcul-ture," *Mediaevalia* 13 (1989 [1987]): 83–118. Part of my book is a response to Bond's chal-lenge: "While the legacy of the Virgilian voice/person to the Middle Ages has been studied in great detail and with great subtlety, that of Ovid—as many critics have noted—still awaits definitive work" ("Composing Yourself," 85).

Ovid's text and explores his notion of a sequence. It also explores his modes of intertextuality, especially those that would in turn be used on him by his medieval and Renaissance successors. Just as Ovid pays homage to (and subverts) the rhetoric of Cicero and the poetics of Propertius, Ovid is imitated and challenged by the troubadours, Dante, Petrarch, and Shakespeare.

Chapter 2 traces the fragmentary transmission of the *Amores* into monastic Latin literary culture before the twelfth century. Since many of these "fragments" cohere into the poetic conventions that become the stuff of the much discussed and disputed concept of *fin' Amors,* I thought it important to examine their source in the *libri manuales* of the medieval schoolroom and the use of such conventions by Maximianus, Theodulf, and Baudri de Bourgueil. They too were fully conscious of what a persona was, because they learned it from Ovid.

Chapter 3 explores the use of the *Amores* by poets in the century in which the text is first widely available in manuscript, the twelfth. Most of the chapter concerns Guillaume IX and Bernart de Ventadorn, since they are probably the most Ovidian of the troubadours, with a glance at Wilibald Schrötter's ancient (and perfectly respectable) hypothesis of Ovid as a source for *fin' Amors.*[2] However, a substantial portion is devoted to the Latin poetic love dialogue, because of its similarity to the troubadour *tenso,* and because such dialogues invariably discuss the merits of Ovid, reflect a knowledge of his personae, and are sometimes critical of the *desultor* and *magister Amoris.*

Chapters 4 and 5 treat Dante's *Vita nuova* and Petrarch's *Rime,* respectively. I examine the *Vita* as a sequence that contradicts itself as a critique of Ovidian troubadour erotics, since Dante appropriates and updates the Protean persona for his epoch, in the manner of his thirteenth-century contemporaries Jean de Meun and the author of *de Vetula,* as well as the *stilnovisti.* The Petrarch chapter analyzes the *Rime* as a type of "exorcism" of the Ovidian persona, establishing Petrarch's thorough knowledge of the *Amores,* their conventions, and their speaker, and the poet's deliberate refashioning of his classical *auctor* as he establishes his own poetics.

Chapter 6 analyzes Shakespeare as heir to Ovid and his medieval imitators in Sonnets 127–54, with Marlowe's translation as intermediating paradigm. Shakespeare's speaker, whom he names Will, is a reanimation and revision of the Ovidian-Marlovian *desultor Amoris.* A broader purpose of

---

2. *Ovid und die Troubadours* (Halle: Niemeyer, 1908). I reinvestigate Schrötter's ideas in a sidelight in chapter 3.

the chapter is to define, by the example of Marlowe's *Elegies,* a "formative intertext": one that literally helps to form another by its very existence. It encourages competitive imitation, or even parodic subversion.

A minor function of this book is to explore the meaning of intertextuality and to see if one can apply such a modern conception to old poems. Although I avoid rehashing the poststructuralist debates of Derrida, Barthes, and Miller on the matter, I also attempt to avoid fulfilling M.H. Abrams' reductive definition of the term as a depersonalization of "influence" into "a reverberation between ownerless sequences of signs."[3] My sense of an "intertext" is probably a more encompassing version of an "influence" (just as it is for Barkan and Bate), because for our medieval and Renaissance authors, Ovid was never a sign but a person, as Chaucer suggests in his phrase "Venus clerke Ovyde" (*The House of Fame,* 1487).

Thomas M. Greene's landmark *The Light in Troy* (New Haven: Yale University Press, 1982) discusses the phases of Renaissance *imitatio* regarding the classical tradition: reproductive, exploitative, heuristic, and dialectical. I explore these phases and presume to call them into question when necessary. For example, although Greene admits that the heuristic and dialectical modes of imitation are sometimes indistinguishable, I have found that the exploitative mode, in which an author such as Guillaume IX basically "cannibalizes" Ovid, is simply another form of dialectical competition. And, in some respects, all *imitatio* of Ovid is dialectical: his poetics encourage his imitators to compete with him and to overtake him in a phenomenon I call *subversive submersion.*

It is almost as fashionable now to bash contemporary critical schools and to deride their terminology as jargon as it once was to pretend to understand the theorists by parroting their phrases and habits of mind. But what is jargon to one person is a tool for another. When no phrase exists for a critical concept, one must be invented and used (i.e., "subversive submersion"; "formative intertext"). Though I am a fairly unvarnished close reader, and though I focus on the authors and the scholarship that accounts for their imitative poetics, I could not have written my own text without contemporary critical notions as (sublimated) background. My exploration of Ovid's use of personae owes something to persona theory. The poststructuralist notion of the arbitrary and indeterminate nature of language informs my analysis of the persona's sophistical and self-subverting nature. My reading of the *desultor Amoris* as an essentially male

---

3. "How to Do Things with Texts," in *Critical Theory since 1965,* ed. Hazard Adams and Leroy Searle (Tallahassee: Florida State University Press, 1986), 436.

animal who degrades women with his mocking male voice would be impossible without current critical concepts concerning gender and sexuality. Finally, poetic sequences and their parts should not be viewed as still-unravished brides of quietude. Cultural and linguistic factors across centuries help authors form texts, and can provide unity within a given text. We would do well to remember that formative unity is Ovid's business, accomplished by him and his successors with what he called *ars*—not just "art," but skill, craft, guile.

Acknowledgments

Many of us who comment on literature may resemble Nabokov's Professor Charles Kinbote in *Pale Fire* more than we realize. If I have been fortunate enough to avoid this somewhat universal predicament, it is only because of my many colleagues with sharp eyes. I wish to acknowledge my debt to Elizabeth Morley Ingram of Eastern Michigan University and William Ingram of the University of Michigan for two decades of intellectual support and encouragement and parental love. I would also like to thank John Velz of the University of Texas at Austin, my mentor in the classical tradition. I am also indebted to Charles Witke of the University of Michigan for first stimulating my interest in Ovid and medieval Latin literature, an interest that has paid me many dividends.

My two readers at the University of Michigan Press made many comments on chapter 1 that I took to heart, and which I used to improve this part of my book. Some of the material on Ovid and *fin' Amors* in chapters 2 and 3 appeared in different form in *"Venus Vituperator:* Ovid, Marie de France, and *Fin' Amors," Classical and Modern Literature* 13 (1993): 283–95. Special thanks must also go to my many readers of chapter 6 on Shakespeare and the *Amores:* Debora Kuller Shuger of the University of California, Los Angeles; Heather Dubrow of the University of Wisconsin-Madison; Lars Engle of the University of Tulsa; and Stephen Booth of the University of Calfornia, Berkeley, whose encouragement has been a singular honor. My readers at *PMLA* and *Shakespeare Quarterly* were also very helpful in their comments on this section.

I also thank my editor at the University of Michigan Press, Ellen Bauerle, who cushioned me from every bump in the road.

Contents

CHAPTER 1

"Non sum desultor Amoris": The *Amores* and Personae

crede mihi, distant mores a carmine nostro
(vita verecunda est, Musa iocosa mea)
magnaque pars mendax operum est et ficta meorum:
plus sibi permisit compositore suo,
nec liber indicium est animi, sed honesta voluntas.

(Ovid Tr. 2.353–57)[1]

[believe me, my conduct differs from my poetry (my life modest, my poetry immodest), and the better part of my work is fictive, unreal: it has permitted itself more license than its creator has enjoyed. A book is not the index of one's soul but an honorable manifestation of the will.]

In his complex poems of lamentation, the *Tristia,* Ovid indignantly laments his permanent exile at the mouth of the Danube, where he stood shaking from the unfamiliar dank cold, his joints swollen, his marrow frozen. The Getic tribespeople baffle and depress him with their rotten food, sour water, and moronic feuding. To them, *ars* and *cultus* can mean nothing, which is a form of barbarism that galls him even more than finding himself marooned in a place where the seas, *horribile dictu,* actually freeze. In response, he stubbornly exemplifies *cultus* by utilizing *ars* to weave his flawless reams of elegiac couplets.

---

1. Throughout, Latin quotations from Ovid are from the following editions: for the erotic poetry, *P. Ovidii Nasonis Amores Medicamina faciei feminae Ars amatoria Remedia amoris,* ed. E.J. Kenney, 2d ed. (Oxford: Clarendon Press, 1994); for the poetry of exile, *P. Ovidi Nasonis Tristium libri quinque Ibis Ex Ponto libri quattor Halieutica Fragmenta,* ed. S.G. Owen (Oxford: Clarendon Press, 1978); for the *Metamorphoses, Ovidius Metamorphoses,* ed. W.S. Anderson (Leipzig: Teubner, 1993). All translations of Ovid are my own.

Ovid may seem to grovel before Augustus for his notoriously obscure "duo crimina, carmen et error" (*Tr.* 2.207).[2] Yet he more frequently defends himself by subtle criticism of his emperor, who, he claims, did not even read the *Ars amatoria* before imposing exile.[3] If Augustus had merely glanced at it, Ovid assures him, he would have found nothing objectionable: "nullum legisses crimen in Arte mea" (*Tr.* 2.240). Ovid becomes bolder as he progresses to his main defense at the epicenter of *Tristia* 2. Poetry differs enormously from the poet who creates it; Ovid describes his art as immodest ("iocosa") and himself as modest ("verecunda"). So his poetry is fictive, a construct created by an act of the will, "honesta voluntas." However one wishes to translate that fiendishly difficult phrase, one may infer that Ovid, in distinguishing between himself and the voice in his erotic poetry, explains the use of the orator's tool that we call *persona,* a device meant to help charm the ear: "plurima mulcendis auribus apta" (*Tr.* 2.358).

That Ovid uses the language of oratory to discuss his poetry is not surprising, because he formed his poetics within the classical rhetorical tradition, one that was simultaneously fluid and well defined concerning the divergence between the speaker and his speech. For example, Plato and Aristotle disagree as they discuss the discrepancy between an orator and the rhetorical tools he utilizes to establish credibility. In the *Gorgias,* Socrates waxes polemical against the Sophists by branding oratory as *kolakeutikós,* or "pandering." It "pays no regard to the welfare of its object, but catches fools with the bait of ephemeral pleasure and tricks them into holding it in the highest esteem."[4] The dichotomy between speaker and technique occasions Plato's virulence. To him, orators are, like poets, liars. In the *Rhetoric,* Aristotle advises that an orator "must dis-

---

2. The standard work on Ovid's banishment to the Black Sea is John C. Thibault's *The Mystery of Ovid's Exile* (Berkeley: University of California Press, 1964). A more recent study is Christine Korten's *Ovid, Augustus und der Kult der Vestalinnen: Eine religionspolitische These zur Verbannung Ovids* (Frankfurt: Lang, 1992).

3. In the *Tristia,* Ovid asks Augustus: "mirer in hoc igitur tantarum pondere rerum / te numquam nostros evoluisse iocos?" [Should I then be surprised that under the weight of state affairs you have never unrolled my jesting treatise?] (2.237–38). The clear implication from context is that the exiled poet means the *Ars.* Despite Augustus' literary pretensions, such as quoting Homer and Virgil at opportune moments (as recorded by Suetonius), there is no reason to suppose that he had read the *Ars.*

4. *Gorgias* 464, ed. and trans. Walter Hamilton (Harmondsworth: Penguin, 1960), 46. Ernst Robert Curtius explains that "rhetoric" was "transfer[red] to Roman poetry," which "was Ovid's accomplishment." See *European Literature and the Latin Middle Ages,* trans. Willard R. Trask (Princeton: Princeton University Press, 1954), 66.

guise his art and give the impression of speaking naturally and not artificially. Naturalness is persuasive, artificiality is the contrary; for our hearers are prejudiced and think we have some design against them, as if we were mixing their wines for them."[5] Aristotle hesitates to make moral judgments, and he gives his speaker almost unlimited license. The dichotomy between speaker and technique is unavoidable, not evil, so a good orator simply closes the gap. Although master and pupil disagree about the morality of this art, they agree that an orator seeks to gain his audience's trust by persuasion and that he can do so most effectively by disguising himself with speech.

Cicero is heir to both traditions, but his bent is distinctly Aristotelian. At the end of the *Orator,* he reminds us that "ipsum illud verum tamen in occulto lateret" [the truth itself lurks in obscurity] (71.237).[6] This maxim is especially useful in oratory, because, as the *Brutus* states, "nec res ulla plus apud animos hominum quam ordo et ornatus orationis valet" [nothing has such an effect on men's souls as ordered and ornate speech] (51.193).[7]

Although Cicero attempts to distinguish poetry from oratory, he often uses one genre to explain the other, since he wrote poetry himself. In composing, "ipsa collocatio confirmatioque verborum perficitur in scribendo, non poetico, sed quodam oratorio numero et modo" (*de Oratione* 1.33.151); that is, the very collocation and arrangement of words is perfected in writing appropriate to the rhythm and measure of oratory, not poetry.[8] Yet he constantly advises his public speakers to use poetry as rhetorical fodder, and he praises any poet who seeks the virtues of an orator: "est eo laudabilior quod virtutes oratoris persequitur" (*Orator* 19.67).[9]

As John of Garland implies as early as the thirteenth century, Cicero's Gorgian rhetorical works foretell Ovid's ultrasophisticated use of

---

5. *Rhetoric* 3.1 (1404b), trans. W. Rhys Roberts, in *The Rhetoric and Poetics of Aristotle,* ed. Friedrich Solmsen, trans. W. Rhys Roberts and Ingram Bywater (New York: Modern Library, 1954), 167. See Robert M. Durling's excellent discussion of the influence of Aristotle on Roman rhetoric in *The Figure of the Poet in Renaissance Epic* (Cambridge: Harvard University Press, 1965), 13–14. Durling also remarks: "Ovid's presentation of the role [of Poet] . . . is profoundly different because it is primarily facetious, and it is here . . . that his greatest originality lies" (28).

6. Throughout, quotations of Cicero are from the Loeb Classical Library's *Cicero in Twenty-Eight Volumes* (Cambridge: Harvard University Press). The text and H.M. Hubbell's translation of the *Orator* is from *Brutus and Orator,* trans. G.L. Hendrickson and H.M. Hubbell (Cambridge: Harvard University Press, 1962), 509.

7. Trans. G.L. Hendrickson, in *Brutus and Orator,* 165.

8. Cicero, *De oratore, De fato, Paradoxica Stoicorum, De partitione oratoria,* trans. E.W. Sutton and H. Rackham, 3 vols. (Cambridge: Harvard University Press, 1967), 1:105.

9. Cicero, *Brutus and Orator,* 359.

personae.[10] This is especially true in the matter of *modus,* or decorum. Indeed, "poeta fugit ut maximum vitium qui peccat etiam, cum probam orationem affingit improbo stultove sapientis" (*Orator* 22.74); that is, the greatest sin that a poet can commit is to affix the speech of a good man to a villain, or of a wise man to a fool.[11] Yet, on decorum or *modus* itself: "magis offendit nimium quam parum" (*Orator* 21.72); too much is more offensive to an audience than too little.[12] Much of Ovid's poetry is a violation of Cicero's first maxim and a celebration of the second.

In the treatise attributed to Cicero for almost a thousand years, the *ad Herennium,* the author echoes many of his illustrious predecessors with this advice: "in dicendo, ne possit ars eminere et ab omnibus videri, facultate oratoris occultatur" [In speaking, let the art be hidden by the skill of the orator, lest it obtrude and be seen by everyone] (4.7).[13] In turn, one of Ovid's most noted lines in the *Metamorphoses,* "ars adeo latet arte sua" (10.252), echoes pseudo-Cicero and demonstrates Ovid's love of poetical sophistry.[14] To Ovid, a poet is a kind of orator whose art should conceal his art, as he argues in the *Epistulae ex Ponto,* poetry from exile addressed to an orator:

> distat opus nostrum, sed fontibus exit ab isdem:
> artis et ingenuae cultor uterque sumus.
>
> . . . .
>
> ambobus debet inesse calor:
> utque meis numeris tua dat facundia nervos,
>   sic venit a nobis in tua verba nitor.
> iure igitur studio confinia carmina vestro
>   et commilitii sacra tuenda putas.
>
> (2.5.65–66; 69–72)

---

10. "In stilo Tuilliano non est attendenda dictionum cadencia sed sola sentencie gravitas et uerborum florida exornacio, qua vtuntur antiquiores tam prosaice quam metrice scribentes, sicut . . . Ovid" [In Cicero's style, the sound of the delivery ought not to be heeded, but the gravity of sentences and the florid embellishment of words alone, which ancient writers used in poetry as well as prose, such as Ovid] (*The "Parisiana Poetria" of John of Garland,* ed. Traugott Lawlor [New Haven: Yale University Press, 1974], 329; my translation).

11. Cicero, *Brutus and Orator,* 361.

12. Ibid., 359.

13. Trans. Harry Caplan, in *Ad Herennium* (Cambridge: Harvard University Press, 1981), 250–51.

14. For an excellent discussion of Ovid's rhetorical sophistry in the erotica, see Leslie Cahoon, "A Program for Betrayal: Ovidian *Nequitia* in *Amores* I.i, II.i, and III.i," *Helios,* n.s., 12 (1985): 29–40.

[our work differs, but it springs from the same sources: each of us is the cultivator of a noble art. . . . both of us should be passionate: just as your eloquence gives strength to my numbers, so splendor comes from me into your words. Thus in principle you think my poetry connected to your profession and that the rites of our common battle ought to be observed.]

Ovid does not mention sophistry, but he demonstrates plenty of it, because the poem itself was written to be read by someone who would think him trustworthy enough to liberate from his Pontic prison. He is, of course, writing for an audience whom he wants to convince of the interdependence, in eloquence and splendor, between poetry and oratory, a type of formal argument that he had learned in school.

A rhetorical education was standard for a typical Roman schoolboy, especially the *declamationes,* in which young men practiced persuasive modes, such as *suasoriae* and *controversiae.* According to the Elder Seneca, young Ovid preferred the former: "libentius dicebat suasorias." This exercise often involved assuming the voice of another person who would give advice to a hero of myth or story.[15] One can certainly see the *suasoria* at work in *Tristia* 2, with Augustus serving as hero to be persuaded.

Yet Ovid's sophistical powers appear to have had no efficacy. Although the persona functions "as a means of obscuring the *ascription* of meaning,"[16] one can still ascribe these meanings to the poet himself. Therefore, to Augustus, Ovid was his poetry, "iocosa," and was deserving of exile. Besides, if the emperor had not read the *Ars,* he would not have bothered to peruse the *Tristia,* nor would he have understood the persona, cared that the truth lurks in obscurity, or seen art concealing art.

1

Even in the *Tristia* and *Epistulae ex Ponto,* Ovid is *magister personae,* posing as *Ovidius paenitens* as he argues tenaciously for his innocence. I suspect that such sophistry has fooled those commentators who fail to distin-

---

15. See John T. Davis, *Fictus Adulter: Poet as Actor in the "Amores,"* (Amsterdam: Gieben, 1989), 5, 12.

16. Gerald R. Bond, "Composing Yourself," 87. Robert Elliot, *The Literary Persona* (Chicago: University of Chicago Press, 1982): "Sincerity . . . can mean many things, but in most definitions it clashes inevitably with ideas of the persona, whether employed functionally by the poet or analytically by the critic. Masks, irony, dissimulation, artifice—all associated with the persona—are suspect when sincerity holds sway" (32).

guish between the poet and his voices, or who write that the erotica exemplifies Ovid's "confessional style."[17] Yet other critics have noted his pervasive and brilliant use of personae, sometimes in the parody of his predecessors (in whose conventions he is nonetheless steeped) or in his knack for "satirizing the third person in the first."[18] Some see the *praeceptor Amoris*

---

17. L.P. Wilkinson, *Ovid Surveyed: An Abridgement of "Ovid Recalled"* (Cambridge: Cambridge University Press, 1962), 14. He does not discuss the persona per se, but he hints at it: "Naturally Ovid pretended that his poetic world was real, and himself its hero; but he pathetically abandoned his *bravura* when trouble forced him to do so" (15). Peter Green sometimes acknowledges Ovid's use of personae, and he surveys the matter in *Ovid: The Erotic Poems* (New York: Penguin, 1982), 60–62.

Some commentators conflate poet and persona, which creates the fallacy that one can make suppositions about an author's life from his or her work. For example, Georg Luck writes: "Ovid pretends to be puzzled by his own nature"; "To be in love, to make love, is for Ovid a natural activity, provided that it leads to mutual pleasure. It is unnatural, however, to seek in love a purely selfish satisfaction" (*The Latin Love Elegy* [New York: Barnes and Noble, 1960] 159, 167). I argue that Ovid's *speakers* (as opposed to the poet himself) are not the slightest bit interested in the mutuality that Luck seems to attribute to Ovid; this is the point of the *Amores*. Therefore I also disagree with W.R. Johnson, who claims that the "central delusion" of the *Amores* is "that love is the most important thing in life" ("Ringing Down the Curtain on Love," *Helios*, n.s., 12 [1985]: 24).

Niall Rudd discusses the use of personae by Roman poets in his refutation of Lionel Trilling's contention that Renaissance England invented sincerity. See "Theory: Sincerity and the Mask," *Lines of Enquiry: Studies in Latin Poetry* (Cambridge: Cambridge University Press, 1976), 145–81. Brooks Otis is also instructive concerning the elegiac persona, who is "most incongruously represented as a Catullan ego whose *servitum* or servile devotion to his girl is both a career and a passion" (*Ovid as an Epic Poet* [Cambridge: Cambridge University Press, 1970], 10). See also Paul Veyne, *Roman Erotic Elegy: Love, Poetry, and the West*, trans. D. Pellauer (Chicago: University of Chicago Press, 1988).

18. E.K. Rand, quoted in Florence Verducci, *Ovid's Toyshop of the Heart: "Epistulae Heroidum"* (Princeton: Princeton University Press, 1985), 293. I.M. Le M. Du Quesnay writes that in the *Amores,* there is "a caricature of the elegiac lover generally." See "The *Amores,*" in *Ovid,* ed. J.W. Binns (London: Routledge, 1973), 1–48. Green focuses on the lover's Protean personality, which varies in the *Ars amatoria* between "devoted lover, social butterfly, [and] avuncular rake" (*Ovid,* 65). Bond suggests that Ovid used personae to explore "the immanence of self and the plurality of voice" ("Composing Yourself," 84–85). Molly Myerowitz writes extensively about Ovid's *praeceptor Amoris* in *Ovid's Games of Love* (Detroit: Wayne State University Press, 1985): that speaker's confessed lack of control is always undercut by our knowledge that Ovid is always in control (37). Davis sees the persona in the *Amores* as a Protean Don Juan who satirizes Propertian fidelity (*Fictus Adulter,* 37). Cahoon uses the term *amator* for the *Amores* persona. She also sees his gradual decline, so that he becomes "a bawd's bawd." See "A Program for Betrayal," 37. See also Verducci's article, "The Contest of Rational Libertinism and Imaginative License in Ovid's *Ars amatoria,*" *Pacific Coast Philology* 15 (1980): 29–39.

For Ovid and his predecessors in the use of personae, see A.L. Wheeler, "Propertius as *Praeceptor Amoris,*" *Classical Philology* 5 (1910): 28–40; Durling, "Ovid as *Praeceptor Amoris,*" *Classical Journal* 53 (1957): 157–67. Wilkinson writes, "We are being introduced to

of the *Ars amatoria* (1.17) as Ovid's "true *persona*,"[19] as if the professor character is somehow a more valid creation than the mythographer, calendar maker, or exile.

Few discuss the "student," Ovid's speaker in the *Amores*, but he merits attention as an original character in elegiac poetry whom medieval and Renaissance poets imitated and revised extensively. He is a truly "unreliable narrator"[20] who discovers his own foolishness in a sequence of love poems, a megalomaniac who becomes everything he despises. I shall name him *desultor Amoris*, despite his protest to the contrary: "non sum desultor Amoris" (*Am.* 1.3.15).[21]

Although the five-book *Amores* were published before the *Ars amatoria*, and though the three-book version must have been finished some time before *Ars* 3.343 (when the *magister* recommends it to women), commentators have long noted the interdependence between the two texts. The

---

a new mood of Latin elegy; we are to be entertained, not moved" (*Ovid Surveyed*, 17). Verducci discusses the "wit, parody, and irony" in the *Heroides* that "seem capricious violations of an obligatory decorum," all of which "function as integral to both . . . motive and significance" (*Ovid's Toyshop*, 6). These principles, I think, apply to the *Amores* as well, whose author, Verducci says, well knew "the gulf between lyric license and real life" (163).

Other works on the Ovidian persona include Bardo Maria Gauly, *Liebeserfahrungen: Zur Rolle das elegischen Ich in Ovids "Amores"* (Frankfurt: Lang, 1990); Meike Keul, *Liebe im Widerstreit: Interpretationen zu Ovids "Amores" und ihrem literarischen Hintergrund* (Frankfurt: Lang, 1989).

19. The phrase is Green's. Du Quesnay ("The *Amores*," 10) and Wilkinson (*Ovid Surveyed*, 143) see the *Amores* as superior to the *Ars*.

20. Peter Allen uses Wayne C. Booth's famous term from *The Rhetoric of Fiction* (Chicago: University of Chicago Press, 1961) for the *Ars* narrator in *The Art of Love: Amatory Fiction from Ovid to the "Romance of the Rose"* (Philadelphia: University of Pennsylvania Press, 1992), 27. Allen maintains, "Credulitas is not . . . what the *Amores* ask for; rather, they encourage their readers to maintain a conscious understanding . . . that those poems play out a conventional game" (23).

21. On the idea that the *Amores* character is indeed *desultor*, see the brilliant close reading of *Amores* 1.3.14 by Leo C. Curran, who explains that the OR sounds in repertOR, amOR, mORes, pudOR, and amORis emphasize the disingenuous disavowal that the speaker is desultOR. See "*Desultores Amoris:* Ovid's *Amores* 1.3," *Classical Philology* 6 (1966): 48. More recent articles on this crucial elegy include J.A. Barsby, "*Desultor Amoris* in *Amores* 1.3," *Classical Philology* (1975): 44–45; E. Burck, "Ovid, *Amores* 1.3 im Rahmen der römischen Liebesdichtung," *Der altsprachliche Unterricht* 20 (1977): 463–81; J.F. Davidson, "Some Thoughts on Ovid *Amores* 1.3," *Collection Latomus* 168 (1980): 278–85; Francis Cairns, "Ovidio, *Amores* 1.3.: Dipendenza Letteraria vs. Independenza Intellettuale," *Cultura, Poesia, Ideologia nell' Opera di Ovidio*, ed. Italo Gallo and Luciano Nicastri (Napoli: Edizioni Scientifiche Italiane, 1991), 27–40.

desultor seems designed to have been the student of the *praeceptor,* a relationship noted as early as the twelfth century. A medieval *accessus* (preface) to the erotica delineates this intertextuality:

> Ovidius de Amatoria arte dat precepta amantibus
> ut sint cauti, hic autem de Amore et in semetipso
> complet precepta.

> [Ovid's *Art of Love* gives precepts to lovers so that they may be on their guard, and in the *Amores,* he puts these very precepts into practice.][22]

These *precepta* have been enumerated and analyzed elsewhere, and, anachronism aside, it is not difficult to blame the misadventures of the *desultor* on the later advice of the *Ars.* Much more significant is the poetic inheritance. The *praeceptor* explains to all circus-riders-in-training that an intelligent poet never changes his essence while adopting as many poses as possible:

> qui sapit, innumeris moribus aptus erit,
> utque leues Proteus modo se tenuabit in undas.
>
> <div align="right">(<i>AA</i> 1.760–61)</div>

> [he who would be wise will adopt numerous guises, just as Proteus will preserve himself in the slippery waves.]

The *praeceptor Amoris* also knows, just as Aristotle, Cicero, and Pygmalion in the *Metamorphoses* all know, that art should conceal art: "si latet, ars prodest" (*AA* 2.313). Therefore, to him, the art of deception in love is normative, because he believes that women are deceivers who deserve to be deceived: "fallite fallentes" (1.645). The *desultor* uses such amoral or mercenary logic in the *Amores* as he speaks to his mistresses, to his adversaries, and to us. Yet this logic is based on advice provided by a *praeceptor* whom a recent critic correctly labels "a pedantic fool," advice

---

22. For the *accessus,* see Hexter, *Ovid and Medieval Schooling,* 16 n. 4 (my translation). John M. Fyler also thinks of the *Amores* narrator as the student of the *Ars praeceptor.* See "*Omnia Vincit Amor:* Incongruity and the Limitations of Structure in Ovid's Elegiac Poetry," *Classical Journal* 66 (1971): 201.

that is doomed to fail for fairly obvious reasons.[23] Despite his frequent boasting, the *desultor* is an ordinary man who makes ordinary mistakes.

2

As the *Amores* begin, even the persona seems ordinary. The lover is Cupid's captive (1.2.19–20); love is by nature humiliating, an emotion that literally leads one in triumph. Therefore every lover must soldier on as Cupid holds the fort: "Militat omnis amans, et habet sua castra Cupido" (1.9.1). Yet such Propertian conventionality establishes a rhetorical posture to be violated. One implicit parody may lie in the absence of Corinna, the (sex) object of affection; readers of Roman elegy often compare Propertius, whose *Monobiblos* begins "Cynthia prima." Also, her absence prefigures the tone of the ensuing *Amores,* because the *desultor* always focuses on himself, not the woman in question. Still, the speaker's initial pose is predictable. Like Chaucer's Troilus after him,[24] he mocks the little love god for his pretense of sovereignty in poetry—"'quis tibi, saeue puer, dedit hoc in carmina iuris?'" (1.1.5)—which necessitates an attack:

> me miserum! certas habuit puer ille sagittas:
>   uror, et in uacuo pectore regnat Amor.
>
> (1.1.25–26)

[Woe is me! That boy had sharp arrows: I burn, and love reigns in the empty breast.]

The heavy consonance of *r* exaggerates the emotion of the second line so that one may hear Ovid's burlesque of the burning lover. Yet the adjective "uacuo" distinguishes the persona from Propertius and Tibullus. Amor fills a figurative void. To characterize one's heart or breast as empty reveals more than one would want to reveal. As conventional as it may be for love to reign in the empty (hence idle) breast, it is also

---

23. For the comment on the foolishness of the *magister* in the *Ars,* see Fyler's *Chaucer and Ovid* (New Haven: Yale University Press, 1979), 11. The observation concludes, "we err greatly if we identify him with Ovid or take his self-characterization seriously."

24. "'O veray fooles, how nyce and blynde be ye!' . . . At which the God of Love gan loken rowe" (*Troilus* 1.202, 206). See also *Metamorphoses* 1.456: "'quid,' que 'tibi, lasciue puer, cum fortibus armis?'" See Durling, "Ovid as *Praeceptor,*" 157, for a discussion of Ovid's violation of convention.

possible that there is no "there" there. So, although the speaker's breast
is pierced with sharp arrows, Ovid subtly modulates the conventional
pose of giving in:

sic erit: haeserunt tenues in corde sagittae,
   et possessa ferus pectora uersat Amor.
cedimus, an subitum luctando accendimus ignem?
   cedamus: leue fit, quod bene fertur, onus.

(1.2.7–10)

[so it will be: slim arrows will stick in the heart, and wild Love twists in
the captive breast. Shall I yield, or kindle the hidden fire by struggling?
I'll yield: the burden borne lightly is borne well.]

Such banal protestations invite scrutiny; the passion is crystallized, frozen
like the faces in a mosaic. Particularly indicative is the jarringly epigrammatic last line. As the speaker himself later admits (2.4.6), no lover would
be able to bear this burden lightly. Still, he will repeat this image and
remind us of his helplessness in the face of "indignate Cupido" (2.9.2).[25]
Yet it is simply a posture, a face to meet the faces that he meets, grandiose,
even camp.

For a short time, the initial banality of the *desultor* hides his unscrupu-
lous virtuosity. *Amores* 1.3 also seems cliché until we examine its premises
and compare it to the ensuing elegies. It begins with an entreaty to Venus
to intercede for the speaker with the as-yet-unnamed Corinna:

accipe, per longos tibi qui deseruiat annos;
   accipe, qui pura norit amare fide.

(1.3.5–6)

[Accept one who will serve you zealously for many years; accept one
who will love with perfect fidelity.]

---

25. In *Le roman de la rose,* Guillaume de Lorris may have had this in mind when he portrayed his lover pierced with three arrows "par l'oel ou cors m'entra" (1743): "la saiete bar-
belee / Qui Biautés estoit appelle" (1715–16); "Simplece" (1736); and "Cortoisie" (1767). I
quote here from *Le roman de la rose,* ed. Daniel Poirion (Paris: Garnier-Flammarion, 1974).

What appears to be an intense declaration of feeling actually undercuts itself with bland diction and predictably anaphoric rhetorical structure.[26] This paradoxical effect continues and increases in ironic intensity:

> et nulli cessura fides, sine crimine mores,
>> nudaque simplicitas purpureusque pudor.
> non mihi mille placent, non sum desultor amoris
>
>> (1.3.13–15)

[I have fidelity without end, morality without spot, naked simplicity and blushing modesty. Thousands do not please me; I am no circus-rider of love]

No one who is actually this praiseworthy would feel the need to tell us so. Such declarations are the antithesis of *virtus*. In fact, if the lover feels compelled to claim that his fidelity cannot cease and that his *mores* are without flaw, he may worry that his auditor may suspect a faithlessness and unsavory character that will somehow be revealed. Thus the speaker sets himself up as unreliable, even in his most intense declaration of fidelity. He is no sexual circus-rider who leaps from mount to mount only because he lacks the opportunity; a thousand women would please him very much. In such duplicity, the *desultor* resembles the *magister* of the *Ars,* who insists that he is a sacred poet who knows no crime or stratagem ("uera canam," 1.30; "inque meo nullum carmine crimen erit," 1.34; "insidiae sacris a uatibus absunt," 3.539), so that he may lie more convincingly.

Amores 1.4 confirms the speaker's duplicitous nature. The man who has recently assured us that his *mores* are "sine crimine" clearly acts as *magister* in teaching his married lady friend how to deceive her *vir,* or husband. The speaker is thus faithful to faithlessness. Two elegies earlier, he gives himself permission to lie:

> Mens Bona ducetur manibus post terga retortis
>> et Pudor et castris quicquid Amoris obest.
>
>> (1.2.31–32)

---

26. Green sees the speaker's declaration as "genuine" (*Ovid,* 270). See also Katherine Olstein, "*Amores* 1.3 and Duplicity as a Way of Love," *TAPA* 105 (1975): 241–58.

[Let Conscience be led with her arms tied behind her back, and Modesty and everyone else who marches on the field of Love.]

The *desultor* uses this "allegory of love" to explain or predict his later deceptions. Conscience and Modesty are led captive in what may be a profane analogue to Virgil's "omnia vincit amor; et nos cedamus Amori" (*Eclogues* 10.69), or even a reversal of Plato's metaphor of the charioteer and horses in the *Phaedrus*. Appetite is the charioteer.

One would assume that the persona would be pleased with himself in the successful planning and execution of his amoral strategy. But 1.4 does not find him gloating:

> multa miser timeo, quia feci multa proterue,
>   exemplique metu torqueor ipse mei
>
> (1.4.45–46)

[I'm afraid of everything, miserable, because I've done many things impudently, and I'm tormented with the fear of my own example]

In explaining his perverse jealousy of the man he is attempting to cuckold, the speaker mutes his bravura at his present success. His diction is not triumphant but agonized ("miser," "timeo," "metu," "torqueor"). In this, he is strongly self-critical. He also seems to understand that he cannot possess in toto the woman for whom he lusts. For now, he must content himself with "footsie," raised eyebrows, and tugs of the earlobe (1.4.15–16). He is thus reduced to making snide declarations to Corinna:

> sed quaecumque tamen noctem fortuna sequetur,
>   cras mihi constanti uoce dedisse nega.
>
> (1.4.69–70)

[but whomever fortune may bless you with tonight, tomorrow, with a steady voice, deny that you have done it.]

In essence, he is a liar who wants to be lied to, or at least spared the knowledge that the woman for whom he burns will be physically possessed by another on the same evening he has been flirting with her. This idea recurs in the second book of the *Amores,* in which the persona knows that his *amica* lies to him constantly and completely:

> me modo decipiant uoces fallacis amicae
>   (sperando certe gaudia magna feram),
> et modo blanditias dicat, modo iurgia nectat
>
>   (2.9b.43–45)

[sometimes the words of a faithless mistress deceive me (I can make myself very happy by hoping), and sometimes she flatters me, and tightens my yoke]

Yet he enjoys it; the hope and the sublimation of desire serve as erotic spur to his flank. So the *desultor* who would possess a thousand *feminae* (no Propertius) uses a misogynist maxim to melt them all down into a single shapeless mass. All women are one girl, and this one girl is a sweet evil: "dulce puella malum est" (2.9b.26).

The twisted logic of 1.4 becomes normative in the *Amores* as the speaker tells us more about himself. In 2.4, he abjures all declarations of fidelity and purports to reveal his "true" self:

> Non ego sum mendosos ausim defendere mores
>   falsaque pro uitiis arma mouere meis.
> confiteor, siquid prodest delicta fateri;
>   in mea nunc demens crimina fassus eo.
> odi, nec possum cupiens non esse quod odi:
>   heu quam, quae studeas ponere, ferre graue est!
>
>   (1–6)

[I won't venture to defend my mendacious behavior, or wage war to protect my vices. If it is useful to confess, I'll confess; still, it's crazy to confess crimes against myself. I hate, yet I'm unable not to desire what I hate: how heavy the burden is that you're eager to set down!]

The "onus" of 1.2.10 is not "leue" but "graue." This poem truly reverses the saccharine declarations in 1.3: he would love a thousand women in bed or anywhere else. He no longer defends his *mores* as "sine crimine" but confirms them as "mendosos." He "confesses," and is more sharply self-critical here than in 1.4: "noster in has omnis ambitiosus amor" (2.4.48)—he wants them all. He hates himself because he can be nothing but what he hates, a lustful fool who has leaped into a net of his own weaving, which Ovid emphasizes by placing "odi" at the beginning and ending of line 5.[27] This strange quadruplex of elegies (1.3, 1.4, 2.4, 2.9) serves as a lens through which to view the *Amores* and their duplicitous, whining lover. He "deconstructs" himself in much the same way as does the *magister* of the *Ars,* whose neutral pose, "ego sum praeceptor Amoris" (1.17), eventually encrusts itself with the nasty residue of the adjective "lasciui."[28]

3

Amores 1.4 also reveals the personality of the *desultor,* maintained throughout the sequence. In comic contrast to the virile and suave Propertian model or the elegantly damaged Tibullus, the persona of the *Amores* is a "little" man in every sense—petty, jealous, nasty. He remains in an annoying state of pursuit, as if he had been tongue-lashed by the *magister* of the *Ars,* who barks out imperatives such as "persta" (1.477), and "perfer et obdura" [stand firm, persist, and be obdurate] (2.178). To worsen his disagreeable state of mind, the lover saddles himself with a nightmarish imagination, asking Corinna if she will warm another man's lap by sitting in it: "alterius sinus apte subiecta fouebis?" (1.4.5). That this other man is "Vir tuus" (1.4.1) is beside the point; his own persistent jealousy makes him obdurate in his imagining and vitriol. He is even "little" enough to mention all of this to the still-unnamed Corinna directly. If she initiates physical contact with her husband at the banquet, the *amans perferens* will declare his love publicly:

---

27. See Luck, *The Latin Love Elegy,* 160.

28. For example, Apollo labels the speaker "'lasciui . . . praeceptor amoris'" (2.497). Compare also "nil nisi lasciui per me discuntur amores" [nothing except lascivious loves are learned through me] (3.27); "sit in infida proditione fides" [let fidelity be kept in proditious infidelity] (3.578); "fiet amor uerus, qui modo falsus erat" [love becomes true, which once was false] (1.618); "ut fallas, ad mea sacra ueni" [so that you might deceive, attend to my rites] (3.616); "cunctas / posse capi" [all [women] are able to be caught] (1.269–70); "nomen amicitia est, nomen inane fides" [friendship is [but] a name, fidelity is a meaningless name] (1.740); "audiat optatos semper amica sonos" [a mistress should always hear speech that she wishes to hear] (2.156). See also E.D. Blodgett, "The Well-Wrought Void: Reflections on the *Ars amatoria,*" *Classical Journal* 68 (1973): 322: "the artist's role is to dissimulate, to cheat, to counterfeit, to fake, to make, in a word, the incredible credible."

oscula si dederis, fiam manifestus amator
et dicam "mea sunt" iniciamque manum.

(1.4.39–40)

[if you give him kisses, I'll announce that I'm your lover, and I'll say,
"Those are mine," and lay hands on you.]

Possession is everything, as his little outburst indicates; even her kisses
should belong to him, and he will lay hands on her in a legal claim.[29] His
logic continues to twist as his anger rises. He snidely accuses the woman of
hypocrisy in his suggestion that she only gives to her *vir* by law what the
desultor should be receiving secretly: "quod mihi das furtim, iure coacta
dabis" (1.4.64). Yet his own unattractive irrationality would preclude any
genuinely enthusiastic "favors" that she might grant. He thus destroys the
efficacy of the relationship as it begins.

To say that the relationship is "purely physical" does not explain the
sexual fixation of the *desultor* well enough: "uix a te uideor posse tenere
manus" (1.4.10). He really cannot keep his hands to himself. The entire
scope of the relationship is physical, even the communication:

uerba superciliis sine uoce loquentia dicam;
    uerba leges digitis, uerba notata mero.

(1.4.19–20)

[I'll utter silent words spoken with the eyebrows; you'll read words in
my fingers, words written in wine.]

Surely the need for secrecy (and its effect as aphrodisiac) dictates the need
for silent communication and heightens the eroticism of writing in wine on
the table. But this little tableau becomes an overriding metaphor for the
relationship: it is literally "sine uoce" where the woman is concerned, as
transient as writing in wine, and entirely dependent on fleshly contact.

The emptiness of the relationship is the lover's own fault. (That Ovid
stresses the wordlessness of his lovers' communication in such conversational poetry is yet more irony to be noted.) The mode of evidence for
Corinna's later unfaithfulness is particularly galling to the lover; it too is
physical:

---

29. To Green, Ovid's speaker epitomizes "a man to whom women are, fundamentally,
sexual objects" (*Ovid*, 68).

ipse miser uidi, cum me dormire putares,
  sobrius apposito crimina uestra mero:
multa supercilio uidi uibrante loquentes;
  nutibus in uestris pars bona uocis erat.

(2.5.13–18)

[Miserable, and very sober, I saw your misdeeds with wine at the table
when you thought me asleep: I saw many things spoken with a raised
eyebrow; the better part of your voice was in your nods.]

This is the code that the speaker taught Corinna so she could maneuver
around her husband in 1.4. Now she employs the same methods to carry
on with her new lover when she thinks the *desultor* is asleep. And now he
is the *vir,* the cuckold, an oaf to be gulled.

This phase in the lover's ironic metamorphosis begins in book 1. He
gradually makes himself unattractive, a man that any woman would want
to cashier. If he is, as he claims, no longer attracted to Corinna, it must be
her fault:

nec facies oculos iam capit ista meos.
  cur sim mutatus quaeris? quia munera poscis:
haec te non patitur causa placere mihi.

(1.10.10–12)

[that face no longer captures my eyes. Do you ask why I've changed?
Because you ask for gifts: this cause does not allow you to please me.]

Obviously, his perception of Corinna's beauty is far from altruistic. If
she grants sexual favors to the *desultor,* he will reward her with praise,
poetic immortality (1.3.9f). That she would prefer more tangible benefits
surprises him, which underscores his naïveté. If Corinna would have
bracelets rather than poems as a measure of the lover's esteem, "stat
meretrix certo cuiuis mercabilis aere" [she must be a whore who can be
bought with hard cash] (1.10.21). However, the *desultor* has created this
dynamic and achieved the shallow relationship that he has sought, albeit
unwittingly. Therefore, when he asks what seems to be a completely
valid question,

quae Venus ex aequo uentura est grata duobus,
altera cur illam uendit et alter emit?

(1.10.33–34)

[when sex is shared equally between two people, why should she sell it
and he buy it?]

his own actions have undercut his argumentative reliability, even when he
makes this "valid point." There is nothing *aequus* about the relationship.
It is all for him. So Corinna is not a whore; the *desultor* has simply affixed
the concept of recompense to her sexuality. He has forced her to sell what
he wishes to buy.

4

In the *Amores*, Ovid often clusters poems around the same theme to illustrate the contradictory processes of his speaker's mind and to underscore
his unreliability. Like the speaker of the *Ars*, the *desultor* cannot adhere to
his own precepts: "monitis sum minor ipse meis" (*AA* 2.548). *Amores* 1.3
and 1.4 delineate his poor logic and dreadful personality. *Amores* 1.5 can
be read as a companion piece; although notable for its brevity, it is a
steamy tour de force that describes a seduction, with a fiendish touch on
the speaker's part: "ecce, Corinna uenit tunica uelata recincta" (9).
Corinna is not hitherto named, but now that she is practically naked and
in a position of sexual vulnerability, she receives this "personalizing
touch," an identity.[30] But this is virtually all; the rest of her consists of
body parts, physical description. Furthermore, the comparisons with
Semiramis and Lais seem indicative, given the propensity of these women
for accommodating "multis . . . uiris" (12).

Actually, this encounter seems overdone, even fantastic. The persona
begins the elegy describing his siesta, then "ecce, Corinna." The moment
could not have been better scripted. How does she appear? Also,
Corinna's behavior here is the stuff of predictable male fantasy, at odds
with her portrayal elsewhere in the *Amores*, in which she seems madden-

---

30. In contrast to Ovid, Propertius repeats Cynthia's name almost sixty times. See *Sextii
Propertii Carmina*, ed. E.A. Barber (Oxford: Clarendon Press, 1953), 173.

ingly elusive and capricious. As the potential lovers assume their erotic clinch, she fights (predictably) as one who does not wish to conquer: "ita pugnaret tamquam quae uincere nollet" (15). This may be an early stage in the relationship, where illicit passions and novelty provide much heat but little flame. This may simply be an extension of the lover's megalomania that he is a man no woman can resist.

A key to interpretation may be the speaker's description of Corinna's body—lovingly detailed yet heavily stylized, his catalog of her charms proceeding systematically down her body, as proscribed by the rhetorical textbooks.[31] He then pauses: "singula quid referam?" (23). Surely "Why should I enumerate particulars?" is meant to be ironic, because the speaker has been engaging in precisely this rhetorical activity, titillating his audience by listing and describing her parts. His second question, "cetera quis nescit?" [Who doesn't know the rest?] (25), magnifies the irony. He has carefully framed the part that he does not describe, below the *uenter* and between the *femora*, a triangular void. Then he abjures his description of *mons Veneris*.

In the manner of a Renaissance painter, such as Ghiberti or Donatello, the speaker has created a "vanishing point." In reading the poem, the reader disappears into the undescribed cleft that Ovid has encouraged us to imagine. This metaphorical gap functions as an emblem for the *Amores:* a physical *pudendum* and symbolic vacuum on which the *desultor* focuses his entire being. He longs to vanish into it; perhaps it was never there for him to vanish into. Hence the subjunctive mood of the last line, "proueniant medii sic mihi saepe dies" (26), may reflect a desire for a similar event on a similar afternoon; it may also reflect wishful thinking about an encounter that never occurred.

Even if *Amores* 1.5 recounts an actual occurrence and is not simply the stuff of male fantasy, the *paraklausithuron*, 1.6, undercuts the smugness of the previous poem (or suggests that it is indeed fantasy). For we find the persona reduced to begging the Ianitor who guards the household of Corinna's *vir*, like the *gardador* who serves as enemy to all troubadours. What keeps the lover out of doors? From the refrain, "tempora noctis eunt; excute poste seram" (24), one would guess that the Ianitor simply performs the duty that the man of the household has assigned him, which is to make sure that the door-bolt does *not* open at night. However, it is possible that Corinna has given the order, if the following poem is truly

---

31. See *Ovid: Amores: Text, Prolegomena, and Commentary,* ed. J.C. McKeown, 4 vols. to date (Wolfeboro, N.H.: Francis Cairns, 1987–) 1:63–64.

part of a sequence: "furor in dominam temeraria bracchia mouit" (1.7.3). The lover becomes abusive and strikes the woman with whom he may have enjoyed his siesta in 1.5 (although he blames *furor,* not himself, for the abuse). He never explains his physical violence; perhaps it was because of the entry denied in 1.6.

The persona renews his posture of self-excoriation that began in 1.4: "mihi quam profitebar amare / laesa est" (1.7.33–34). He understands that one ought not injure the woman one professes to love. But just as he thought of himself as love's captive (1.2.19–20), he thinks of Corinna in the same terms, regardless of his pretensions to contrition; she is "effuso tristis captiua capillo" [a sad captive with disheveled hair] (1.7.39). Although he comprehends his behavior well enough to regret it, he advises her to think in his vengeful terms: "minuet uindicta dolorem" (1.7.63). And, at poem's end, his sympathy and sorrow have clearly evaporated. In what one critic has described as the "coda," the speaker commands Corinna to compose herself by reassembling her hairdo: "pone recompositas in statione comas" (1.7.68).[32] Yet this "coda" is no reversal; it simply builds to the climax that one expects: selfishness, brutality, insincerity.

Therefore, that Corinna would seek the advice of the old woman Dipsas and that the speaker would eavesdrop says a great deal about the character Ovid builds for our perusal. What else should one who has suffered a nasty beating do but seek advice? What else should the abuser do but attempt to listen in?

"ludunt formosae: casta est quam nemo rogauit;
        aut, si rusticitas non uetat, ipsa rogat."

(1.8.43–44)

[beautiful women enjoy themselves: a virgin is one whom no one has solicited; or, if rusticity does not prohibit her, she solicits for herself.]

Ovid's speaker vilifies the old woman (the Roman forebear of Jean de Meun's Vieille in *Le roman de la rose*).[33] Yet her advice about sexual pleasure, the male ego, and the politics of adultery in Augustan Rome seems familiar and makes much sense. It is, in fact, virtually the same counsel that the *praeceptor Amoris* later gives women in *Ars* 3. If one must lie, one should, suggests Dipsas, lie well:

32. Douglass Parker, "The Ovidian Coda," *Arion* 8 (1969): 80–97.
33. For the Vieille's discourse, see *Roman* 12381–14718.

"nec, si quem falles, tu periurare timeto:
commodat in lusus numina surda Venus."

(1.8.85–86)

[if you wish to trick him, don't be afraid to lie: Venus ignores promises
made in passion.]

Again, as much as the speaker decries such female bonding in duplicity, it
describes his amatory philosophy completely. Hence his admission "me
mea prodidit umbra" (1.8.109) invites scrutiny. His shadow really does
"give him away." He is not clever enough to remain unobserved, by the
reader or by the two women, despite all his stated savoir faire about love.
More important, Dipsas' advice really is his "shadow," in that it doubles
his own counsel, and it "exposes" him for what he is.

5

As the *Amores* proceed into their second book, the speaker's motives
become more transparent, his helplessness more pronounced. Ovid's first
ten elegies demonstrate that his lover is a liar who beats his *amica,* cannot
gain access to her when it pleases him, and must spy on her as a result.
Thus the use of the intermediary Nape in 1.11 suggests that the lover lacks
what Chaucer's Wife of Bath will call "maistrye." As conventional as the
tablet-bearing Nape may be for elegiac poetry and its adulterous skuldug-
gery, she also symbolizes the speaker's lack of control over his love affair,
which Ovid underscores in 1.12. Corinna refuses his invitation *via tabula*
for an assignation. His address to Aurora (the predecessor of the troubadour *alba* or trouvère *aubade*), his proud recounting of (and longing for)
the familiar pleasures of his mistress, contains a slight hitch:

nunc iuuat in teneris dominae iacuisse lacertis;
si quando, lateri nunc bene iuncta meo est.

(1.13.5–6)

[now it would please me to have enjoyed the tender embraces of my mistress; if she can ever be joined to my side, let it be now.]

Hidden in the seeming ease of this reverie is "si quando," which suggests a
wish contrary to fact. Has he ever actually been with Corinna? If so, how

often? The doubt and frustration of 1.6 and 1.12 continue as the second book opens, as does the idea that Corinna has shut him out: "clausit amica fores" (2.1.17). The *desultor* confesses his own failure, yet he insists, "mollierunt duras lenia uerba fores" (2.1.22). But his words have not been gentle, nor have they softened many hard doors.

The amount of advice that the speaker dispenses is remarkable, if we consider his lack of success with the woman he pursues. His confidence in decrying the stupidity of Corinna's *vir* to Bagoas, the eunuch assigned to guide her, is disarming:

uir quoque non sapiens: quid enim seruare laboret
    unde nihil, quamuis non tueare, perit?

(2.2.11–12)

[also her husband is unwise: why labor to protect something from which nothing would be lost, even if you didn't protect it?]

Here he intimates that the *vir* does not care whether Corinna violates her married chastity or not. Yet a few lines earlier (6–8), the persona suggests that the eunuch's strict guardianship of Corinna necessitated the rebuff of 1.12. If these things are true, then who has given Bagoas his orders? Perhaps his *domina,* Corinna. As the speaker's arguments build in this elegy, a note of shrillness is not undiscernible: "quod uoluit fieri blanda puella, facit" (2.2.34). The husband fulfills his wife's every whim. If the woman that Bagoas is assigned to guard can manipulate her *vir* this easily, perhaps we should ask why she is not doing so now, or why the speaker should devote sixty-six lines to argument with a slave. This casual reference to Corinna's manipulativeness will redound on the lover cruelly:

ut faciem uidi, fortes cecidere lacerti:
    defensa est armis nostra puella suis.

(2.5.47–48)

[As I saw her face, my strong arms fell: my girl was defended with her own type of arms.]

At the lover's expense, she indulges in the same deception with another man that the lover and Corinna had practiced against the *vir* in 1.4, and he witnesses it. But his anger dissipates at her hurt, "innocent" gaze, her *arma.* So, she can manipulate him as easily as she can her husband. The speaker has become the *vir.* In fact, as she kisses him to the equipoise of forgiveness, he reveals an embarrassing fact: "nescio quis pretium grande magister habet" (62). Some other "magister" has schooled her in the proper bestowing of "oscula." An Elizabethan writer of "emblemes" might tag Ovid's lover *vir insipiens.*

Some critics maintain that the speaker does not reveal his capacity to deceive until the midpoint of book 2.[34] This is obviously untrue: the *desultor* is self-revelatory from the first line of *Amores* 1.1. Yet *Amores* 7 and 8 function with the symmetry of total deceit. They are companion pieces in which the persona first addresses Corinna and hotly denies his unfaithfulness to her with her maid, Cypassis—"ecce, nouum crimen" (2.7.17)— then addresses Cypassis and berates her for allowing Corinna to learn of their tryst, about which he was forced to lie to protect them both: "sensit concubitus unde Corinna tuos?" (2.8.6). His directive to Cypassis is predictable:

> pro quibus officiis pretium mihi dulce repende
>   concubitus hodie, fusca Cypasi, tuos.
>
> (21–22)

> [dusky Cypassis, for these duties, reward me sweetly today with your sex.]

Sex is simply a means of asserting domination. There is no "mutuality," no pleasure, simply an impersonal transaction. Perhaps one should expect no less from Ovid's Roman persona, whose culture regarded slaves, male and female, as subhuman.[35] Yet this same dehumanizing impulse informs the adulterous relationship that the persona attempts to maintain. His frequent references to Corinna in terms suitable to a prostitute (e.g., 1.5, 3.14) further equate *domina* and *ancilla,* and they recall his concept of

---

34. See Parker, "Ovidian Coda"; Green, *Ovid;* and Nicholas P. Gross, "Rhetorical Wit and Amatory Persuasion in Ovid," *Classical Journal* 74 (1979): 305–18.

35. For further reading, see Sarah Pomeroy, *Goddesses, Whores, Wives, and Slaves: Women in Classical Antiquity* (New York: Schocken, 1975); J. Peradotto and J.P. Sullivan, eds., *Women in the Ancient World* (Albany: State University of New York Press, 1984); Paul Veyne, ed., *A History of Private Life,* vol. 1, *From Pagan Rome to Byzantium,* trans. Arthur Goldhammer (Cambridge: Harvard University Press, 1987).

female sexuality as a reward for the man yet something for which the woman is to be recompensed (1.10.3–4). Corinna and Cypassis are the same woman because all women are the same to this speaker.

The maid's reward for allowing herself to be seduced is to be forced into unwanted sex in order to protect the reputation of her seducer with her mistress. Her refusal will necessitate an itemized list of assignations to Corinna, real or imagined: "narrabo dominae quotque quibusque modis" (2.8.28). *Amores* 2.8 is certainly a naked statement of male hegemony, informed by the principle of transactional sex. Yet it is nothing new; it confirms what Ovid has already shown us about this lover. He lacks the requisite social finesse and erotic charisma to keep his bored married lady coming back for more on a regular basis, so he must blackmail her poor maid, lash-scarred side and all, for forced *concubitus*. Thus his concessive "nec maior Achille" (2.8.13) is a significant understatement. That he feels at liberty to entertain such a comparison to Achilles is ludicrous.

Yet the elegies that immediately follow emphasize epic sexual bravado: "non erat in curas una puella satis?" (2.10.12). Since there appears to be more than one *puella* to worry about, the sexuality denied the *desultor* in book 1 now cascades on him (if he can be believed). Apparently there is at least one other woman involved besides Corinna and Cypassis. Sleeping alone should befall one's enemies; may they sleep alone: "hostibus eueniat uiduo dormire cubili" (17). Like the *magister* of the *Ars,* the lover's technique is one to be imitated, even trumpeted about:

> decepta est opera nulla puella mea;
> saepe ego lasciue consumpsi tempora noctis,
>   utilis et forti corpore mane fui.
>
>   (26–28)

[no girl has been disappointed in my technique; often I have consumed the night lasciviously, and have been hale and hearty in the morning.]

Regardless of the metrical exigency that his pentameter demands, Ovid makes us wait for his speaker's "nulla" in the first line. Perhaps "decepta" is a pun. No girl is disappointed in his "opera"; no girl is deceived by them either, which we know to be blatantly untrue. And, as is the case with the *magister* (cf. *AA* 2.497), the word *lasciue* clings to the lover like smoke.

6

Like *Amores* 1.3–1.8, Ovid intends elegies 2.12, 2.13, and 2.14 to function as a thematic cluster. We can watch the lover's psychology develop. He finds himself embroiled in what John Donne will later call "Loves Warre":

> Here lett mee warr; in these armes lett mee lye;
> Here lett mee parlee, batter, bleede, and dye.
>
> (*Elegies* 20.29–30)[36]

Ovid allows his lover to boast of his sexual prowess, then he undercuts him. In this case, the reversal, or "coda," signals the descent into self-loathing and self-abasement. *Amores* 2.12 reflects the lover's narcissism. He congratulates himself for the conquest of Corinna; in fact, the poem might as well be subtitled *Corinna concubita,* because the language of triumph and captivity that marches throughout the *Amores* peaks here:

> uicimus; in nostro est ecce Corinna sinu,
> quam uir, quam custos, quam ianua firma (tot hostes!)
> seruabant, ne qua posset ab arte capi.
>
> (2–4)

[I have conquered; behold Corinna in my embrace, whom husband, keeper, and closed doors (so many enemies!) have guarded.]

The lover's early declaration "nuda simplicitas purpureusque pudor" (1.3.14) sounds especially hollow now. If modesty was necessary or if ingenuousness was an ideal, the lover has dissipated both, as he had intimated he would from the first. Despite his seeming joy in his mistress and her embraces, he shows us that he is not "happy" at all. Actually, the elegy reveals a bitter undercurrent in its tone of exultation. Corinna could be anyone, as long as she was difficult to procure, or to collect. The lover crows over his ingenuity in conquering his "hostes"—husband, ianitor, closed doors:

---

36. My quotations from Donne are from *The Complete English Poems of John Donne,* ed. C.A. Patrides (London: Dent, 1985).

at mea seposita est et ab omni milite dissors
gloria, nec titulum muneris alter habet

(2.12.11–12)

[but my glory is different from any other soldier's: no other holds the title of this prize]

Corinna is dehumanized here as elsewhere; she is a prize, something monetary, a thing. The elegy is a paean to self-love. How impressed with himself the *desultor* is! *Amores* 2.12 ends with the image of Cupid urging him to bear his standards "sine caede" (27), or without bloodshed, in love's war. What makes this fit of boasting singular is the severity of the coming reversal.[37]

The next two elegies reveal that the *bellum amoris* is not "sine caede." Corinna has shed her own blood in an attempted abortion. In keeping with the lover's vituperative insensitivity, he berates Corinna for killing *his* child. Regardless of the concern expressed for her life, he thinks his anger hath a privilege: "ira digna mea" (2.13.4). His second impulse is to ascertain whether or not the child she has attempted to abort is his: "sed tamen aut ex me conceperat, aut ego credo" (5). The lover's high moral tone is quite ironic here, since he has no thunderhead of *mores sine crimine* from which to throw *fulmina*.

The *desultor* never clarifies whether the abortion was accomplished, but he reveals himself as so insensitive and unsympathetic that the outcome of Corinna's action hardly matters. In 2.14, he suggests that Corinna's only reason for probing her entrails was to prevent stretch marks (7), and then he proceeds to lambaste her. Clearly Corinna did not want to be pregnant—certainly not with the child of the lover. What also seems apparent is that Corinna's act is one of repudiation, a disavowal of the relationship itself.

If Ovid has made this discrepancy between his persona's self-image and reality so blatant to us, it must be more blatant still to the Corinna who inhabits the fictive world of the *Amores*. Few women in any age would keep a lover of such deficiency, one who lies, gossips, bothers the help, sleeps with one's maid, threatens to reveal the affair to one's husband, begs and whines for sex, is physically abusive, boasts, depersonalizes, impreg-

---

37. This military boasting will redound on him later as he laments his lack of amatory success: "nos odimus arma" (3.2.49). See also Mary-Kay Gamel, "'Non sine caede': Abortion Politics and Poetics in Ovid's *Amores*," *Helios*, n.s., 16 (1989): 183–206.

nates, and always, always, always *blames*. Fewer still would keep a lover who refuses to bear any responsibility for the guilt with which he attempts to saddle Corinna, and his parting words constitute another indignity. He has been harsh enough, he implies, but the gods will punish similar immorality: "satis est: poenam culpa secunda ferat" (2.14.44). If Corinna is as shallow and as capricious as the lover claims, she will certainly not stay around for this sort of self-righteous abuse. Nor does she.

Two elegies at the end of book 2, 17 and 18, reveal the lover's sense of defeat and signify his preparation for his farewell to Corinna. Read by themselves, they might provoke empathy for a man who finds himself conquered by his love for a woman who defies consistency. Yet set in context with the rest of the *Amores,* especially the "abortion cluster" that precedes them, 2.17 and 2.18 may make him sound contemptible:

> Si quis erit, qui turpe putet seruire puellae,
>   illo conuincar iudice turpis ego.

(2.17.1–2)

> [If anyone judges it base to serve a girl, let me be convicted as base in such a judgment.]

The high moral tone of 2.14 has vanished. Instead, the lover vanishes into a pit of self-loathing from which he is never to emerge. He is his mistress' thrall, base and servile, subordinated to his own lust. He feels debased because he cannot free his mind from one who treats him with disdain:

> dat facies animos: facie uiolenta Corinna est;
>   me miserum, cur est tam bene nota sibi?

(2.17.7–8)

> [beauty provides spirit: Corinna is violent in her beauty; miserable me, why does she know this so well?]

Her beauty makes her haughty toward him. Although he asks why Corinna is cognizant of her effect on him, he has spent most of the *Amores* explaining why her hard-earned power over him is her only defense against his deceitfulness. So he is truly the foolish *vir* of 1.4, except without any of the legal recourse of a husband. She can control him with the sexual power with which he has endowed her:

implicuitque suos circum mea colla lacertos
et, quae me perdunt, oscula mille dedit.
uincor

(2.18.9–11)

[she wrapped her arms around my neck and gave me a thousand kisses,
which destroyed me. I'm conquered]

The lover begs for pity, but what reason should we find to pity him? He has
sought a loose bond with Corinna: shallow, impersonal, sexually oriented,
one without emotional consequences for at least one partner. One might
say that he has been supremely unlucky, only because he has attained
exactly the relationship he desired, with one exception: the "wrong" person (Corinna) now enjoys the lack of emotional consequences. Ovid
devotes the rest of the *Amores* to a series of reflections on this theme, one
in which the lover discovers, to some extent, who he is and what he is not.

7

Commentators often discuss *Amores* 2.19 and 3.4 together, but as diamet-
ric opposites, for fairly obvious reasons. In the first elegy, the speaker
warns the *vir* that unless he strengthens his marital control over his wife,
the speaker's attentions will cease; in the second, the speaker tells the same
husband that such strictness will only make the wife's desire for illicit sex
more intense. It is also evident that the woman in question is not Corinna,
but a *femina nova* (2.19.19), although Corinna's name is mentioned and
her spirit lurks throughout.

Peter Green argues that 2.19 and 3.4, despite their opposing rhetorical
stances, function together quite well as commentary on the speaker's state
of mind, much as 2.7 and 2.8 do. The lover's outward mendacity is bound-
less, and he reveals himself and his methods most conclusively. In arguing
against the idea of naive contradiction, Green suggests that 2.19 and 3.4
"emphasize . . . the excitement of deprivation, the boredom of free indul-
gence," and that the speaker dislikes husbands who are overly restrictive
or indifferent and who thus "spoil the fun by refusing to take on the roles
conceived for them."[38]

---

38. *Ovid,* 316, 309.

Strangely, however, it is here that Green objects most strongly to the idea of a persona in the *Amores*. "Ovid is *homo ludens* in person: we do his character less than justice if we reduce its varied literary manifestations to a mere bundle of masks."[39] I object on a number of grounds. Ovid's very nature as *homo ludens* is embodied, quite self-consciously, in his personae. This "mere bundle of masks" constitutes his "literary manifestations." In fact, as Ovid himself argues in the passage from the *Tristia* that began this discussion, these masks allow his literary consciousness to manifest itself, particularly in *Amores* 2.19 and 3.4.

The only "character" that need concern us is the one who speaks to us in the *Amores* and is consistently inconsistent. *Amores* 2.19 and 3.4 distinguish themselves for their relative candor concerning such dubiety. Forbidden passion waxes in intensity because of its very illicitness:

> indignere licet, iuuat inconcessa uoluptas:
> sola placet, "timeo" dicere si qua potest.

> (3.4.31–32)

[you're free to be angry, but forbidden pleasure brings happiness: she is only happy if she is able to say, "I'm afraid."]

Yet satisfaction wanes because of the mutability of the liaison. The challenge of a seduction made difficult by circumstances, forbidden, "inconcessa," is the speaker's single pleasure, which is why he would seduce Cypassis, deny it to Corinna, and then blackmail more sex from Cypassis under her mistress' nose (2.7, 2.8). Although the two elegies in question constitute conflicting (if disingenuous) directives, both only heighten the husband's awareness of the lover's presence and hence the lover's importance as someone to be reckoned with.

To some extent, this attitude of self-importance accounts for the allusions to Danae and Jupiter in these two poems (2.19.27–28, 3.4.21) and elsewhere. Fittingly, the same allusion strengthens both arguments, as contradictory as they may seem. Danae epitomizes a woman who needs to be watched yet whose desire for unfaithfulness will increase if she is watched overzealously. In keeping with the speaker's megalomania, he dares to imagine himself as Jupiter—who never had to beg a eunuch for

---

39. Ibid., 309. The term *homo ludens* is Johan Huizinga's. See *Homo Ludens: A Study of the Play Element in Culture,* trans. George Steiner (London: Paladin, 1970).

entry. Most important, the idea of a young woman impregnated by a shower of gold cascading into her lap implicitly communicates certain cynical attitudes about money, sex, and women that are expressed more explicitly elsewhere in the *Amores*.[40] This *femina nova* will birth no Perseus; she may, like Corinna, abort all traces of her "Jupiter" if the need arises.

As the persona posits two lies to the husband to make his wife a bit easier to seduce, he expresses a kind of truth about himself. He flees what follows him, yet he follows what flees him: "quod sequitur, fugio; quod fugit, ipse sequor" (2.19.36). Surely we have known this all along. Although the phrase is intended to make the *vir* guard his wife more vigorously so that seducing her will be more stimulating, it epitomizes the speaker's mind-set, the theme with which he commences this elegy. What is lawful is unsought, but what is illegal entices more keenly: "quod licet, ingratum est; quod non licet, acrius urit" (2.19.3).

For the *desultor,* such a concept as "licet" is merely an obstacle to be overcome. If there were no obstacle, he should have to invent one, and if it were not challenging enough, he should become bored and have to invent another. Thus, in attempting to make himself sound trustworthy to the *vir,* he underscores his unreliability to the reader. This paradox also informs the companion poem, where the lover argues the opposite point. His object of conquest, he suggests, is equally fickle. She will only do something if it is forbidden to her: "quae, quia non liceat, non facit, illa facit" (3.4.4). In her fine disregard for "licet," she would seem to be a perfect companion. However, which statements can be true? Perhaps only those that clearly delineate the lover's enjoyment of pain. Hence, the suffering inherent in maintaining such a relationship rings truest, reminiscent of the admission of the *magister* in the *Ars:* "en ego, confiteor, non nisi laesus amo" (3.598). Love is pain, and pain is happiness. The statement concerning the wife's fickleness, intended as untruth to deceive the husband, foreshadows the contemptuous attitude of the *femina nova* toward the speaker throughout book 3. Like Corinna in book 2, she will see him as a husband to be cuckolded.

The *desultor* modulates his address from the *vir* to his wife and "others" in these two elegies. As part of his argument to the husband, he explains that the threat of infidelity is yet another aphrodisiac:

---

40. In the *Eunuchus,* Terence uses the same image for comic effect (589). See Augustine's scathing condemnation of the fable in *Confessions* 1.16. Oddly enough, Ovid does not describe the incident graphically in the *Metamorphoses.*

> quo mihi fortunam, quae numquam fallere curet?
>   nil ego, quod nullo tempore laedat, amo.
> uiderat hoc in me uitium uersuta Corinna,
>   quaque capi possem, callida norat opem.

(2.19.7–10)

[what good is Fortune if she never deceives me? I cannot love something that never hurts me. Crafty Corinna saw this flaw in me, and knew that I could be captured by false hope.]

The lover explains that a woman who never hurts him provides precious little excitement. He enjoys deception, whether he practices it or it is practiced against him. In fact, Corinna (who now occupies the past tense) used it as bait. In a rhetorical formation nearly identical to 2.19.7 in the companion poem, "quo tibi formosam, si non nisi casta placebat?" (3.4.41), the speaker posits a shopworn dichotomy: why pick a beauty if you wanted her to be faithful? In defending himself, he cynically indicts the character of his new woman. And, by the similarity of the construction, Ovid links the lover's sense of *fortuna* and the husband's sense of his wife's beauty; these are, of course, carefully linked in the lover's mind. Although this phase of argument purports to trick the husband, it also seems to serve as the lover's defense against being patronized as a bachelor cuckold and as his assurance to us that being so patronized does not affect him. His pose is unconvincing, because he has scarcely more success with his new mistress, who must be trained to be loved: "daque nouae mentem dominae, patiatur amari" (3.2.57).

One of the more remarkable statements in 2.19 is the lover's bravura conclusion in his warning to the husband:

> iamque ego praemoneo: nisi tu seruare puellam
>   incipis, incipiet desinere esse mea.

(2.19.47–48)

[and now I must warn you: unless you begin to guard your girl, she'll begin to cease to be mine.]

As ridiculous as this may sound, it makes perfect sense in the mind of the lover, where adultery is a kind of virtue. The rhetorical posture of addressing the husband whose wife the lover is attempting to seduce, and even the pseudomilitary verb *seruare* (i.e., to guard, defend, serve), are inherited from Tibullus:

> at tu, fallacis coniunx incaute puellae,
>   me quoque *servato,* peccet ut illa nihil.
> . . . .
>   tua si bona nescis
> *servare* frustra clavis inest foribus!
>
> (Tibullus 1.6.15–16; 33–34; my emphasis)[41]

[but you, careless husband of a deceitful girl, guard me as well, so that she will not be unchaste. . . . if you cannot guard your own good things, the key in the door is useless!]

In the first passage, Tibullus desires to keep Delia, the *puella fallax,* "chaste" for himself, and thus he debases the *coniunx* by ordering him to perform this Ianitor-like function. The second passage stresses the impossibility of keeping Delia from unchastity in any sense, and it reinforces the necessity of monitoring her behavior for the lover's sake. To Tibullus, this idea is ancillary to his elegy, but Ovid makes this concept central to his lover's psychology:

> nec corpus seruare potes, licet omnia claudas:
>   omnibus occlusis intus adulter erit.
> cui peccare licet, peccat minus: ipsa potestas
>   semina nequitiae languidiora facit.
>
> (3.4.7–10)

[you'll be unable to guard her body, although you may close all doors: the adulterer will be within, with everything closed up. For whom it's permissible to sin, she'll sin less: this power makes the seeds of sin more languid.]

Although Ovid's speaker seems to purvey the same good-natured effrontery in such commentary as does Tibullus, his conception of himself and the current object of his quest become more global: everyone desires to sin,

---

41. The text is quoted from *Tibullus: A Commentary,* ed. Michael C.J. Putnam (Norman: University of Oklahoma Press, 1979), 27. The translation is mine.

but only if the sin has consequences. One cannot guard any woman; therefore, one ought not to bother. The triumphant use of *seruare* (2.12.4) is now reversed. Yet once again, such worldliness is also a pose. The *desultor* is no more comfortable with such élan than the husband whom he attempts to gull, as book 3 of the *Amores* demonstrates.

8

Throughout the *Amores,* the pronouncements of the *desultor* erode as subsequent events redound on him, and he is buried in a veritable avalanche of reversals. As late as the last elegy of book 2, he still advises, *magister-*like, on the art of trickery. She who would rule her lover for any length of time should delude him: "si qua uolet regnare diu, deludat amantem" (2.19.33). In one of the many perplexing ironies that support the infrastructure of the *Amores,* the *desultor* boasts ceaselessly about his efficacy in deception, although his deceit has provided little benefit to him. In fact, Corinna and the *femina nova* reign over him with the sort of trickery he himself has tried to employ.

Similarly, the speaker affects the pose of superior knowledge in his relationship with Corinna. Because of him, she has learned to deceive her keeper: "per me decepto didicit custode Corinna" (3.1.49). He even uses the language of the *Ars* ("didicit") and boasts about what he has taught his capricious mistress. Yet what has this profited him? He now describes her in the third person and uses the past tense. The lover has only taught Corinna how to leave him. The same principle applies to the *femina nova:*

Esse deos, i, crede: fidem iurata fefellit,
    et facies illi quae fuit ante manet.

(3.3.1–2)

[Go and believe that the gods exist: she who has pledged her faith has been deceitful, though her beauty remains as it was before.]

He is immensely satisfied with his skills in teaching the art of deception, yet he is shocked and dismayed when his new mistress uses such art against him. He has also discovered, contra 1.10, that a woman's behavior does not affect her beauty. Therefore, such pronouncements as the one in 2.19 simply confirm that he has succeeded in deluding himself. All he can say is

"Spare my eyes": "oculis certe parce, puella, meis" (3.3.48). He now epitomizes the flaccidity that he has despised all along.

Ovid graphically symbolizes such limpidity in 3.7. His speaker devotes this elegy to his impotence, and comedy is operative on two fronts. The speaker admits his inadequacy, but then, true to form, he attempts to blame it on someone or something besides himself, wildly and unconvincingly:

> exigere a nobis angusta nocte Corinnam,
>   me memini numeros sustinuisse nouem.
>
> (3.7.25–26)

> [I can remember when Corinna demanded that I satisfy her nine times in one short night.]

In a passage that recalls Catullus' plea to Ipsitilla ("nouem continuas futu-tiones," 32.8), Ovid's lover recalls a time when his services were required and tendered ninefold. But there is no such occurrence in the *Amores,* and furthermore, Corinna is no more. The lover has failed now with a new woman, and his failure to perform has had two discernible results. The first is that he is alone, a condition he seems to dread. The second is that he has been replaced:

> ecce recens diues parto per uulnera censu
>   praefertur nobis sanguine pastus eques.
>
> (3.8.9–10)

> [behold, a knight recently made rich, gorged on blood, is preferred to me.]

This is a fate that he dreads more, but one that his behavior has predicted, even necessitated. Worse, he has been supplanted by a nouveau-riche soldier, one who is even more a parvenu than he but who leaves the side of the *femina nova* in a state of sexual exhaustion that the speaker desires but never attains (3.11.13–14), regardless of the tentative success implied in book 2.

Amores 3.11 and 3.14 constitute the last cluster, the speaker's farewell to love. He attempts no grand conclusions but hints that he may have learned something:

Multa diuque tuli; uitiis patientia uicta est:
cede fatigato pectore, turpis amor.

(3.11.1–2)

[I have borne many things for a long time; patience is conquered by
vice: base love, leave my wearied breast.]

He has borne much, victimized by a base love that exhausts the heart. He
blames the object of his lust, whose *vitia* lead him captive in the same way
that Amor conquers his modesty and conscience in 1.2. So, he has learned
that Amor can be "turpis," and that beauty admits no discourse to honesty:

Non ego, ne pecces, cum sis formosa, recuso,
sed ne sit misero scire necesse mihi

(3.14.1–2)

[Since you're so beautiful, I don't ask that you don't sin, only that I'm
not forced to know about it]

Accordingly, love has made him "turpis," one who cannot check his mistress' excesses and who must beg her to keep him ignorant of them. In his
subtle yet constant comparisons of this *femina nova* to Corinna, the
speaker suggests that the former is afflicted with a gracelessness that the
latter is not. *Quod erat demonstrandum:* all women are not the same.

Eventually, Ovid's speaker admits, "non ego sum stultus, ut ante fui"
(3.11.32). He has been a fool. However, what precisely is he less *stultus*
about? How is he less a fool? Perhaps he is less ignorant about himself and
his own capriciousness, which would constitute a type of self-knowledge:

hac amor, hac odium; sed, puto, vincit amor.
odero, si potero; si non, invitus amabo.
nec iuga taurus amat; quae tamen odit, habet.

(3.11b.34–36)

[here's love, here's hate; but, I think, love conquers. I'll hate if I'm able;
if not, I'll love unwillingly. The bull doesn't love the yoke; yet he
endures what he hates.]

Here, perhaps, is the best case for renaming the *Amores* the *Odia.* Now that the lover has become the cuckolded bachelor *vir* he has dreaded metamorphosing into, love is not a desirable state. It is, in fact, less preferable than its corresponding state, hate. A lover is vulnerable, exposed, a yoked bull. If love can be said to conquer, it only conquers partially and hesitantly. Since the speaker cannot decide whether he is lover or hater, all that remains to him is desire, timeless and irremediable—"similar to an endless movement, an ever new beginning or, perhaps, a series of new beginnings, where each is more startlingly new than the previous one."[42]

9

Again, as the speaker bids love farewell, he begs his mistress to spare him further embarrassment, even if she has no regard for her own reputation: "si dubitas famae parcere, parce mihi" (3.14.36). The key term, *fama,* is important for a motif that underlies the *Amores* and the persona who narrates them: poetic immortality. The sequence has dramatized the psychology of a lover who keenly desires to be a famous poet and who compresses his reflections into elegiacs. This lust for fame informs virtually every elegy and accompanies the speaker's more recognizable lust for women. He enjoys public recognition or at least deludes himself into thinking that he has attained it: "aliquis . . . ait 'hic, hic est, quem ferus urit Amor'" (3.1.19–20). Ovid pumps his speaker full of egotism. He seeks, but has not earned the right to claim, as "Ovid himself" does at the end of the *Metamorphoses,* "iamque opus exegi" (15.871).

Like the ethereal ladies who later inhabit the sequences of Renaissance sonneteers, Corinna has no reason to exist except as fodder for elegiacs. She is subject and object, *materia.* Although poetic immortality would be an honor for a mortal person, such a promise is a strange mode of seduction:

te mihi materiem felicem in carmina praebe:
prouenient causa carmina digna sua.

(*Amores* 1.3.19–20)

---

42. Luck, *The Latin Love Elegy,* 164.

[let yourself be fertile material for my poetry; my poetry will then grow
worthy of its inspiration.]

Far from complimentary, the statement foretells a bloodless and transactional relationship, not unlike the one to come with Cypassis in book 2. If
Corinna offers herself as material, the speaker's poetry will rise to her
worth. Or perhaps the woman whom he desires will rise to the worth of his
poetry: "quam uolui, nota fit arte mea" (1.10.60). This is a backhanded
compliment, indeed. The lover's clumsiness, even gaucheness, overflows
the measure. A love poet usually hopes to get his mistress' favors by the act
of devoting poetry to her or by pretending to such devotion. He ought not
offer verses as bait, like a pretty bracelet. Needless to say, this dissipates
the illusion of sincerity. Furthermore, his ensuing mythological catalog in
1.3 of women who have been raped is dubious company for Corinna, or
any woman, to find herself in. The speaker's real interest throughout is
poetic immortality. He seeks the perennial fame that will make him cele-
brated throughout the world as the glory of his homeland: "mihi fama
perennis / quaeritur, in toto semper ut orbe canar" (1.15.7–8); "Paelignae
dicar gloria gentis ego" (3.15.8).

Such egotism is as prevalent in the *Amores* as the lover's constant boasting about his sexual prowess. However, that he must repeat these arguments to the women he attempts to seduce is part of the ironic distance
that Ovid keeps from his persona. His amatory strategy does not work:

> et multae per me nomen habere uolunt:
> noui aliquam, quae se circumferat esse Corinnam;
>   ut fiat, quid non illa dedisse uelit?

(2.17.28–30)

[many women wish to gain fame through me: I know of one who tells
everyone she is Corinna. What wouldn't she have done to make it come
true?]

The speaker uses the same argument on the *femina nova* here as he does on
Corinna elsewhere. If other women seek a name through his poetry, and if
another claims that she is the Corinna sung in his *carmina*, why should this
woman not desire the same fame? Ovid's silent answer is simple, one that
never dawns on his persona. Perhaps most women would be thrilled to be
made immortal in verse, as long as their abortions, failed hair-dyeing, and

adulteries did not live forever, as Corinna's have. The new mistress has no desire for such fame, to be prostitute to genius: "ingenio prostitit illa meo" (3.12.8). If she has listened to the poet's vituperation against Corinna, she probably wishes to avoid this as well.

So, this gambit has also redounded on the lover. He has used women to immortalize himself, but in a way that confers no dignity:

> mea debuerat falso laudata uideri
> femina; credulitas nunc mihi uestra nocet.
>
> (3.12.43–44)

[my woman ought to seem to be praised falsely; your credulity has harmed me.]

We are now to believe that all praise for his women should be discounted. Yet why should we accept this directive more than any other? Because of the "accelerating process of involuntary self-revelation,"[43] our "credulitas" has dissipated; we have known all along what the speaker tentatively admits here: he is a liar.

In *Chaucer and Ovid,* John M. Fyler asserts, "Of all Ovid's legacies to later medieval poetry, probably the most important is his self-conscious, obtrusive narrator, who refuses to be a clear medium for the poem he recites."[44] This legacy of the narrator, especially that of the *Amores,* helps medieval and Renaissance poets invent the concept of persona for their own poetics. In their imitation and subversion of Ovid, they reprocess and reanimate him for their own time. Yet this medievalization of the *desultor* was necessarily controlled by the availability of the *Amores* in the early Middle Ages. Only then could poets process and pass on the elegiac topoi that would develop into the conventions of *fin' Amors: ianitores,* love's war, the speaker who undercuts himself, perhaps even the idea of sequence. Essentially, Ovid's poetry was seen as a paradigm that encouraged its own subversion.

---

43. This is Verducci's phrase to describe Hypsipyle's epistle to Jason (*Her.* 6). See *Ovid's Toyshop,* 63. The concept applies equally well to the *desultor.*

44. *Chaucer and Ovid,* 19.

CHAPTER 2

Ovidius sine titulo: The *desultor Amoris* before 1100

Distat autem hoc opus ab opere artis amatorie, quia in arte amatoria dat precepta. In hoc opere ludicra tractat et iocosa. Intentio sua est quedam de amoribus suis iocose exponere. Causa intentionis duplex est: vel ut delectet vel ut prosit. Vnde Oratius: *Aut prodesse volunt* et cetera. Vtilitas est delectio uel apud Corinnam sui ipsius conmendatio. Ad ethicam spectat quia de moribus suis loquendo succubarum, ancillarum, iuuenum et puellarum, riualium, maritorum et etiam lenonum mores insinuat . . . .Contigit a longe tempore post artis amatorie tradicionem, opus artis amatorie ab Augusto dampnari et a publico armario reici. Poete vero timentes librum amorum amittere, titulum deleuerunt, et ita liber iste caruit titulo.[1]

[Moreover, this work [the *Amores*] differs from the work of the *Ars amatoria,* because in the *Ars amatoria,* [Ovid] bestows precepts. In this work [the *Amores*] he treats ludicrous and jocose matters. His intention is to relate certain things about his love affairs in a humorous way. The

---

1. Cited from Hexter, *Ovid and Medieval Schooling,* 224. The translation here is my own, as is the case throughout this chapter, unless otherwise noted. For comparison's sake, here is another *accessus* on the *Amores* with a different twist, translated by A.J. Minnis: "In his *On the Art of Love* Ovid gives certain precepts to lovers to put them on their guard. But here, in the *Amores,* he puts these precepts into practise in his own case. The reason why this book [i.e. the *Amores*] has no title must be understood as follows. Before he wrote it, he had written *On the Art of Love* and had made adultresses of almost all the married women and maidens. This had made the Romans hostile towards him, and so, in case this book should incur even greater disfavour, he did not give it a title, and we readers call it Ovid's *Book without a Title.*" See A.J. Minnis and A.B. Scott, eds., *Medieval Literary Theory and Criticism, c. 1100–c. 1375: The Commentary Tradition,* rev. ed. (Oxford: Clarendon Press, 1991), 28. It should be noted that no commentator refers to the *liber sine titulo* as the *Amores.*

motivation of his intention is twofold: either that he may delight or that
he may be useful. Hence Horace, "[Poets] either wish to be useful," etc.
[*Ars Poetica* 333]. The utility is pleasure or praise of himself in the eyes
of Corinna. He attends to ethics because according to his practices he
introduces morals in speaking of assignations, maids, boys and girls,
rivals, husbands, and even of pimps. . . . It happened that a long time
after the composition of the *Ars amatoria,* this work was condemned by
Augustus and cast out of the public library. The poets, truly fearing to
lose the book of *Amores,* deleted the title, and therefore this book was
without a title.]

The manuscript *clm* (*codex latinus monacensis*) 631, compiled between
1100 and 1400 and now housed at the Bayerische Staatsbibliothek,
Munich, is a diverse collection of Latin texts and quotations from classical
and medieval authors. In it are these excerpts from an *accessus,* or preface,
to the *Amores.* They may tempt us to generalize about medieval hermeneutics concerning this work and others, since some of these strategies have
passed down to us unaltered. Many modern readers also see the *Amores*
and the *Ars* as interrelated, associate Corinna with Ovid, and imply that
the author documented a real-life adulterous love affair. Such readers
seem to have inherited John of Garland's thirteenth-century appreciation
of Ovid's elegiac comedy, which he classifies as *comoedia,* a versified comic
tale. At the same time, some moderns dismiss the sequence as light fare
precisely because it is comic.[2]

There is a minor difference between this particular medieval view of
Ovid and the modern view: the *clm* 631 commentator thinks that the *Ars*
predates the *Amores,* and that Ovid intended his love poems to complement the *precepta* that the *Ars* narrator offers to his readers; moderns
think that the *Amores* were written first, since the *Ars* mentions them
(3.343). Moderns refer to them as early work, even juvenilia, as if Ovid

---

2. For John of Garland's comment on *comoedia* and Ovid, see F.J.E. Raby, *A History of
Secular Latin Poetry in the Middle Ages,* 2 vols. (Oxford: Oxford University Press, 1957),
2:54. For an amusing misreading of Ovid and his intentions, see Grant Showerman's preface
to the Loeb edition of *Heroides and Amores* (1914), which G.P. Goold, the editor of the second edition of that text (Cambridge: Harvard University Press, 1986) puckishly reprints:
"The reader will not look to the *Amores* for profundity of any sort, whether of thought or
emotion. . . . It is exactly this absence of the serious that gives the *Amores* their peculiar charm
. . . here and there [they] display offences against even a liberal taste. The translator has felt
obliged to omit one poem entire, and to omit or disguise a few verses in other poems where,
in spite of the poet's exquisite art, a faithful rendering might offend the sensibilities of the
reader, if not the literary taste" (316–17).

were self-consciously preparing himself for a poetic career, like Mr. Pope or Lord Tennyson. Yet the medieval commentator includes his own bit of mythmaking to demonstrate that the *Ars* predates the love poems. The *Amores* were known interchangeably as *Ovidius sine titulo, liber sine titulo,* or *de sine titulo,* because of Ovid's well-known persecution by the emperor over the *Ars.* His fellow poets did not want the *Amores* lost or censored, so they gelded the title.

However, as the *clm* 631 commentator distinguishes the *Amores* from the *Ars* more sharply, his hermeneutics seem quite medieval in comparison with our own, because he was forced to entertain a question that would not trouble a modern critic. How is one to justify the study of pagan texts in a Christian society, texts that an authority as venerable as Augustine would surely condemn? As an answer, the commentator may have kept in mind Tertullian's question: "Quomodo repudiamus saecularia studia, sine quibus divina non possunt?"[3] Since secular study made divine study possible, one ought not repudiate the former—instead, one should justify secular study by reading ethically.

Therefore, the commentator suggests one do just this with the *Amores,* to which he applies the familiar medievalized Horatian formula, reminiscent of the four causes (efficient, formal, material, final) in what A.J. Minnis calls the "Aristotelian prologue": *materia, intentio, utilitas, ethice.*[4] *Ovidius mores insinuat,* even when discussing pimps and assignations. Such schematization may seem fantastic. Yet there is no particular condemnation of fornication or adultery in the excerpts, nor is there the allegorizing or bowdlerization that a modern might expect from a medieval interpreter of an erotic classical poet. The moralizing is subtle and not altogether specious, with a peculiarly modern twist: a quiet emphasis on the pleasure and enjoyment that a reader might gain from Ovid's work.

Nevertheless, the postmodern reader may note with disappointment that Ovid's medieval commentator does not cherish what many now believe *ought* to be cherished. There is no notion of the *Amores* as sequence, nor is there any consideration of their protean narrative voice, the persona. Such concepts may have been unknown to our *magister* or too sophisticated for his audience of schoolboys, who were blundering through their Latin. Some medievalists assure us that the twelfth century

---

3. Raby, *A History of Christian Latin Poetry from the Beginnings to the Close of the Middle Ages,* 2d ed. (Oxford: Oxford University Press, 1953), 6.

4. *Medieval Theory of Authorship: Scholastic Literary Attitudes in the Later Middle Ages,* 2d ed. (Philadelphia: University of Pennsylvania Press, 1988), 28–29.

had no conception of "the individual,"[5] which would surely nullify the existence of the literary persona, in Ovid or elsewhere. Others cite medieval evidence to the contrary concerning both the idea of the individual and, by implication, the persona. These too could have been inherited from antiquity and transmitted by schoolmasters.[6]

Whether these schoolmasters in turn fomented a medieval Ovidian poetics remains unclear. Yet commentators who produced *accessus* and presided over the compilation of *libri manuales* (schoolbook anthologies) such as *clm* 631 must have taught poets about Ovid and how to read him. Medieval poets surely imbibed the *Amores* and *Ars* in some fashion and then reprocessed such texts in their own poetry, perhaps through the process of "dialectical *imitatio*," as Thomas M. Greene describes it, a poetics that is at once reverential and competitive.[7] Ovid seems to have

---

5. Two noted scholars who dismiss the idea that twelfth-century people possessed a conception of "the individual" are Caroline Walker Bynum, "Did the Twelfth Century Discover the Individual?" in *Jesus as Mother: Studies in the Spirituality of the High Middle Ages* (Berkeley: University of California Press, 1982), 82–109; John F. Benton, "Consciousness of Self and Perceptions of Individuality," *Renaissance and Renewal in the Twelfth Century*, eds. Robert L. Benson and Giles Constable (Cambridge: Harvard University Press, 1982), 263–95. To Benton, the twelfth century "was not a time of the 'discovery of the individual' . . . there did occur, however, a renewed commitment to the examination and a development of modes of thought about the self and others which have profoundly affected our civilization" (264).

6. Colin Morris is the leading proponent of the theory that the twelfth century knew what an "individual" was; it is his theory that Bynum and Benton attack. See *The Discovery of the Individual: 1050–1200* (Toronto: University of Toronto Press, 1972). Direct literary support for Morris is provided by no less an authority than Robert W. Hanning, in *The Individual in Twelfth-Century Romance* (New Haven: Yale University Press, 1977). The genesis for such literary thinking was no doubt the historian R.W. Southern, who argues that the twelfth century saw "the emergence of the individual from his communal background." See his monumental *The Making of the Middle Ages* (New Haven: Yale University Press, 1953), 221.

I think that the medieval inheritance of the idea of the literary persona indirectly supports Morris' thesis. For the voluminous literature on the medieval conception of persona, see the following works and the bibliographies imbedded in their endnotes: Thomas M. Greene, *The Light in Troy;* Gerald Bond, "*Iocus amoris*" and "Composing Yourself."

7. In *The Light in Troy*, Greene's "four types of strategies of humanist imitation" (38) are as follows: "*reproductive* or *sacramental*," which "celebrates an enshrined primary text by rehearsing it liturgically" (38); "*eclectic* or *exploitative*," which "treats all traditions as stockpiles to be drawn upon ostensibly at random" (39); "*heuristic*," which "advertis[es]" its "derivation from the subtexts" and then shows distance from such subtexts (40), essentially a poetics of "imitative discovery" (198); and "*dialectical*," a more competitive and aggressive form of the heuristic model that sometimes borders on parody (45–46). Although Greene's term *humanist* implies that these types of *imitatio* (especially the latter two) are a Renaissance phenomenon, many other critics have used his concepts, especially the "dialectical," to explain medieval imitation as well. See Robert W. Hanning, "Courtly Contexts for Urban

spawned a medieval taste for elegies of love and exile and their worldly ironies, as well as a poetic consciousness of the narrative ego and its possibilities. There are enough medieval love treatises for which to blame the *Ars*. Ovid's tableaux of courtship and adultery in the *Amores* seem to have been responsible for many of the "courtly" conceptions of love in the Middle Ages, since they surface in lyric and narrative form. Wounded by Amor, Ovid hunts Corinna; in the throes of *fin' Amors,* Bernart and his fellows pursue the elusive *midons.*

1

However, before we explore the influence of the *Amores* on the love poetry of the Middle Ages, it would be useful to discuss some aspects of the "medieval Ovid." Surely one is well advised not "to tease out the threads of a secret pagan tradition running through the medieval world," but divergence from a perceived ethics and aesthetics of chilling Augustinian rationality is neither sporadic nor isolated.[8] The best evidence of this is Ovid's pervasiveness at the root of medieval culture, the schools, as the scrupulous work of E.H. Alton, E.W. Wormell, R.B.C. Huygens, James McGregor, and Ralph Hexter demonstrates conclusively. Ovid's essential role in medieval education is suggested in his appearance in the *libri manuales* and in the sheer number of commentaries and their *accessus* to his work, such as the one that begins this chapter. He was a "school author" in the fifth, sixth, eighth, and ninth centuries; his entire opus was incorporated into the French curriculum by the eleventh century.[9]

Cultus: Responses to Ovid in Chrétien's *Cligès* and Marie's *Guigemar,"* *Symposium* 35 (1981): 34–56; and Leslie Cahoon, "The Anxieties of Influence." Greene's categories are not rigid; they are somewhat interchangeable and are easily amended.

8. The quotation is from James H. McGregor, "Ovid at School: From the Ninth to the Fifteenth Century," *Classical Folia* 15 (1961): 29. D.W. Robertson is the most notable proponent of Augustine's centrality to medieval art and culture: "Medieval man, who inherited the implications of Augustine's doctrine of illumination, looked inward, not to find the roots of emotion, but to find God. The last poem of Petrarch's *Rime* [addressed to the Blessed Virgin, not Laura] is just as "sincere" and just as moving as are the early sonnets. For Petrarch it was undoubtedly the most moving of them all" (*A Preface to Chaucer: Studies in Medieval Perspectives* [Princeton: Princeton University Press, 1962], 16). For an antidote to such thinking, see Leonard Barkan, *The Gods Made Flesh.*

9. For the adaptation of Ovid into the French school curriculum, see Bond, "Composing Yourself," 85. Alton and Wormell set the groundwork with a two-part article, "Ovid in the Mediaeval Schoolroom," *Hermathena* 94 (1960): 21–38; 95 (1961): 67–82. R.B.C. Huygens' definitive edition of many *accessus* is *Accessus ad auctores* (Leiden: Brill, 1970). For an

Still, we may ask: why use Ovid in school? Hexter suggests that the answer is quite simple: the purpose of literature was held to be avowedly didactic. In fact, didactic poetry was "prized and cultivated" to an extent that seems confusing to us. Since Ovid explicitly refers to the use of exempla in the erotica, these works would have been model teaching texts for the rhetorical technique of argument by example, despite their subject matter.[10] A certain eleventh- or twelfth-century commentator is very frank indeed in his discussion of the end of *Ars amatoria* 3. Even Ovid blushes to delineate coital positions that are most pleasurable for women, but the commentator glosses one of them candidly in idiomatic Latin, without Christian moralizing: "*Parua* [*uehatur*] *equo* [*AA* 3.777]. idest ascendat amicum suum.*" Therefore, the idea that Ovid was recommended "*always* with affection and *always* with distrust" bears rethinking.[11] The idea that one can teach ethically and do justice to the spirit of the *materia* gradually gained force. In the early twelfth century, the schoolmaster Conrad of Hirsau defended Ovid because he knew of the One God; by the 1530s, Erasmus, Cardinal Wolsey, and Thomas Elyot institutionalized Ovid in English schools.[12]

I suggest some more prosaic reasons for Ovid's utility as a teaching text. His elegiac poetry (the *Heroides, Amores, Ars amatoria, Epistulae ex Ponto,* and *Tristia*) is composed in relatively "easy" Latin. Its simple diction and closed couplets may have been more fathomable to schoolboys than was Virgil's labyrinthine hexameter. Yet the Horatian model of the

---

exhaustive bibliography on the *accessus* tradition, see Minnis, *Medieval Theory of Authorship*, 294–311. Quintilian's grudging praise reads: "Lasciuus quidem in herois [i.e., hexameters] quoque Ouidius et nimium amator ingenii sui, laudandus tamen partibus" (10.1.88); "Ouidius utroque lasciuior [i.e., than Tibullus and Propertius], sicut durior Gallus" *Institutionis oratoriae,* ed. M. Winterbottom, 2 vols, (Oxford: Oxford University Press, 1970), 1:93.

10. Hexter, *Ovid and Medieval Schooling,* 20, 57. Marilynn Desmond writes, "If Ovid did not quite *embody* classical authority, his texts were nonetheless read for their wisdom, learning, and even their potential as moralized *exempla*" ("Introduction," *Mediaevalia* 13 [1989 (1987)]: 2).

11. The quotation concerning the universality with which Ovid was loved and distrusted belongs to McGregor ("Ovid at School," 30; my emphasis). For a similar formulation, see Jean Leclercq, *The Love of Learning and the Desire for God,* trans. C. Misrahi (New York: Fordham University Press, 1961), 140. The sexual position alluded to by the commentator is "the little horse," or female-superior; see Hexter, *Ovid and Medieval Schooling,* 72, 77.

12. For Conrad, see Minnis, *Medieval Literary Theory,* 56–57. For a general discussion of Ovid in Tudor and Elizabethan schools, see Caroline Jameson, "Ovid in the Sixteenth Century," in *Ovid,* ed. J.W. Binns (London: Routledge, 1973), 212. See also J.W. Binns, *Intellectual Culture in Elizabethan and Jacobean England: The Latin Writings of the Age* (Leeds: Francis Cairns, 1990), 741.

poet who "miscuit utile dulci, / lectorem delectando pariterque monendo" (*Ars poetica* 343–44) may have also informed the teaching of Ovid, as the *clm* 631 commentator's allusion to the same text suggests. It is not untoward to suggest that the boys may have learned their Latin with more vigor if the subject matter was to their liking.[13]

Nevertheless, early twentieth-century scholarship found it paradoxical that the ferociously Catholic Middle Ages admired and imitated an erotic poet of antiquity: hence we have the phrase "Ovid misunderstood," for which C.S. Lewis is so often blamed.[14] Yet subsequent research demonstrates that the paradoxes and misunderstandings exist not in the Middle Ages but in the early twentieth-century scholarship that attempted to account for the use of Ovid by medieval makers.

First, the use and imitation of source material was different from our own. We might call it plagiarism. However, Colin Morris explains that the twelfth century itself

> had not developed a critical historical sense. . . . There was no conception of the difference between Roman society and the contemporary world. . . . Since contemporaries were scarcely aware of classical writers as a phenomenon foreign to themselves, they were able to absorb easily those parts of their message which were appropriate to the new needs.[15]

Thomas M. Greene ("heuristically imitating" Gerald R. Bruns) is more specific:

> for the medieval writer, the inherited text is tacitly unfinished. . . . [Medieval] intertextuality is metonymic because the later text touches, connects with, grows out of, the earlier one. All writing enjoys a neighborly community. Thus there is no perceived threat of anachronism, . . . no itinerary from one concrete historical moment to another.[16]

---

13. Hexter writes, "Certainly the range of medieval testimonies on Ovid's erotic poetry gives one the impression that the two things medieval readers and writers liked most were to love and to learn" (*Ovid and Medieval Schooling,* 17).

14. See Lewis, *The Allegory of Love: A Study in Medieval Tradition* (Oxford: Oxford University Press, 1936; reprint, 1977), 8, 20, 43.

15. *The Discovery of the Individual,* 54, 56.

16. *The Light in Troy,* 86. Compare Bruns, "The Originality of Texts in a Manuscript Culture," *Comparative Literature* 32 (1980): 113–29.

Accordingly, those who appropriated Ovid felt a kinship with him: the twelfth century did not erect the same obstacles between itself and antiquity that we erect in the twentieth century. In Jean Leclercq's ringing declaration, "Ovid, Virgil and Horace *belonged* to these men as personal property; they were not an alien possession to which to refer and quote with reverence—and with bibliographical references."[17] This is why the *Eneas* poet can so easily continue and reconfigure the *Aeneid* as a pseudo-Ovidian chivalric romance, in which "dame Dido . . . tornot et retornot sovant" on her bed (1220–29), just as the *desultor Amoris* toils and roils on his bed in *Amores* 1.2.[18]

Second, medieval Catholic culture may have been less puritanical than our own. Ernst Robert Curtius argues that "the Middle Ages were much less prudish than the Modern Period." Joan Cadden explains that sex was widely discussed as a moral and scientific issue by authors as respected as Isidore of Seville and Constantinus Africanus, both of whom wrote about "sexual anatomy and desire" as "part of the divine plan for the perpetuation of natural kinds."[19] Naturally, then, Ovid would be an important physiological and psychological authority on this subject, eminently worth reclaiming regardless of his "immorality."[20]

Indeed, the adoption and refashioning of Ovid is evident throughout the Middle Ages in both Latin and the vernacular. In the fifth century, Martianus Capella raids the *Metamorphoses* and *Heroides* with impunity to create his neoplatonic Latin prose tract on the seven liberal arts, *De nuptiis Philologiae et Mercurii*. Within the next one hundred years, the Christian North African Fulgentius reconfigures and moralizes Ovid's mythological and erotic material completely in his *Mythologiae*. The Carolingian

---

17. *The Love of Learning*, 124.

18. J.J. Salverda de Grave, ed., *Eneas: Roman du XIIe Siècle*, 2 vols. (Paris: Champion, 1964), 1:38. In a related thought, Robert W. Hanning suggests that the monologues of Chrétien's character Enide wax Ovidian (i.e., imitate the *Heroides*). See *The Individual in Twelfth-Century Romance*, 69.

19. Curtius, *European Literature*, 50; Cadden, "Medieval Scientific and Medical Views of Sexuality: Questions of Propriety," *Medievalia et Humanistica*, n.s., 14 (1986): 157–59.

20. For Ovid as medical authority on matters of sexuality, see Peter Green, "Venus Clerke Ovid," in *Essays in Classical Antiquity* (London: Murray, 1960), 112. For information on medieval medical sexuality in general, see Helen Rodnite Lemay, *Women's Secrets: A Translation of Pseudo-Albertus Magnus' "De Secretis Mulierum" with Commentaries* (Albany: State University of New York Press, 1992), especially her bibliography. Other crucial works that delineate a more tolerant Middle Ages include Friedrich Heer, *The Medieval World*, trans. Janet Sondheimer (New York: New American Library, 1962); John Boswell, *Christianity, Social Tolerance, and Homosexuality: Gay People in Western Europe from the Beginning of the Christian Era to the Fourteenth Century* (Chicago: University of Chicago Press, 1981).

court poets Theodulf and Einhard write in elegiac couplets and echo the erotica; Alcuin quotes Ovid in the *Praecepta vivendi.*[21] The *Carmina Burana* overflows with Ovid, and twelfth-century Goliardic poets utilize him in their work. Walter Map mentions him, and the Archpoet alludes to the *Amores.*[22] Walter de Châtillon finishes seven strophes of his twenty-strophe *Missus sum in vineam* with quotations from Ovid. Many medieval Latin poems imitate the *Amores* or are imbued with the worldly wisdom of the *Ars amatoria* and *Remedia amoris,* such as the dialogue *Conqueror et doleo de te* between an *amicus* and *amica* in the late eleventh-century Spanish Ripoll manuscript, which Peter Dronke classifies as a *tenso* between Ovidian morality and *fin' Amors.*[23] The second sentence of John of Salisbury's innovative treatise on grammar and logic, the *Metalogicon,* is a paraphrase of *Epistulae ex Ponto* 3.4.74.[24] Myriad Ovidian passages inform the poetry of the troubadours and trouvères—Guillaume IX, Marcabru, and Bernart de Ventadorn foremost among them. As the philologist Wilibald Schrötter concludes: "Ovid sagt: Liebe erniedrigt. Die Troubadours sagen: Liebe veredelt."[25]

Some thirteenth-century authors, such as John of Garland in his *Integumenta Ovidii,* distill Ovid and recast him typologically.[26] The anonymous *Les echecs amoureaux* and *La clef d'amors* translate and rework the *Ars*

---

21. Raby, *Secular Latin Poetry,* 1:178–208; Jessie Crossland, "Ovid's Contribution to the Conception of Love Known as '*L'amour courtois,*'" *Modern Language Review* 42 (1947): 199.

22. There is some controversy over the Archpoet's intentions. He allegedly fuses *Amores* 2.10.38, in which the *desultor* expresses his wish to die in the midst of orgasm, with Luke 15.10, Christ's injunction to the Pharisees about the joy in heaven over one repentant sinner. See Paul Gerhard Schmidt, "The Quotation in Goliardic Poetry: The Feast of Fools and the Goliardic Strophe *cum auctoritate,*" in *Latin Poetry in the Classical Tradition: Essays in Medieval and Renaissance Literature,* ed. Peter Godman and Oswyn Murray (Oxford: Clarendon Press, 1990), 49–65.

23. Dronke, *Medieval Latin and the Rise of European Love-Lyric,* 2 vols. (Oxford: Oxford University Press, 1965), 1:256.

24. See C.C.J. Webb, ed., *Metalogicon* (Oxford: Oxford University Press, 1929).

25. *Ovid und die Troubadours,* 48. Schrötter finds four areas of correspondence between Ovid and the Provençal poets: love as coercion, sickness, war, and art. "Bei Ovid findet sich oft wörtlich Entsprechendes für nicht weniger als vier Vorstellungskreise der Troubadours; Liebe als Zwang, Liebe als Krankheit, Krieg und Dienst, Liebe als Wissenschaft" (110). A word of caution from Dronke: "it is seldom profitable to speculate on specific borrowings, where these are not plainly evident. Thus it would be absurd to claim that . . . Bernart de Ventadour . . . *derived* [his] language of love-worship from [Ovid] . . . but it would be equally absurd to pretend that these poets would have written exactly as they did if such poetry had never existed" (*Medieval Latin,* 1:180).

26. For a discussion of *integumentum,* see Minnis, *Medieval Theory of Authorship,* 21, 140, 142–43.

amatoria and *Remedia amoris* and equate contemporary Paris with Ovid's Rome. Boncompagno da Signa's *Rota veneris* is a pseudo-Ovidian love treatise in the manner of Andreas Capellanus' *de Amore* from the previous century. The anonymous *de Vetula,* sometimes attributed to Ovid in the Middle Ages, dramatizes the master's last love affair and ends with his conversion to Christianity and a hymn to the Blessed Virgin. By the fourteenth century, John of Garland's *integumentum* becomes full-blown Christian allegory, in the tradition of Fulgentius and the Vatican mythographers before the turn of the first millenium. Apollo and Perseus are equated with Christ. The anonymous vernacular poem *Ovide moralisé* and the prose *Ovidius moralizatus* of Petrarch's friend Petrus Berchorius (Pierre Bersuire) are finished by the time Chaucer is born. Even in the Renaissance, the medieval mode of moralization is still the preferred method of Ovidian exegesis, which that exciting new invention, movable type, spreads through Europe. Giovanni di Bensignori's *Metamorfoseo volgare* (c. 1370) was published in Venice in 1497 and reprinted seven times before the mid-sixteenth century.[27]

Yet even those who can be said to bowdlerize Ovid justify their appropriation of him just the same. The author of the *Ovide moralisé,* like William Caxton in the next century, defends his reading of Ovid (not merely his own "moralization" of the *Metamorphoses*) by alluding to "l'escripture," Romans 15.4: "Quaecumque enim scripta sunt, ad nostram doctrinam scripta sunt; ut per patientiam, et consolationem Scripturarum, spem habeamus."[28] "Quaecumque," then, signifies *everything* sacred and profane under the sun, even Ovid, which is an aggressive defense of Tertullian's position on the impossibility of cogent religious study without the framework of secular pedagogy.

So, to apply the formulation "Ovid misunderstood" to the Middle Ages makes no sense. The age understood him well enough to justify its reading of him. And this phenomenon does not merely apply to the mythological poetry. Again, some medieval commentators are "erotodidactic"; they use the erotica to teach ethics.[29] One commentator recommends that the *Heroides* be studied in this way, so that the student may be able to distinguish between lawful and illicit love: "de ipso amore, scilicet de legitimo, de illi-

---

27. See Daniel Javitch, "Rescuing Ovid from the Allegorizers," *Comparative Literature* 30 (1978): 97–107. On the Vatican mythographers, see Barkan, *The Gods Made Flesh,* 104, 124, 126–27.

28. See Minnis, *Medieval Theory of Authorship,* 206.

29. Hexter, *Ovid and Medieval Schooling,* 17.

cito, et stulto . . . et sic commendando legitimum, stultum et illicitum reprehendit."[30] Thomas the Cistercian discusses the *Ars* to explain the Song of Songs.[31] Apparently, not everyone agreed with St. Augustine, who stigmatizes such literature as a "flumen tartareum" because "per haec verba turpitudo ista confidentius perpetratur."[32]

2

This list of references, allusions, and imitations suggests that the most influential Ovidian texts were the *Metamorphoses* and the *Ars amatoria,* with the exile poems and *Heroides* a distant second. The clerks hardly mention the *Amores,* nor do these poems seem to have been broadly imitated much before 1100. This seems odd, given their sanguinary temperament, amusing nature, sophisticated manipulation of tone, and subtle craftsmanship, qualities congenial to medieval poetics, fit for *imitatio*—reproductive, eclectic, heuristic, or dialectical. One would expect sequences of elegiac or lyric love poems to spring up, blooming with Corinnae.

Perhaps such an enterprise would have been considered too worldly (i.e., erotic) and prideful to undertake. The exemplum of the solitary man who narrates his adventures and confesses his sins was Augustine. Who would be so arrogant as to secularize and versify such a spiritual journey, substituting the *desultor Amoris* for the Augustinian *ego*?[33] But this explanation reflects modern misdiagnosis of the "puritan" Middle Ages and betrays a disappointment in medieval authors for "failing" to anticipate the modern critical adoration of sequences and unreliable narrators. Surely individual troubadour *cansos* and medieval Latin lyrics are very worldly indeed, even if they do not cohere into sequential form. And Abelard's horrifying autobiography, *Historia calamitatum,* may be a darkly parodic version of the *Confessions* in its conception.

A better explanation is twofold: the *Amores* were not widely known in their complete form, and early medieval Latin writers were literary canni-

30. Huygens, *Accessus ad auctores,* 33.

31. Minnis, *Medieval Theory of Authorship,* 182; D.W. Robertson, "Chrétien's *Cligés* and the Ovidian Spirit," in *Essays in Medieval Culture* (Princeton: Princeton University Press, 1980), 175.

32. *St. Augustine's Confessions,* trans. W. Watts, 2 vols. (Cambridge: Harvard University Press, 1912; reprint, 1989), 1:49.

33. Benton argues that Augustine was a model whom no one dared imitate. See "Consciousness of Self," 265.

bals who raided the Ovidian body for the parts they needed. Prudentius (fl.
380) Christianizes Ovid's erotic phraseology and allegory. In the *Psychomachia,* Luxuria mocks the seven virtues—Iustitia, Honestas, Sobrietas, Ieiunia, Pudor, Simplicitas, and Mens Humilis (243–44), some of
which Amor leads in triumph in *Amores* 1.2. Later, Sobrietas harangues
her troops against Luxuria:

paeniteat, per si qua movet reverentia summi
numinis, hoc tam dulce malum voluisse nefanda
proditione sequi.

(394–96)

[Repent, I beseech you, by the fear of the high God, if at all it moves
you, that you have desired to follow after this pleasant sin, committing
a heinous betrayal.]³⁴

Here, "dulce malum" is lifted from the *Amores* (2.9b.26), in which the
desultor distills all women into one girl who is a sweet evil. Evidently, Prudentius uses Ovid's very words to criticize the pagan habits of thought that
such terminology epitomizes, just as St. Jerome does when he cites the
Amores in one of his letters to underscore the dangers of beautiful dark-
eyed women and the physical desire they can kindle.³⁵ The poet Dracontius (fourth century) simply lifts a line from Ovid in which the *desultor* glories in Corinna's nakedness—"ut stetit ante oculos posito uelamine
nostros" (*Am.* 1.5.17)—and reprocesses it to make his Christian point
about the glories of naked Scriptural revelation (*de Laudibus Dei* 1.393).³⁶
If the sentiment offends thee, cast it out—but keep the rhetorical form.

Similarly, in Martianus' *de Nuptiis,* the chaste Terpsichore advises the
chaster Euterpe to observe a "cura vigil," strangely echoing a phrase from
the *magister Amoris,* who advises his pupils not to forgo their erotic pur-

---

34. *Prudentius,* ed. and trans. H.J. Thomson, 2 vols., (Cambridge: Harvard University
Press, 1969), 1:296–97, 306–7.
35. The line that Jerome quotes in *Epistola* 123 is "risit, et argutis quiddam promisit ocel-
lis" (*Am.* 3.2.83). See M. Manitius, *Beiträge zur Geschichte des Ovidius und andrer römischer
Schiftsteller im Mittelalter* (Leipzig: Weicher, 1900), 727; Sigmund Tafel, *Die Ueberlieferungsgeschichte Ovids Carmina amatoria verfolgt bis zum 11. Jahrhundert* (Tübingen: Heckenhauer, 1910), 64.
36. Dracontius' line reads, "Constitit ante oculos nullo velamine tecta" (Tafel, *Die Ueberlieferungsgeschichte,* 63).

suits (*AA* 3.411).[37] Moralizing Fulgentius, "occupied . . . with lust and its sadness," begins his vision of Orpheus' mother, Calliope, with "nox erat," the opening formulation of the *somnium Ovidii* (*Am.* 3.5.1), and paraphrases the *desultor* elsewhere.[38] These prescriptive authors differ from such Gallic poets as Paulinus and the author of *de Providentia Divina* (c. 410), who mention Corinna or write in Ovidian elegiacs. Venantius Fortunatus (c. 600) is similarly unencumbered in his adaptive imitation, even though he addresses a nun as if she were Corinna.[39]

Such information is heartening to the literary detective. Yet two questions remain. Where did our poets get their *Amores*? And why did they simply pirate the phrases of the *desultor* and fuse them into their own? Though sumptuously illuminated "complete" editions of such authors as Virgil survive from as early as the fifth century, there were many other texts that contained individual lines and passages of *auctores* that the poets and compilers appropriated into their own works, source books that predate the *libri manuales* of the eleventh and twelfth centuries. Of course, Virgil appears in such anthologies, and Ovid's erotic poetry surely existed in relatively complete form before the ninth century. However, I would suggest that the "cannibalized" codices were an important means of transmission for fragments of the *Amores* and that this compositional technique may have inspired a more sophisticated appropriation of the erotic Ovidian corpus by Prudentius and his fellows, even if more "complete" texts were available. Such poetics seem natural if one accepts the assumption of Greene and Bruns that medieval intertextuality is metonymic, that one text grows into and out of another without fear of plagiarism or anachronism.[40]

One such source book that may have been of importance is the *Anthologia latina,* that crazy quilt of classical, late, and early medieval Latin fragments from the *auctores.* The oldest surviving manuscript is the North African *Codex Salmasianus.* Although it dates from the eighth century, it was probably compiled around 533–34 (just as the Vandal kingdom was collapsing), and its poetry could have been written three centuries

---

37. *Martianus Capella,* ed. Adolph Dick (Leipzig: Teubner, 1925; reprint, 1969), 43.

38. George Leslie Whitbread, *Fulgentius the Mythographer* (Columbus: Ohio State University Press, 1971), 19–20. He suggests the following passages from the *Amores* as echoes in the *Mythologiae:* 1.5.9–10, 3.5.3–7.

39. For Paulinus see Raby, *Secular Latin Poetry,* 1:67–68; for Venantius Fortunatus see Manitius, *Beiträge zur Geschichte des Ovidius,* 728.

40. See note 16 in this chapter.

earlier.[41] A possible dateline of six hundred years is a significantly long time in which a text may be written, collected, copied, garbled, recopied, read, reread, imitated, burned, and preserved.

Ovid is heavily represented in the *Anthologia*. Surprisingly, there are thirty separate fragments from the *Amores,* more references than its modern editors attribute to the *Heroides* (twenty-six), *Ars* (six), and *Remedia* (one). The codex quotes from all three books of the *Amores* and reprocesses the lines like this:

Candida me docuit nigras odisse puellas.

Odero si potero, si non, invitus amabo.

(Anthologia latina 354)[42]

As neo-Catullan as the first verse may sound, the second is a definite hit. It is one of Ovid's most widely quoted phrases in the Middle Ages and Renaissance, one that epitomizes the *desultor Amoris* and his misadventures with women (*Am.* 3.11b.35). Many of the other tags from the *Amores* that, in embryonic form, seem to anticipate the stuff of troubadour poetry appear in the *Anthologia:* the lover as soldier, the cruelty of the lady, the protestations to the *ianitor* or eunuch who guards her, and so on.[43] If one considers the rather wide parameters of composition, compilation, and publication of such manuscripts as the *Codex Salmasianus* (e.g., 150–750),

---

41. See L.D. Reynolds and N.G. Wilson, eds., *Texts and Transmissions: A Survey of the Latin Classics* (Oxford: Clarendon Press, 1983), 9–12. The codex is named for the man who owned it, Claude de Saumaise (Salmansius, 1588–1653), who held the chair at Leiden. See Reynolds and N.G. Wilson, *Scribes and Scholars: A Guide to the Transmission of Greek and Latin Literature,* 3d ed. (Oxford: Clarendon Press, 1992), 182. An excellent bibliography on the *Codex Salmasianus* is Maddalena Spallone, "Il Par. Lat. 10318 (Salmasiano): Dal Manuscritto Alto-medievale ad una raccolta enciclopedica tardo-antica," *Italia medievale e umanistica* 25 (1982): 1–71.

42. F. Buecheler and V. Riese, eds., *Carmina Latina Epigrapha: Anthologia Latina,* 3 vols. (Leipzig: Teubner, 1895–1926), 1:167.

43. The only text more frequently raided than the *Amores* is the *Tristia* (thirty-six references). In their three-volume edition of the *Anthologia* (vol. 1, 1895; vol. 2, 1897; vol. 3, 1926), Buecheler and Riese list these tags from the *Amores* (with three added from Manitius, *Beiträge zur Geschichte des Ovidius,* 725–27):

1.6.59	2.6.55	2.19.57	3.5.40	3.9.25
1.8.77	2.7.15	3.1.9	3.6.2	3.9.66
1.9.1	2.9.41	3.1.51	3.6.45	3.9.67
1.10.55	2.10.11	3.2.1	3.6.87	3.9.70
1.10.62	2.11.36	3.2.29	3.6.105	3.11.5
2.1.38	2.16.47	3.5.11	3.9.18	3.11.35

the *Anthologia latina* may have helped transmit the unmistakable voice of the *desultor* in fragmentary form, as well as Ovid's own erotic conventions in the *Amores*, which, transmogrified by later medieval poets, make up the much disputed concept of *fin' Amors*, "courtly love," or "amour *courtois.*"[44]

3

Maximianus (fl. 550) may be the first dialectically imitative Ovidian, one who applies the poetics of the *desultor* to his source as well as to the composition of his own text, gleefully subverting as he imitates. Ernst Robert Curtius stresses the importance of this undervalued poet to the later Middle Ages. F.J.E. Raby suggests (cursorily) a valid and useful parallel between the fifth elegy of Maximianus and *Amores* 3.7, the infamous "impotence poem" in which a woman bewails "nostri languorem membri."[45]

Maximianus 5 demonstrates a thorough knowledge of other elegies from the *Amores* besides 3.7. Its physical description of the "Graia puella" (6)[46] practically paraphrases *Amores* 1.5, the afternoon tryst with Corinna. Its first-person narrator, an old man, bewails his inability to perform in bed. Like *Amores* 3.7, a good part of Maximianus' elegy consists of male-oriented comic apostrophes to the fiendishly recalcitrant *membrum*, by its user as well as by its owner.

Maximianus' *puella,* far from understanding and tender, vents her bitter disappointment and jealousy, suspecting that another woman has primed the pump. His narrator, like the *desultor,* also provides us with an amusing, semipornographic attempt at reanimation, doomed (alas!) to failure:

> Contractare manu coepit flaccentia membra
>   Meque etiam digitis sollicitare suis.
> Nil mihi torpenti uel tactus profuit illis:
>   Perstitit in medio frigus ut ante foco.
> "Quae te crudelis rapuit mihi femina?" dixit.
>
>   (56–61)

---

44. Ovid's influence on *fin' Amors* is discussed at length in chapter 3.

45. Curtius says that the early Middle Ages read Maximianus "zealously" (*European Literature,* 50). Raby discusses the fifth elegy in *Secular Latin Poetry,* 1:121 n. 2.

46. My text of the *Maximiani elegiae* is from Emil Baehrens, *Poetae Latini minores,* 5 vols. (Leipzig: Teubner, 1883), 5:313–48.

[She began to manipulate the flaccid member with her hand and even stroked me with her fingers. No touching of the inert thing proved useful for her purposes: it lay cold before that hearth as before. "What cruel woman has snatched you away from me?" she said.]

Ovid's poem reads:

hanc etiam non est mea dedignata puella
  molliter admota sollicitare manu;
sed postquam nullas consurgere posse per artes
  immemoremque sui procubuisse uidet,
"quae me ludis?" ait . . . .

. . . .
. . . "alio lassus amore uenis."

(*Am.* 3.7.73–77, 80)

[at this point my girl did not hesitate to manipulate me gently with a firm hand, but after she saw that it would be roused by none of her arts and that it lay flaccid, unmindful of her, she said, "Why do you play with me? . . . [perhaps] you come here exhausted from another's love."]

At first, the imitation of the *desultor Amoris* seems reproductive by one who learned to write elegiacs by reading the neoteric elegists. Yet Maximianus provides his own study in sexual egocentricity to rival his Ovidian source, in which the author keeps his ironic distance from the bumbling *desultor*. Also, in contrast to Ovid's *femina nova* (who is nasty, brutish, and short), the *Graia puella* in Maximianus 5 takes over the elegy in her lament for the flaccid member, addressing it and its kind like a fallen Priapus.

Such revisions of Ovid may parody certain "fertility rites" and underscore the excesses of self-gratifying male fantasy. Yet, penile worship aside, Maximianus makes some effort to account for a woman's sexual psychology, as well. She is not some inert love-doll. The agonized and humiliated old man whom the poet creates, in his wisdom and maturity, seems to be a critique of Ovid's young buck, who, drunk on his own testosterone, never blames himself for his failings.[47]

---

47. The infamous Elizabethan poem *The Choise* [sic] *of Valentines* attributed to Thomas Nashe is very much in the manner of Maximianus 5. For discussion of the *Choise* as neo-Ovidian imitation-parody, see my article "Nashe and the Poetics of Obscenity: *The Choise of Valentines*," *Classical and Modern Literature* 12 (1991): 29–48.

4

The three centuries between the death of Maximianus and the rise of the
Carolingian makers in the ninth century constitute a veritable black hole
for the complete text of the *Amores*.[48] The most learned authors provide
mere fragments. In his discussion of the Minotaur in the *Etymologiarum*
(11.3.38), Isidore of Seville quotes *Ars* 2.24 and would seem to allude to
the *somnium Ovidii, Amores* 3.5, with "semibovemque virum, semi-
virumque bovem." Although Charlemagne's court poets Florus and
Walafrid are said to have known of and alluded to this part of the Ovidian
opus, how much of it they knew and in what form they knew it is still con-
troversial.[49] In the following passage, Theodulf seems to be raiding and
imitating the *Amores:*

> Esto et sollicitus propriae de parte iugalis,
>   Ne mentem maculet inliciendo tuam!
> Oscula quae genibus, manibus, colloque, genisque
>   Blanda dabit, miscet lenia verba quibus,
> Sueta preces tali proprias armare veneno,
>   Armat ut architenens inpigra tela suo.

[Watch out for your own wife, let her not corrupt your mind with temp-
tations! On your knees, hands, neck, and cheeks she will press sweet
kisses mingled with soft words, practised at spiking her prayers in the
poison with which the archer tirelessly equips his shafts.][50]

The poet has read the *Amores,* and for his courtly audience he reconsti-
tutes its situations: the bravura warning by the *desultor* to the husband he

---

48. Bond discusses the rise of the "New Ovid" between the ninth and eleventh centuries,
caused, to some extent, by the new attitudes toward persona ("Composing Yourself," 85).
Ludwig Traube's famous definition of the spirit of the age that succeeds the use of Virgil (c.
600–800) and the use of Horace (c. 800–1100) follows: "Es ist das Zeitalter, das ich die *aetas
Ovidiana* nennen möchte, die Zeit, did der aetas Vergiliana, dem 8. und 9. Jahrhundert, folgt"
(*Vorlesungen und Abhandlungen,* vol. 2, *Einleitung in die lateinische Philologie des Mittelalters*
[1911; reprint, Munich: Beck, 1965], 113).
49. On Florus and Walafrid, see Raby, *Secular Latin Poetry,* 1:234. The quotation from
Isidore is from *Isidore Hispalensis Episcopi Etymologiarum sive Originum Libri XX,* ed. W.M.
Lindsay, 2 vols. (Oxford: Oxford University Press, 1911), 2:38.
50. The text and translation of Theodulf is from Peter Godman, ed. and trans., *Poetry of
the Carolingian Renaissance* (London: Duckworth, 1985), 166–67.

plans to cuckold (*Am.* 2.19), the loving description of Corinna's physical affection (1.4), and the misogynous sentiment concerning women and their "deceitful wiles" (3.4). The elegiacs are impeccable.

The "complete" three-book *Amores* survive in only four manuscripts dated between 800 and 1100, and only three separate lines in three separate manuscripts appear in the *libri manuales* between 1100 and 1350.[51] The first group of *accessus* that mentions the *Amores* does not begin to surface until c. 1130. So, although the idea of poems like the *Amores* was probably not unknown, the conception of an extended sequence of secular love poems may not have existed before the twelfth century. Poets can hardly be expected to imitate or allude to texts that they have not read.

It has been argued that because of feudalism and its hierarchical structure, the medieval poet lacked the "virtually autonomous ego" to create a sequence. Yet this concept of order was not unknown; it had simply not been secularized. The Psalms were thought of as a group of sacred poems that *lacked* a chronology. One would need to possess the notion of a sequence to perceive such a lack of order. In fact, some *accessus* discuss the category *ordo* quite extensively.[52] The *Consolatio* of pagan Maximianus' Christian acquaintance Boethius, with its interrelated verses and prose meditations, could be considered sequential. (It is probably significant that this text was translated into Provençal as early as the tenth century and thus was available for the perusal of troubadours in their vernacular.) Also, the *sequentia cum prosa* that developed in the Mass between the eighth and tenth centuries, in which the *iubilus* or *sequentia* (a complex melody) was divided into *clausulae* interspersed with Scripture,[53] suggests a knowledge of both the term and its potential.

Although classical precedent was served by groups of related poems treating erotic themes and written in the first person, such as Horace's *Odes* and the poetry of Catullus, the first erotic sequence in elegiacs known to medieval Europe was the *Amores* in the eleventh and twelfth centuries. (Propertius and Tibullus do not appear widely until the fourteenth century.) Since the *Amores* were inevitably read with the *Ars*, one must con-

---

51. See Hexter's detailed analysis in *Ovid and Medieval Schooling,* 16, 19.

52. On feudalism as a bar to the idea of sequence and virtual autonomy, see Paul Allen Miller, "Sidney, Petrarch, and Ovid, or Imitation as Subversion," *English Literary History* 58 (1991): 499–522. On the Psalms, see Minnis, *Medieval Theory of Authorship,* 55. For *ordo,* see Minnis and Scott, *Medieval Literary Theory,* 2, 32, 151, 198, 364. The term usually refers to the overall outline of a work, such as the table of contents.

53. On the Provençal translation of Boethius and the account of the *sequentia,* see Raby, *Christian Latin Poetry,* 114, 210, respectively.

sider the pair a complementary influence. Poets frequently mention the doctor of love who "in arte amatorie dat precepta," but the voice of the *desultor* in the *Amores,* who "ludicra tractat et iocosa," served as an example for the lyric male voice.

Many of the twelfth-century borrowings seem superficial but are integral to the poetics. Cupid is the lord of terrible aspect, leading his processions and triumphs. The lover who scoffs at the god's power finds himself pierced with arrows, a punishment emblematic of revenge for disdain. Love is, then, suffering, pain, and war. There are wounds and symptoms of lovesickness, what Schrötter grandiosely titles *Krankheitssymptomen.*[54] Even so, Amor is an entity to which one can attempt to bid farewell in order to untangle oneself from adulterous passions, the nail-biting secrecy and the mutual deceit. There are the annoying intermediaries: *los gardadors* who prevent entry, and *ancillae* who prevent a different sort of entry by walking in on one at opportune moments. Again, such Ovidian commonplaces, which may have been transmitted initially through such manuscripts as the *Codex Salmasianus* as well as more integral texts, may have calcified into the conventions of *fin' Amors.*

Another inheritance is more significant: the attitude toward women. Just as the *desultor Amoris* idealizes and debases Corinna, twelfth-century poets invest the *midons* with a similar dualism. She is a feudal lord to be revered, yet a capricious vixen whom one castigates because she exercises the very superiority that her admirer has thrust on her. This phenomenon foments a particularly pernicious sexual psychology. Men who attempt to regain the *maistrye* by resubordinating women are themselves subordinated—by their own agency.

Perhaps the most significant legacy of the erotica is the persona and the authorial notion of ironic distance from this speaker. Thanks to Ovid, the Middle Ages understood that when a poet claims, "I am," he or she makes an infinite number of characters and poses possible. Ovid's preferred speaker is the *amans,* or lover, who is also *poeta,* possessing the godlike power to make himself, as well as his subject, immortal. Yet this speaker tells lies as well as the truth. He is self-critical, angst-ridden, angry, and masochistic, not just glib, worldly, and charming. As a result, the focus in the *Amores* and *Ars* is on the speaker, not on his subject, a concept that

---

54. *Ovid und die Troubadours,* 64. Edmond Faral also holds to the Ovidian hypothesis for *fin' Amors,* although he applies it to the trouvères north of the Loire. See "Ovide et quelques autres sources du roman d'Enéas," *Romania* 40 (1911): 161–234.

medieval makers grasped completely, because they knew what a persona was.[55]

5

Baudri de Bourgueil (1046–1130) is one of the first poets whose name we know who truly internalized Ovid's erotic conventions. Medievalists usually discuss him in tandem with other members of the "Loire" or "Cathedral" school of early twelfth-century Franco-Latin poetry: Marbod de Rennes, Hildebert de Lavardin (who uses the imagery and diction of *Amores* 1.5 in his *Versus de sancta Susanna* ["aestus erat"]), and Bernard Silvestris. Bernard wrote,

> militat in thalamis, tenero deservit amori
>   tactus, et argute saepe probare solet
> aut castigato planum sub pectore ventrem,
>   aut in virgineo corpore molle femur.[56]

[one soldiers in the bedroom, his touch zealously serving tender love, and is most often subtly successful [by touching] either the flat belly beneath the agitated breast, or the virgin's soft thigh.]

One can only guess which elegies from the *Amores* (1.9?) or sections of the *Ars* Bernard is imitating in his neo-Theodulfian manner. Yet Baudri's conscious and deliberate Ovidianism distinguishes him from his peers. In this, he seems to anticipate the erotic vernacular poetics of his troubadour compatriots.

Twentieth-century criticism has given us two Baudris. There is Raby's polite and rustic churchman, warbling his woodnotes wild: "the charm of river and field and of all the natural things amid which his youth was spent held him throughout the years"; "His verse was the relaxation of his

---

55. In *Medieval Theory of Authorship,* Minnis cites the discussion of the literary persona in the exegesis of the Psalms and Song of Songs by Gerhoh of Reichersberg (22); Origen, Bede, William of St. Thierry, and Bernard of Utrecht (57–58); Aquinas (90); and Bonaventure on Solomon in Ecclesiastes: "Sometimes he speaks in his own person, sometimes in the persons of others (*in persona aliorum*)" (189).

56. For the quotation from Bernard, see Raby, *Secular Latin Poetry,* 2:13 (my rough translation). Raby discusses Marbod, Hildebert, and other Loire poets in this volume and throughout *Christian Latin Poetry.* For Hildebert's imitation of *Amores* 1.5, see E.K. Rand, *Ovid and His Influence* (Boston: Longmans, 1925), 113.

leisure, written at night or while he was travelling." Baudri does not strike Raby as an accomplished religious poet and is therefore a lightweight: "he had none of that spiritual and intellectual conviction which guided an Anselm or a Hildebert."[57] Far from Raby's "wounded victim of sin who has need of the medicine of salvation," there is Gerald Bond's Baudri, a guerrilla Ovidian whose poetry is "explicitly ludic and continually self-ref-erential" and who actively participates in an "Ovidian subculture." Since Baudri's work is somewhat unspectacular and conventional, yet so thor-oughly informed by the *magister Amoris,* Bond intimates that Ovidianism was widespread in the Loire valley well before Guillaume and Marcabru.[58]

For my own purposes, one of Bond's most significant observations is that Baudri, like the love poets who follow him, ingests the idea of the per-sona from Ovid and creates poetry that one might call "personal." In this, Bond builds on the work of Martin Stevens, who labels the twelfth-century persona the "performing self" or "poetic 'I.'"[59] The need for a monastic poet to use this device seems implicit, especially if his subject matter is sex-ual love. Hence Baudri defends himself and explains his aesthetics as fol-lows:

Quod uero tanquam de certis scriptito rebus
Et quod personis impono uocabula multis
Et modo gaudentem, modo me describo dolentem
Aut puerile loquens uel amo uel quidlibet odi,
Crede michi: non uera loquor magis omnia fingo.
Nullus amor foedus michi quidlibet associauit.

(85.35–46)[60]

[When I write about things as if they were real, and when I compose words using many masks, and describe myself in one instance as joyous, in another as grieving, or childishly say "I love" or "I hate" something,

---

57. Raby, *Secular Latin Poetry,* 1:337; *Christian Latin Poetry,* 279, 285.

58. Raby, *Christian Latin Poetry,* 284; Bond, *"Iocus amoris,"* 144, 189–90, 155.

59. Bond writes that Ovid "portrayed the unity (and necessary duplicity) of the poet and lover" (*"Iocus amoris,"* 155). Stevens' article is "The Performing Self in Twelfth-Century Cul-ture," *Viator* 9 (1978): 193–212. John M. Fyler mentions the Ovidian legacy of the unreliable narrator to the Loire poets in *Chaucer and Ovid,* 19.

60. Quotations of Baudri are from *Baldricus Burgulianus Carmina,* ed. Karlheinz Hilbert (Heidelberg: Carl Winter, 1979). All translations of Baudri's texts are my own unless other-wise stated.

believe me: I don't tell the truth but fabricate everything. No love has
actually tainted me.]

Bond uses this passage to explain the influence of the *Heroides* on the *ars
dictaminis,* or poetic letter, in France and the corresponding development
of the notion of persona.[61] I suggest that, given Baudri's subject matter,
this very passage indicates the influence of Ovid's *amans* from the *Amores*
on twelfth-century culture as well.[62] Therein lies the notion that something
needs to be defended or excused, something more dangerous than imitating verse epistles written *in persona feminae nobilis.* It is probably not accidental that in Baudri's first elegy, a thoroughly conventional poem in
which he bequeaths his book to the world and defends it "contra obtrecta-
tores," he describes "liber . . . meus" as a "carmen sine nomine" (1.2–3), a
description similar to the one that our aforementioned schoolmaster and
his contemporaries often used for the *Amores.*

Clearly, Baudri's explanation of persona echoes Ovid's defense of his
erotic poetics in the passage from the *Tristia* cited at the beginning of this
study (2.353–58). The French poet's "loquens uel amo uel quidlibet odi"
may be an allusion to Catullus 85. However, given the context, Baudri
could just as well be alluding to that very famous line from the *Amores* that
will have resonance for medieval and Renaissance poets:

> hac amor hac odium; sed, puto, vincit amor.
> odero, si potero; si non, invitus amabo.
>
> (3.11b.34–35)

Baudri, in the words of the exiled *magister* with whom he felt such kinship,
explains that this anguish is simply a mask. In the passage that immediately precedes his explanation of persona, one in which he delineates his
audience, he seems to allude again to the *Amores:*

---

61. Bond, "Composing Yourself," 85.
62. Peter Allen explains that the *Amores* were thought of as *epistulae* in the twelfth century, but he cites no evidence for this; he also speculates that Baudri knew the *Amores* (*The
Art of Love,* 50). Tafel implies that the *Ovidius sine titulo* was also known as *Ovidius epistu-
larum amatoriarum* (*Die Ueberlieferungsgeschichte,* 62). For more on the interplay between
the *Heroides,* the idea of the verse epistle, and medieval poetics, see Florence Verducci, *Ovid's
Toyshop,* 83–84. She does not mention the *Amores* in her discussion.

Et cur scribatur, nisi scriptum forte legatur?
Ergo, quod pueros demulceat atque puellas,
Scripsimus, ut pueris id consonet atque puellis,
Sicque meum relegatur opus uolitetque per orbem,
Illud dum relegent pueri relegentque puelle.

(85.30–34)

[And why should one write, unless by chance what has been written may be read? Therefore, I write what may stimulate boys and girls, that which may be agreeable to boys and girls, and thus my work may be studied and travel through the world, while boys and girls reread it.]

Never one to resist repeating himself, Baudri verifies that he writes for "pueri" and "puelle." In this, especially in the choice of the verb *demulceat* (lit. "caress") and its erotic overtones, he pays homage to Ovid's disingenuous self-defense in *Amores* 2.1: "me legat in sponsi facie non frigida virgo, / et rudis ignoto tactus amore puer" (5–6). Yet one would never classify Baudri as an advocate of free love. In fact, he commands the reader to interpret his discourse with a spotless heart: "Sermones nostros intellige pectore fido" (85.47). Even more forcefully, he admonishes us not to pander his words: "Non sis uerborum scurrilis leno meorum" (85.49). Here, Baudri divides poet from persona decisively, like his beloved Naso—even though Baudri wittily blurs the distinction between the two in his revision of *Tristia* 2.354 from "vita verecunda est, Musa iocosa mea" [my life is modest, my Muse jocose] to "Vita iocosa michi placet, ergo Musa iocosa" [the jocose life pleases me, therefore my Muse is jocose] (86.42).

In a pair of complementary verse epistles (*carmina* 97 and 98), Baudri constructs a correspondence between Florus, a young admirer of the exiled Ovid, and the poet himself, who hopes that the youth will intercede for him in Rome with Augustus. (In assuming the *persona Ovidii,* Baudri anticipates *de Vetula* in the next century.) In these elegiacs, the French poet amplifies his defense of erotic poetry, Ovid, and himself begun in *carminum* 85. Florus assures Ovid:

Sexus uterque diu sine carmine nouit amare.
    Quod tenuere prius secula, tu recitas.
Non tu secla doces, sed secula te docuerunt

(97.45–47)

[For a long time both sexes knew how to love without [your] poem; what the previous ages repressed, you recite. You do not teach the ages, but the ages taught you.]

Thus Baudri assures his audience that Ovid merely explains what we already know, so we should not be offended. By implication, Baudri is simply updating the same information.

In a later passage from the same poem, Baudri extends his analogical self-defense more aggressively:

Naturam nostram plenam deus egit amoris.
  Nos natura docet, quod deus hanc docuit.
Si culpatur amor, actor culpatur amoris.
  Actor amoris enim criminis actor erit.

(51–54)

Bond argues that this is "revolutionary syllogizing" between God and Amor, and translates: "God filled our nature with love; Nature teaches us what he taught her. If love is to be blamed, the source of love is to be blamed; For the source of love will be the source of the crime."[63]

At the risk of being impertinent, I suggest that this is a hopeful mistranslation. Is it not also possible that the "deus" is actually *deus amoris,* or the god of love? Might "actor" be glossed as "doer" or "performer" instead of "source"? If the answer to these queries is affirmative, the following translation might serve: "The god of love makes our nature complete; this nature instructs us just as the god [of love] instructs it. If love can be blamed, the perpetrator of love must be blamed; the perpetrator of love would truly be the perpetrator of a crime." Although one should remember the medieval indifference to the concept of anachronism, why would pagan Florus invoke a Christian God? If Baudri, through Florus, defends the nature of earthly, secular love, his monkish syllogizing is even more revolutionary than supposed—or, considering his colleagues and the subject matter of the *libri manuales* they compile, not very revolutionary at all.

Perhaps Baudri defends Ovid as Ovid, not as a forerunner of the Christianized Naso in *de Vetula.* Baudri, in *persona Ovidii,* claims:

Nostra puellares exponunt carmina mentes
  Nosque puellarum non quatit ullus amor.

---

63. Bond, "Composing Yourself," 94.

Quodsi uiuat amor aliqui uiuatque uoluntas,
Horum iam neutrum subcomitatur opus.

(98.57–60)

[My poems explain the dispositions of young women, but no love for young women troubles me. However, if the love and desire for one should arise, neither can be said to have been conceived by my work.]

In this elastic disclaimer that serves as envoi to *carmina* 85 and 97, Baudri-Ovid defends himself against the charge that he is responsible for other people's lust, a defense already advanced by Florus: "Tu recitator eras nec eras inventor amoris" (97.59). One must admit that this seems disingenuous from such a careful and discriminating poet who enjoys his poses and tricks elsewhere, one clever enough to fool Father Raby into thinking him a "wounded victim of sin."

If Baudri can be said to epitomize monkish poetics, then the following facts are clear by 1100: the *milieu* of the troubadours is firmly established; the *desultor* and *magister Amoris* have been medievalized; and Ovid has inspired the dialectical-heuristic imitation of himself that he himself practiced on other poets.

CHAPTER 3

"Dirai vos de con": Ovid and the Troubadours

The *Amores,* along with other Ovidian texts, inform the secular erotics of the troubadours and help form their poetics. To borrow a term from Thomas M. Greene, troubadour imitation of the *desultor* (as well as the *magister*) *Amoris* demonstrates "polyvocality," a plurality of voices and borrowings in a text. Naturally, this borrowing is not haphazard or passive. To use Greene's terminology further, twelfth-century imitations of Ovid are both "exploitative" and "dialectical."[1] In fact, the frequency with which troubadours raid the Ovidian corpus and rewrite it makes them, to some extent, literary cannibals.

If we think of Guillaume IX as a type of cannibal, his ingestion and digestion of Ovid is both parody and revision of the *Amores* Ovid. Simply put, the Count says what the *desultor* and *magister* seem hesitant to say. Other troubadours, authors as diverse as the Ripoll poet and Bernart de Ventadorn, dismantle, rewrite, and medievalize the *auctor* in whom they steep themselves. In their imitations of Ovid, they assert independence and show debt. I call this phenomenon *subversive submersion.*

The troubadours and their fellow poets north of the Loire, the trouvères, produced some 4,000 lyrics. Therefore, it is preposterous to assume that a critic can discuss them systematically or completely regarding any topic, even one as limited as the influence of the *Amores.* Also, since most if not all of these lyrics were set to music (many of whose settings, unfortunately, are lost),[2] it may seem a diminished thing to discuss them at all.

---

1. Greene discusses polyvocality throughout *The Light in Troy.* See especially 75–76.

2. There are many fine recordings of troubadour music; for example, Camerata Mediterranea, *Lo Gai Saber: Troubadours et Jongleurs 1100–1300,* dir. Joël Cohen, Erato 2292-45647-2 (1991); Clemencic Consort, *Troubadours,* dir. René Clemencic, Harmonia Mundi 90396 (1977); Ensemble for Medieval Music, *Trouvères: Courtly Love Songs from Northern France,* Deutsche Harmonia Mundi, 77155-2-RC (1984).

Yet like any other well-represented literary form, *cansos* and *tensos* do not always diverge wildly from one another, and one can discuss representative examples with considerable profit. Furthermore, such discussion is possible because troubadour poetry is not mere doggerel when bereft of its musical accompaniment. That it stands on its own as poetry is demonstrated by the long critical tradition of troubadour scholarship, beginning with Dante's *De vulgari eloquentia,* and extending into our own time with Gaston Paris, Wilibald Schrötter, Alfred Jeanroy, Jessie Crossland, Roger Boase, and others.[3]

Despite this critical tradition and its yoking of Ovid and the troubadours, there is not much written on the *Amores* as an intertext or formative influence; the *Metamorphoses, Heroides,* and *Ars amatoria* have received the most attention. In this chapter, I will use Guillaume IX, the Ripoll poet, and Bernart de Ventadorn to show how twelfth-century poets deploy the *Amores* to widen the guerilla Ovidianism of Baudri de Bourgueil, especially in their use of personae and the accompanying *pelles,* or masks. However, it is appropriate to discuss first *fin' Amors* and the classical *auctor* who is intertwined in it.

1. *Fin' Amors* and Ovid

The lyric and narrative poets of the Middle Ages reprocess Ovid's erotic poetry almost completely. This intertextuality is clearly a part of the phenomenon that Gaston Paris named "amour *courtois*" in 1883 and that C.S. Lewis translated as "Courtly Love" in 1936. Later medievalists, such as D.W. Robertson and E. Talbot Donaldson, disparage these conceptions entirely as anachronistic. More contemporary scholars compromise between the Parisian and Robertsonian paradigms and focus on the

---

3. As the founder of *Romania,* Paris' contribution to scholarship is obviously extensive. His most famous definition is that of "amour *courtois,*" schematized in "Le Conte de Charrette," *Romania* 12 (1883): 459–534. Schrötter's *Ovid und die Troubadours* propounds the "Ovidian hypothesis" as partial explanation for *amour courtois.* For Jeanroy, see *Historie sommaire de la poésie occitane* (Paris, 1945; reprint, Geneva: Slatkine Reprints, 1973). For Crossland, see "Ovid's Contribution" and *Medieval French Literature* (Oxford: Blackwell, 1956). The most valuably concise overview, including an extensive bibliography, is Boase's *The Origin and Meaning of Courtly Love: A Critical Study of European Scholarship* (Manchester: Manchester University Press, 1977).

medieval texts themselves.[4] The terminology they use to describe the love phenomenon ranges between *fin' Amors* and *bon' Amor* to *cortes Amor*, as well as the titles *fin' Amant* and *fin' amador*, since the poets themselves use this terminology to describe the love they are writing about. No two medievalists agree exactly on the defining term for the *spiritus* behind love poetry, but most acknowledge its existence nonetheless and credit Ovid in some way as an influence.[5]

How do the practitioners of *fin' Amors* reconstitute Ovid? As we have seen, the satirical *Ars amatoria* and *Amores* discuss physical love very frankly, detailing sexual psychology and encounters. *Fin' Amors* is also highly erotic, but its adherents seldom use Ovid's sardonic tone, and the sexuality is rarely graphic. Trysts are wrapped in skeins of euphemism, such as that which enfolds Lancelot and Guenevere in Chrétien's *Le chevalier de la charrete* (4633–4736).

In another significant divergence from Ovid, eleventh- and twelfth-century courtly makers do not treat sexual relationships in exclusively masculine terms. To the *magister* and his pupil, *puellae* are indistinguishable beings to be preyed on for the purposes of seduction. With the notable exceptions of Marcabru and Guillaume IX, troubadours purport to have more respect for women than this: *cortezia*. Yet this attitude of sincerity and respect may be a more subtle means of seduction than that proffered by the *praeceptor* in the *Ars*. Perhaps, then, it is mistaken to distinguish

---

4. Lewis' definition occurs in *The Allegory of Love*, 2. Robertson's "The Concept of Courtly Love as an Impediment to the Understanding of Medieval Texts," in *The Meaning of Courtly Love*, ed. F.X. Newman (Albany: State University of New York Press, 1968), 1–18, and Donaldson's "The Myth of Courtly Love," in *Speaking of Chaucer* (New York: Norton, 1970), are highly polemical and dismissive of both Paris and Lewis. Peter Dronke has taken issue with both Robertson and Donaldson, beginning with *Medieval Latin*. So has Jean Frappier, in *Amour courtois et Table Ronde* (Geneva: Droz, 1973) and "Sur un procès fait à l'amour courtois," *Romania* 93 (1972): 145–93. Moshé Lazar's *Amour courtois et "fin' Amors" dans la littérature du XIIe siècle* (Paris: Klincksieck, 1964) mediates between the two positions and attempts to account for and define the term *fin' Amors*. See also the recent article by Edmund Reiss, "*Fin' Amors*: Its History and Meaning in Medieval Literature," *Medieval and Renaissance Studies* 8 (1979): 71–99.

5. Dronke links author and epoch with a rhetorical question: "If Ovid showed the Middle Ages the complete 'Rota Veneris,' how could it fail to include something of the courtly experience?" (*Medieval Latin*, 1:165). Twelfth-century poets who use the disputed love-terminology include Thomas d'Angleterre (*Tristan* 329), Béroul (*Tristan* 2722), the *Eneas* poet (8285), Chrétien (*Lancelot* 3963), Bernart ("Non es meravelha" 34), Blondel de Nesle ("Bien doit chanter" 1), Marie de France (*Chievrefoil* 8, *Eliduc* 944).

between two separate medieval love traditions, the "romantic" and Ovid-
ian-satirical.[6] They are twins, fraternal if not identical.

So the troubadours, ingesting Ovid's conventions, rewrite his erotic
poetry. The *desultor* and *magister Amoris* consider love to be a disease and
therefore pretend no reverence for *puellae*. Any woman in the dominant
position is a cause for alarm: "tunc amo, tunc odi frustra quod amare
necesse est" [now I love, now I hate in vain what I must love] (*Am.* 3.14.39).
The *desultor* in the *Amores* despises the secrecy that his adulterous behavior requires, yet he perversely enjoys the aura of mutual recrimination that
results. He seems to follow the injunction of the *magister* to deceive the
deceivers: "fallite fallentes" (*AA* 1.645). Surely some troubadours describe
love as suffering but not as a disease. And the *domina* in a given *canso* is
sometimes so revered that she is addressed as *midons,* or "my lord," as if
the poet were her vassal. The relationships are also (notoriously) adulterous, but the required secrecy builds mutual trust and foments a sacramental sort of fidelity. Perhaps the much discredited C.S. Lewis is correct in
declaring that *fin' Amors* divests Ovid's erotic conventions of their cyni-
cism and "feudalizes" them.[7]

Yet the troubadours submerge themselves in the Ovidian corpus and
subvert it more than Lewis would be willing to admit. Evidence of this can
be found in the poetry of the *trobairitz* (women troubadours), who often
express their displeasure with their male counterparts, particularly with
their tendency toward objectification. Isabella (c. 1180) denounces the
troubadour Elias Cariel as a *fegnedor* (phony) in her *tenso* with him.[8] The
dames in *Le lay dou lecheor* declare that *cortezia* is no more than "l'entente
du con," a peculiarly modern formulation to those of us trained to think of
medieval literary women as pallid and circumspect phantoms haunting
Gothic castles erected in the nineteenth century.[9]

---

6. For example, see Bernard O'Donoghue, *The Courtly Love Tradition* (Manchester:
Manchester University Press, 1982), 3–7.

7. Lewis, *The Allegory of Love,* 2. A recent defender of Lewis by comparative philology is
Joan Ferrante, "'Cortes Amor' in Medieval Texts," *Speculum* 55 (1980): 686–95. Two books
widely believed to have superseded Lewis' are John Stevens, *Medieval Romance* (London:
Hutchinson, 1973); Lynette Muir, *Literature and Society in Medieval France* (New York: St.
Martin's, 1985).

8. See Meg Bogin, ed. and trans., *The Women Troubadours* (New York: Norton, 1980),
110–11. Texts and translations from the *trobairitz* follow this source.

9. See Paris, "Lais Inédits," *Romania* 8 (1879): 65–66. For an anthology of such writing,
see René Nelli, ed., *L'erotique des troubadours,* 2 vols. (Paris: Union Générale, 1974); Pierre
Bec, ed., *Burlesque et obscénitie chez les troubadours: Le contre-texte au Moyen Age* (Paris:
Stock, 1984).

Surely the concept of "chivalry" does not exist in Ovid's works, although some forms of "courtesy" are quite palpable, particularly its role in the objectification of women.[10] Medieval women writers are quite aware of such misogynistic tendencies in this *auctor*. Heloise does not share Abelard's enthusiasm for the master of love. She cites the passage from the *Ars* on wine as aphrodisiac (1.233–44) with disapproval, and she concludes elsewhere, "Ipse . . . poeta luxuriae turpitudinis doctor."[11] Her fourteenth-century sister Christine de Pizan, engaging in the *querelle des femmes* with the learned doctors of Paris concerning *Le roman de la rose,* shrewdly allows Cupid himself to disclaim Jean de Meun's sourcebook, the *Ars:* "Car homs qui veult selon ce livre faire / N'amera ja, combien qu'il soit amez" [The man who behaves according to that book will never love, no matter how much he is loved].[12] These are not isolated sentiments. In the poetry of the troubadours, a medievalized Ovid surfaces with all of his unreconstructed and stereotypical masculinity.

2. Guillaume IX

Nearly a century of scholarship has confirmed the debt of the first known troubadour to Ovid. Most commentators have attempted to identify passages and themes from the erotica, including the *Amores,* that surface in Guillaume's lyrics and that helped form his poetics. Medieval commentators refer to this sort of *imitatio* as *contaminatio;* Greene classifies it as "eclectic" or "exploitative."[13] If one applies such an idea to Guillaume, he is a type of literary cannibal, a raider of *auctores.* Or, in Douglas Kelly's

---

10. I am thinking of John F. Benton's negative definition of courtesy: "Courtesy was created by men for their own satisfaction, and it emphasized a woman's role as an object, sexual or otherwise. Since they did not encourage a genuine respect for women as individuals, the conventions of medieval chivalry, like the conventions of chivalry in the southern United States, did not advance women toward legal or social emancipation. When men ignored chivalry, women were better off" ("Clio and Venus: An Historical View of Medieval Love," in *The Meaning of Courtly Love,* ed. F.X. Newman [Albany: State University of New York Press, 1968], 35). A contemporary (and, I think, overstated) parallel to such thinking is the outright equation of idealization with misogyny. See Mary Beth Rose, *The Expense of Spirit: Love and Sexuality in Renaissance Drama* (Ithaca: Cornell University Press, 1988).

11. Hexter, *Ovid and Medieval Schooling,* 17.

12. "Epistre au dieu D'Amours." The text and translation are from Thelma S. Fenster and Mary Carpenter Erler, ed. and trans., *Poems of Cupid, God of Love* (Leiden: Brill, 1990), 52.

13. *The Light in Troy,* 39.

pattern of a trouvère, Guillaume does not create a poem but finds its parts and puts them together;[14] Ovid is a component.

Yet those who question the existence of the "Ovidian hypothesis" as a source for *fin' Amors* (or to determine if *fin' Amors* in fact existed) have suggested that Ovid's presence in troubadour poetry is so elusive as to be nonexistent. Indeed, such skepticism is useful physic. When a troubadour or trouvère waxes sexual or satiric, we conclude that he must be Ovidian, since the *Ars* and *Amores* leave a distinct residue in the texts of imitators who acknowledge their debt, such as de Meun. So, when Guillaume's unparalleled coarseness violates our concept of the way a medieval aristocratic poet is supposed to present himself—on his knees before the terrible *midons*—Ovid is an appealing culprit. At the same time, even skeptics invariably reinforce his presence—and rightly so.[15]

Wilibald Schrötter, the first genuine champion of the Ovidian hypothesis for *fin' Amors,* adduces thematic and linguistic parallels, all of which he categorizes after the fashion of his day. He finds the source of Guillaume's line "Greu partir si fai d'amor qui la trob'a son talen" [It is hard to separate from Love for one who finds it to his liking] (1.6) in *Amores* 2.4.5: "odi, nec possum cupiens non esse, quod odi" [I hate, (yet) desiring, am unable to be (anything) except what I hate].[16] This, Schrötter tells us, is the *Naturzwang der Liebe,* or natural pain of love. He explains that Guillaume's verbs, such as *temer* and *auzar,* prove the existence of a love language, derived from Ovid's *timere* and *audere:* the fear and daring of love. In a similar vein, the yoking of love and death constitute a *Tod aus Liebe.*[17] This, too, is from Ovid:

> Si.n breu non ai ajutori,
> Cum ma bona dompna m'am,
> Morrai, pel cap Sanh Gregori!
>
> (Guillaume 8.15–17)

---

14. *Medieval Imagination: Rhetoric and the Poetry of Courtly Love* (Madison: University of Wisconsin Press, 1978), xii.

15. Leslie Cahoon argues, "'Ovid' seems to exist only in the eye of the beholder and 'Ovidian' to be an empty sign of arbitrary signification" ("The Anxieties of Influence," 119). She then demonstrates the Ovidian presence in poems by Marcabru and Guillaume IX (120–44).

16. The text and translation of Guillaume throughout are from *The Poetry of William VII, Count of Poitiers, IX Duke of Aquitaine,* ed. and trans. Gerald A. Bond (New York: Garland, 1982). A recent article on Guillaume's appropriation of Ovid is Peter A. Thurlow, "Ovid's *Amores* III.iv: Its Reception in William of Aquitaine, Sebastian Brant, and Middle High German Literature," *Reading Medieval Studies* 10 (1984): 109–34.

17. *Ovid und die Troubadours,* 52, 58–59.

[If I do not have aid shortly
In order that my Good Lady love me,
I shall die, I swear by the head of St. Gregory!]

Nullus amor tanti est (abeas, pharetrate Cupido),
  ut mihi sint totiens maxima uota mori.

(Ovid Am. 2.5.1–2)

[No love is worth so much—go away, quiver-bearing Cupid—so that
my frequent and greatest wish should be to die.]

Schrötter's Guillaume is Wagner's Tristan, suffering from *Liebesschmerz,*
or love pains.[18] His parallels received their imprimatur in the mid-twentieth century from Dimitri Scheludko (1934), Antonio Viscardi (1939), and
Jessie Crossland (1947), all of whom expanded and revised Schrötter's
work. Scheludko, for one, writes that the implied analogy between lust and
thirst at the end of Guillaume's poem "Compaigno, non pus mudar"
(2.20–21) owes its genesis to Ovid's maxim "nitimur in uetitum semper
cupimusque negata: / sic interdictis imminet aeger aquis" [We seek what is
forbidden and desire what is denied: so the sick person lusts for forbidden
water] (*Am.* 3.4.17–18). Crossland suggests that the same poem, with its
mockery of husbands who think they can guard their wives from adultery,
imitates *Amores* 3.4 almost completely, in the same spirit and with the
same tone.[19]

In themselves, the "parallels" seem excruciatingly inexact. We have no
definite Ovidian quotations comparable to those that one would find in
Walter de Châtillon, who cites *Amores* 2.8.14 at the end of one of his
Goliardic stanzas: "quod decuit magnos, cur michi turpe putem?" [why
should I think base for myself what is fitting for the great?].[20] Perhaps *parallels* is too inexact a word for such hints, soundings, and scraps. Yet if one
takes them together, it becomes apparent that Guillaume inhales the
Amores and fashions his own *desultor Amoris.* Submerging himself in
Ovid, he subverts him.

---

18. Ibid., 65, 77, passim.

19. See Scheludko, "Ovid und die Trobadors," *Zeitschrift für romanische Philologie* 54
(1934): 128–74; Viscardi's more recent work on the subject, "Le origini della letteratura
cortese," *Zeitschrift für romanische Philologie* 78 (1962): 269–91; Crossland, "Ovid's Contribution," 200–201.

20. For Walter's text, see Raby, *Secular Latin Poetry,* 2:192 (my translation). E.J. Kenney's Oxford text of the *Amores, P. Ovidii Nasonis Amores,* has *reges* for *magnos.*

The *Amores* taught Guillaume polyvocality, to complicate his poetry with several voices and moods. One can discern Guillaume's debt by compiling (like Schrötter and his fellows) a florilegium of comparisons between Guillaume's lyrics and the *Amores*. The Count boasts that two women are more than enough for him to manipulate simultaneously, a "problem" that the *desultor* recounts in *Amores* 2.7, 2.8, and 2.10. Then, in a tender moment, the Count laments that his mistress has not recently written to him (10.7–10), the same disappointment expressed in *Amores* 1.13. The *gardadors* who protect married women from such hounds as the *ieu soi*, or "I am," of Guillaume's lyrics (1.7–9, 22–24) can claim Ovid's *ianitor* (*Am.* 1.6) as an ancestor. In another poem, the speaker confides to his comrades that sex with a married woman is no crime against her husband; a felled forest grows back, and a lord loses no revenue from it. Therefore, Guillaume's speaker claims,

> Tortz es c'om [planha la tala,
>   si negun] dan no.i a g[es].

(3.19–20)

> [It is wrong to lament the devastation
>   if there is no harm at all.]

This crystallizes what Guillaume might have called the *razo* or "theme" of *Amores* 2.2, in which the *desultor* tells Bagoas, the eunuch who guards the wife of a prospective cuckold, that protecting his master's spouse will only make the lover desire her more. Even if Bagoas did not bar entrance, nothing would be lost by the tryst that the lover seeks: "nihil, quamuis non tueare, perit" (line 12). Such facetious logic merely underscores the subtext: what is forbidden is more desirable, which a poet-aristocrat adulterously entwined with a woman named Dangerosa-Maubergeonne[21] must have known well.

What our first real vernacular lyric poet imitates in the *Amores* is Ovid's Protean *desultor Amoris*. Guillaume ingests such a persona and medievalizes it. His use of this device reflects twelfth-century practice as a whole, north and south of the Loire, in the vernacular and in Latin, as previously demonstrated by his contemporary Baudri of Bourgueil, who claimed, "quod personis impono uocabula multis . . . non uera loquor magis omnia

---

21. See Bond, *William*, xvii.

fingo" [when I create characters using many masks, I do not speak the truth but fabricate everything].[22]

Since many troubadours used *joglars* (OFr *jongleurs*) to recite their lyrics, the notion of the persona was built into the presentation of the poetry itself. A *canso, sirventes,* or *tenso* was literally performed. Even though a given poem might have been prefaced as "Count William's song," the audience still must have perceived a discrepancy between the *joglar* singing or reciting the poem and its author, because Count William was not in fact presenting it. Since Guillaume's lyrics vary so widely in tone, mood, and audience, this phenomenon must have been all the more pronounced. After all, he learned to make verses from the *magister personae.*

Guillaume may have also been reared with the concept. His father, Count Guy-Geoffrey William VI, brought back women *joglars,* or *joglaresas,* as spoils from the siege of Barbastro in al-Andalus (c. 1064), so they were a fixture of the household in which he was probably reared.[23] In one lyric, Guillaume encourages one "Daurostre," apparently his *joglar,* to sing and not to screech: "chan e [no] bram" (8.36). In another poem, he gives a similar command to "Mon Esteve" (7.47). The directive is clear: recite my work competently; be a credible persona. One might counter that the former poem is now classified "of doubtful attribution," that the role of Esteve in the latter is unclear, and that the chronicler Ordericus Vitalis (c. 1135) implies that Guillaume recited his own *nugas,* or nonsense, to an audience.[24] Yet *joglars* were so customary in twelfth-century Provence as to be unavoidable, and the chronicler, who despises Guillaume, is probably trying to discredit him by describing him capering about like an oaf.

Guillaume's persona is Protean, like the *desultor* of the *Amores:* he is amusing and cannot be trusted. Ironically, his speaker embodies the very description that another hostile chronicler, William of Malmesbury, attributes to the historical Count of Aquitaine: "fatuus et lubricus" [foolish and shifty].[25] Such shiftiness is inherent in the idea of different audiences to whom one gives contradictory information. Ovid's *desultor*

---

22. *Carmina* 85.36, 39.
23. See Bogin, *The Women Troubadours,* 47; Robert Briffault, *The Troubadours* (Bloomington: Indiana University Press, 1965), 53; Maria Rosa Menocal, *The Arabic Role in Medieval Literary History: A Forgotten Heritage* (Philadelphia: University of Pennsylvania Press, 1987), 27, 90.
24. See Bond, *William,* 47, and his appendix A, 10.
25. See Bond, *William,* 120.

addresses mistresses, hairdressers, companions, the "general reader";
Guillaume's *ieu soi* addresses his *companho* (comrades) and *autra gen*
(everyone else). To both poets, the idea of the *pellis,* or mask, is indispens-
able.[26]

The mask's indispensability to Ovid and Guillaume is paradoxically
reaffirmed when they deliberately lift it and allow us to stare into their
faces. One of the most masterful tricks in the *Amores* occurs in book 2. The
persona admits his duplicity, and then, by professions of sincerity, he continues in his attempted deceptions of reader, mistress(es), and self in book
3, as if the original admission had never been made. Even his preliminary
assertions in book 1 that he is one who loves with perfect fidelity ("qui
pura norit amare fide," 3.6) and is not desirous of a thousand conquests
("non mihi mille placent, non sum desultor amoris," 15) sound too cloy-
ingly sweet to be believed. His later admission that his behavior is inexcus-
able ("Non ego mendosos ausim defendere mores," 2.4.1) becomes anticlimactic. Also, the term *desultor* describes him completely.

Guillaume's *ieu soi* is such a man of masks. His statement "Enpero no
vueill c'om sapcha / mon afar de maintas res" [But I do not want people to
know my feelings about things] (3.2–3) is quickly contradicted in the next
line, "dirai vos m'entendensa" (4), because he will tell us his feelings, as
plainly and as crudely as possible: "No m'azauta cons gardatz" (5). In the
operative word, "cons" (cunt), Guillaume both revivifies and explodes the
vaunted "Ovidian spirit," much as one would purposely overinflate a balloon. The *desultor* would prefer that his "cons" be unguarded, but he in
turn hides it from *our* view in his anatomical description of Corinna in
Amores 1.5, "gentleman" that he is. To Guillaume, *cons es cons:* no gentleman is he.

It is tempting at this point to apply Greene's concept of dialectical *imitatio* to Guillaume's reading of Ovid (much as others have done with
Marie de France or Chrétien)—to argue that he is in "creative rivalry with
the Roman master."[27] Perhaps instead Guillaume is, in Ezra Pound's
phrase, simply "making it new." He is a medieval *magister,* as well as a
desultor Amoris, as he describes himself—a "maistre serta" (6.36) who
practices the "joc d'amor" (6.11), his *ludus,* or game of love. Similar to the

---

26. The word *pellis* seems to be a word that Ovid would use in its sense of "mask." However, in *Metamorphoses* 9.266 and *Ars amatoria* 1.516, it simply means "sandal," "strap,"
"leather," or "snakeskin." Since masks were often made from such material, the transference
is obvious. Horace uses *pellis* as "mask": *Satirae* 2.1.64; *Carmina* 1.16.45.

27. Robert Hanning uses this phrase in reference to Marie de France and Ovid ("Courtly
Contexts," 39).

desultor of *Amores* 3.4, the *ieu soi* warns his male auditors that pent-up women will strive to be free (2.13–15). What better method than love poetry to help them achieve this freedom?

> Fait ai lo vers, . . .
>
> . . . .
>
> Que.m tramezes del sieu estui
> La contraclau.
>
> (Guillaume 4.43–48)

> [I've made the song . . . .
>
> . . . .
>
> So that [she] might send me a copy of the key
> To her coffer.]

Similarly, Ovid's *desultor* says,

> at facie tenerae laudata saepe puellae
>   ad uatem, pretium carminis, ipsa uenit.
> magna datur merces
>
> (Ovid *Am.* 2.1.33–35)

> [but [because] the tender beauty of a girl [may be] praised often, she comes to a poet, a reward for his poetry. Great recompense is bestowed.]

Women, suggest the *desultor* and the *ieu soi,* are susceptible to flattery, and, as a happy by-product of such poetry, they are shallow enough to be undone by it and to bestow the requisite sexual rewards. To acknowledge one's power in this respect is to overpay one's artistic, as well as amorous, prowess. When art and nature fail the *desultor* in the notorious and much-imitated-in-the-Renaissance "impotence poem" (*Am.* 3.7), he boasts of his former efficacy in response: "me memini numeros sustinuisse nouem" (26); that is, he performed nine times continuously. The *ieu soi* recounts a similar failure to perform, albeit temporarily (6.50–56), but remembers astonishing success as well: "Cen e qatre vint et ueit vetz!" (5.79–80). He had performed one hundred and eighty-eight times. Here Guillaume bursts the balloon and may be "dialectical" in his imitation after all. He subverts Ovid in much the same way that Naso subverts Propertius.

Yet for the most part, Guillaume is content to reinvent the comic-erotic psychology of the *desultor*. Medieval aristocratic courtliness is just one more mask:

Ja no cera nullis hom ben fis
Contr'amor, si non l'es aclis

(7.25–26)

[No man will ever really be refined
With respect to love, if he is not submissive to it]

This looks ahead to the later troubadours and trouvères. Yet such passages are exceptional, and Guillaume's lyrics in toto flatly contradict them. Most often, the *ieu soi* makes pious professions of "love" to aid him in his pursuit of *cons*—that "don tan gran" that he equates, for obvious reasons, with his "courtly" gift of a ring: "Sa drudari'e son anel" (10.21–22). Ovid also provides the poetic warrant to make this anatomical and fiduciary equation. The *desultor* addresses the gift ring with the directive that it fit Corinna as well as she "fits" him: "tam bene conuenias quam mecum conuenit illi" (2.15.5).

Clearly, Guillaume did not "misunderstand" Ovid at all. Although our first known troubadour was probably a product of an education in which his tutors dissected, exemplified, and occasionally distorted Ovid, the twelfth-century poetic mind was capable of ingesting and processing such fragments and of producing a vernacular *desultor Amoris*. His imprint is unmistakable in Guillaume's poetry: *ecce homo*.

3. Dialogues

Perhaps no other troubadour submerges himself in Ovid in Guillaume's subversively concentrated way. (Marcabru has his own response, as does Bernart de Ventadorn, who will make straight the path of both Arnaut Daniel and, eventually, Dante.) Yet in the very form of the twelfth-century love dialogue, the troubadours, trouvères, *trobairitz*, and Latin authors all participate in a dialectic on the role of the *magister et desultor Amoris* in love and "relationships." Our twelfth-century authors literally work things out in dialogues; *fin' Amors* rewrites Ovid. The age questions him in a way that he cannot question himself, in its Latin writings as well as in the vernacular.

Women's voices constitute part of the revision process, not just in the expected area of *trobairitz* poetry, but in poems and prose *dialogi* written by men—Marcabru, Guiraut Riquier, Andreas Capellanus—in which women get the last word or are allowed to have their opinions prevail. Given modern preconceptions of the woman-hating Middle Ages, the consistency with which women dominate these debates may seem somewhat astonishing to us.

A twelfth-century Spanish text known as "the Ripoll manuscript" features such a love dialogue in Latin verse, titled MACIMADA or MACIMA DA by the scribe (i.e., anagrammatized AD AMICAM); it is better known by its first line, "Conqueror et doleo de te" (R 9.1).[28] It is one of twenty poems in the manuscript in which a lover reflects on the love of

---

28. My text of the Ripoll poet is that established by Therese Latzke, "Die carmina erotica der Ripollsammlung," *Mittellateinisches Jahrbuch* 10 (1974–75): 138–201:

AD AMICAM:
Conqueror et doleo de te, mea dulcis amica.
Quod prohibet facies: nimis exigis esse pudica.
Fac placeas Veneri, Veneris vel desine formam.
Me doctore potes Veneris cito discere normam.
AMICA:
Hoc placet et cupio, meus ut sis semper amicus.
Displicet et doleo, nisi sis quandoque pudicus.
Luxuriam fugias, precor, amplectaris amorem.
Convenit et pulcro iuveni servare pudorem.
AMICUS:
Non te testatur libri didactor amoris:
Non valet ullus amans semper memor esse pudoris.   10
Sed fortassis amans non es? Licet esse fateris.
Lingua sonat, tamen interius producere queris.
AMICA:
Dulcis amice mei, cordis non intima ledas:
Diligo plus nimio te, quamvis non mihi credas.
Non sic fictus amor meus est: si discere velles,
Scire, loqui possint; poterant quod dicere, pelles.
AMICUS:
Non nego me sub veste tua tractasse papillam,
Namque modo simili tractasset quislibet illam.
Crura tui, non sponte tua, sic candida nossem,
Te nisi per nimias vires devincere possem.   20
AMICA:
Simplicis ingenii nimis es, non insipientis:
Virgineae nescis que sit meditacio mentis.
Cum prohibet tactum, vult, ne meretrix videatur.
Condolet interius, nisi, quod negat, illud agatur.

a "pia virgo" (R 3.74). The thirty-two-line poem, set in eight quatrains of two couplets each (i.e., aabb ccdd &c), alternates between an *amicus* and an *amica,* whom the poet or scribe names with the anagrams SUCIMA and ACIMA, respectively. In form and "theme," it resembles the Provençal *tensos* and the French *pastourelles.* Also, like the knights and *tozas* (shepherdesses) in Marcabru's "fontana poems," the sparring lovers in *trobairitz* poetry, and the courtly copulatives in the prose dialogues of Andreas' *de Amore,* the *amicus* and *amica* turn their private debate into a referendum on Ovid and the neo-Ovidianism of troubadours, such as Guillaume. The *amicus* is an apprentice *desultor Amoris.*

Therese Latzke, the most recent editor of the collection, inadvertently demonstrates that "die Carmina erotica der Ripollsammlung" are imbued with the *Amores.* She lists over thirty-four separate instances of borrowing by the Ripoll poet from this Ovidian text. So, by the late eleventh or early twelfth century, the *Amores* were as well known in Spain as the *Heroides,* which Latzke also sees as an imitative model for Ripoll 9.[29]

Peter Dronke suggests that "Conqueror et doleo de te" is "almost a *tenson* between Ovid and *courtoisie.*"[30] I respond in this way: the word *courtoisie* should be widened to include *fin' Amors;* the poem is indeed a *tenso;* most *dialogi* are *tensos.* If we attempt to contextualize "Conqueror" by comparing it to similar twelfth-century material, we will see that the Ripoll poet's Ovidian dialogue is typical and atypical: as *dialogus* becomes *dialectica, amica* and *amicus* turn into *midons* and *servidor.*

AMICUS:
Tunc solet hoc fieri, cum principium fit amoris,
Inprovisus amor cum primis fervet in horis.
Alterius mores alter cum denique noscit,
Si placeant, facit hec, alter quod postea poscit.
AMICA:
Culpa tui, non culpa mei, perturbat amores,
Namque tui varios nequeo cognoscere mores.   30
Evolat hac illac multa tua parte iuventus,
Unde meus merito monstratur amor tibi lentus.

I use Latzke's documentation: capital letter *R* and Arabic numerals to indicate poems and line numbers. Peter Dronke takes issue with some of her editorial practices in "The Interpretation of the Ripoll Love-Songs," *Romance Philology* 33 (1979): 14–42. All English translations are my own, except where noted otherwise.

29. Latzke suggests *Heroides* 16 and 17 (the Paris-Helen debates) as models for Ripoll 9 ("Ripollsammlung," 158).

30. *Medieval Latin,* 1:256.

In the set of alternating quatrains, the man speaks first, and the woman responds by slyly and carefully undercutting him. The *amicus* is a clumsy and aggressive lover who claims to seethe with passion but who simply (and conventionally) lusts. His *amica,* though cautious and tactful, is equally ardent and aggressive as she contradicts, disarms, and attempts to educate—much as the *trobairitz* Alamanda does in her *tenson* with Guiraut de Borneilh:

> plassa vos lo bes e.l mals qu'il manda,
> qu'aissi seretz amatz.

> [accept the good and bad [your mistress] sends, thus shall you be loved.][31]

Like Alamanda, the Ripoll *amica* is conciliatory toward an aggressively male counterpart. Compromise, even submission, she hints, may bring a reward. Her love is as real, "non fictus" (R 9.15), as that of the *amicus* is feigned and phony.

The poem's dialectical interplay is not stichomythic, despite the alternating quatrains that the poet has subdivided into couplets. Its intricacies are in *traductio,* in which a word is repeated in different forms. The *amica* gently but firmly subverts the terminology of the *amicus* by echoing and changing his diction so that its superficiality is immediately apparent. The overall poetic and linguistic effect resembles Romanesque architectural "interlace."[32] A word doubles, contradicts, or connects with another in a different place; what seems to be an apostle is really a gargoyle. And perhaps, through the *amica,* the Ripoll poet engages in a bit of imitative subversion.

Sometimes the gargoyle is Ovid. Since the *amicus* invokes him as an authority ("libri didacator amoris," 9) and the Ripoll poet intimates that the *amicus* is a bit of a dolt, one is tempted to conclude that Ovid is being

---

31. The text and translation are from Bogin, *The Women Troubadours,* 102–3.

32. For the term *interlace* and its literary implications, see Eugene Vinaver, *The Rise of Romance* (Oxford: Oxford University Press, 1971): "since it is always possible, and often even necessary, for several themes to be pursued simultaneously, they have to alternate like threads in a woven fabric, one theme interrupting another and again another, and yet all remaining constantly present in the author's and the reader's mind" (76). This analysis can certainly be applied to wordplay, as well; thematically and lexically, it applies to Ovid, as Vinaver suggests (71).

discredited. Yet one might better deduce whether the *amica* is herself more subtly Ovidian. She may reflect twelfth-century domestication of this *auctor*, whose authority is fatuous when improperly used: he may be an apostle who does not deserve to be a gargoyle.

The *amica* scrutinizes and reverses the terms of address and blandishments of the *amicus*, particularly those that seem the most harmless. The precision of her replies highlights her sincerity and demonstrates her rhetorical skill. By implication, these abilities underscore her companion's imprecision and lack of sincerity. He explains his "grief" at her unwillingness ("doleo . . . nimis . . . pudica," 1–2); she subverts him by repetition and augmentation. Her displeasure at his lust and lack of sincerity ("doleo nisi . . . pudicus," 6) is unfeigned. Even his "mea dulcis amica" [my sweet friend] (1) is undercut. Only gradually is he "meus amicus" (5) and "dulcis amice mei" (13), and the hope is that he will be so "semper." Maria de Ventadorn draws such distinctions between lover and friend in her poetry: "dompna deu a son drut far honor / cum ad amic, mas non cum a seignor" [she should honor him the way she would a friend, but never a lord].[33] The *pia virgo* seeks a similar distance, countering the man's saccharine "amica" with her own guarded "amicus/amice." She has considered the meaning of "friend" and is trying to teach the *amicus* its significance.

The two possess different notions of friendship: he wants a plaything; she wants a companion. They also have divergent ideas about pleasure. What, for example, does it mean to please or be pleasing? Whom should one please? The *amicus*, in his plodding and conventional way, argues that the *amica* is and should be true to the shape and manner of Venus: "fac placeas Veneri, Veneris . . . formam. / . . . Veneris normam" (3–4); that is, she should please *him.* Yet her "displicet" (6) indicates through *traductio* that she can see through him and that she will please herself. Furthermore, the Ripoll poet is careful to balance the "formam" and "normam" as spoken by the *amicus* with the "luxuriam" (7) of the *amica.* It is not accidental that her term agrees in gender, number, and case with the two nouns of his phrase and thus shows his terminology for what it is: the *norma* and *forma Veneris* is simply *luxuria.* She disarms him as easily as the women of Andreas Capellanus' *de Amore* stifle the love calls of their suitors, many of whom say things like "nulla te poterit ratio excusare" [you have no reason not to love me] (51).[34]

---

33. The text and translation are from Bogin, *The Women Troubadours,* 100–101.

34. My quotations of *de Amore* are from *De amore,* ed., E. Trojel (Munich: Eidos, 1964). All references to it are indicated in the text by page numbers in parentheses.

One of Andreas' young swains has enough savoir faire to ask his object of seduction to teach him the ways of love: "te mihi peto magistram et tua doctrina plenius eruditi" (29). Yet the Ripoll *amicus* lacks even this requisite bit of useful insincerity and stretches his opening blunder across two quatrains. He boasts that he will teach his *amica* ("discere," R 9.4) Here he is buffeted by Ovid, the authoritative "libri didactor amoris" (9), who counsels that no lover can always be modest: "non valet ullus amans semper memor esse pudoris" (10).[35] With all modesty aside, suggests the *amicus,* they may both learn what may be "inside" her ("interius," 12). He reveals himself as a *desultor* in training, one whose charms would hardly take root in any woman's mind in any age. The *amica* waits until her second response to overtop him; *he* should learn ("discere," 15) that love cannot be forced.[36] One ought not to rely on "pelles" (17), or masks. Moreover, like her earlier redefinition of *amicus/amica,* her understanding of "interius" (24) and "intima" is much deeper and is less physical.

An anonymous *trobairitz* warns her prospective suitor that he should be frank, noble, discreet, and loving: "francs e fis, celans et amoros."[37] Yet frankness and ardor can be overdone. Andreas explains that one ought to say nothing that would deserve rebuke: "ne aliqua proferat, quae digna reprehensione cernatur" (155). Alas, the *desultor*-apprentice goes to the whip more quickly than even the *magister Amoris* would suggest. Heartened by such Ovidian bromides as "grata est vis ista puellis," the *amicus* lifts his mask:

Non nego me sub veste tua tractasse papillam,
Namque modo simili tractasset quislibet illam.
Crura tui, non sponte tua, sic candida nossem,
Te nisi per nimias vires divincere possem.

(R9.17–20)

[I don't deny that I touched your breast under your garment, for anyone else would have touched it in just this way. Not with your consent

---

35. The Ovid text paraphrased here reads "Pudor . . . castris . . . Amoris obest" (*Am.* 1.2.32); "pudor ipse nocebat" (*Am.* 3.7.37).

36. In "Ripoll Love Songs," Dronke suggests emending *discere* to *dicere,* which would change the tone of the passage. The *amicus* would be asking for permission to speak about love rather than giving himself warrant to teach the *amica* about it.

37. The text is from Bogin, *The Women Troubadours,* 155.

would I know that whiteness of your thighs unless I were able to conquer you with excessive force.][38]

Too frank, and deserving to be rebuked, the *amicus* implies rape as his remaining option. Some would give the lover this verbal license because he "is still so caught up in Ovidian notions of conquest, so impatient, and so imperceptive of her deepest feelings" that he apparently cannot help himself.[39] But *Macimada* belongs to the *amica* hidden in the anagram of the title, and the stress of any analysis of the poem should be on her. Intelligent and perceptive, she seems to have expected her partner's blunder. Her patience is extraordinary:

> Simplicis ingenii nimis es, non insipientis:
> Virgineae nescis que sit meditacio mentis.
> Cum prohibet tactum, vult, ne meretrix videatur,
> Condolet interius nisi quod negat illud agatur.
>
> (21–24)

[You are very naive, but you are not foolish: you don't know what the meditation of a virgin's mind might be. When she prohibits touching, she wishes that she not seem a harlot; she suffers inwardly because she denies that which she might do.]

Perhaps the *amicus* does not deserve such largesse. Yet the reply of the *trobairitz* Garsenda to a lovesick troubadour implies that such magnanimity was customary:

> que ges dompna non ausa descobrir
> tot so qu'il vol per paor de fallir.

[a lady doesn't dare uncover her true will, lest those around her think her base.][40]

---

38. Latzke suggests *Ars amatoria* 1.673 as a parallel ("Ripollsammlung," 159). For help with the translation of this quatrain, I thank Professor Charles Witke of the Department of Classics, University of Michigan.

39. This is Dronke's sympathetic reading of the passage ("Ripoll Love Songs," 37).

40. The text and translation are from Bogin, *The Women Troubadours,* 108–9.

However, the answer of the *amica* is more complex than this, as are the poetics and imitative strategies of the Ripoll poet. Latzke notes that line 21 echoes Paris' admonishment of Helen and her recalcitrance at becoming an adulteress in the *Heroides:* "Ah nimium simplex, Helene, ne 'rustica' dicam" (16.285).[41] Here the *pia virgo* uses the hackneyed language of male seduction to explain, and therefore preserve, her chastity. She uses Ovid to defend virginity, one of the ethical functions that the *Heroides* were supposed to fulfill.

Therefore, *Acima/Amica* is not anti-Ovidian. She simply reads him differently and uses his logic in her own way. She domesticates him, and not only with the *Heroides* that she has reprocessed for him in the manner of an *accessus* commentator. Her frank admission of her inner ardor seems a revision of *Amores* 3.4.8: "intus adulter erit." Her tacit criticism of the lover's technique could easily be summarized by two related Ovidian tags: "si latet, ars prodest" (*AA* 2.313); "ars adeo latet arte sua" (*Met.* 10.252). To paraphrase: the art of seduction is more profitable when subtle; art should conceal art. In this, the *amica* anticipates these noted lines from the *Carmina Burana:*

Artes amatorie	iam non instruunter
a Nasone tradite	passim pervertuntur

(105.7–8)

[The arts of love according to Ovid are not taught now but perverted everywhere.]

Alison Goddard Elliot's comment on this passage is instructive: "Those who believed in the religion of worldly love were not true Ovidians, for they, missing Ovid's tone of mockery, were guilty of treating love with pretentious solemnity."[42] The lines also apply to the blundering *amicus* of the present dialogue. Latzke excellently paraphrases the *amica*'s reply to her lover: "du handelst nicht nach der *norma* des *sapienter amare*, du gefährdest dadurch die Liebe selbst."[43]

---

41. "Ripollsammlung," 181.

42. "The Bedraggled Cupid: Ovidian Satire in *Carmina Burana* 105," *Traditio* 37 (1981): 437.

43. "Ripollsammlung," 159–60. The quotation can be roughly translated "You do not observe the rules of love wisely, but endanger the love itself."

Plainly, the *amica* is truer to the spirit of the *auctor,* even as she modifies Ovid for her own use. Yet *Sucima/Amicus* does not listen; he, apparently, cannot:

Tunc solet hoc fieri, cum principium fit amoris,
Inprovisus amor cum primis fervet in horis.
Alterius mores alter cum denique noscit,
Si placeant, facit hec, alter quod postea poscit.

(R 9.25–28)

[This is customary when love begins; unforeseen love boils in its first hours. When one finally knows the mores of another, let her do what he next entreats her to do, if it pleases them both.]

His last words to her in this dialogue show that he has allowed the opportunity with which she had provided him to pass. Rather than allowing himself to be instructed, he continues to instruct without the requisite authority. So, like the shepherdesses in the six *pastorellas* of Guiraut Riquier,[44] the *amica* gets the last word in what functions in the dialogue as a *tornada* or envoi:

Culpa tui, non culpa mei, perturbat amores,
Namque tui varios nequeo cognoscere mores.

(29–30)

[It is your fault, not mine, that your love troubles you, and I have no desire to understand your fickle mores.]

Her "Culpa tui" echoes and undercuts the "Crura tui" (19) of the *amicus:* that her physical charms distract him is his own fault. She repeats and transforms his *amoris* (25) and *mores* (27), rhyming them together (29–30) to highlight the general incompatibility of the two concepts. (One almost

---

44. For a discussion of Guiraut's *pastorellas* and for the text of the sixth, see Frederick Goldin, ed. and trans., *Lyrics of the Troubadours and Trouvères: An Anthology and a History* (New York: Anchor, 1973), 316–27. Guiraut owes much to Marcabru, on whose shoulders he stands. See Charles Fantazzi, "Marcabru's *Pastourelle:* Courtly Love Decoded," *Studies in Philology* 71 (1974): 385–403; Susan Olson, "Immutable Love: Two Good Women in Marcabru," *Neophilologus* 60 (1976): 190–99; Keith Bate, "Ovid, Medieval Latin, and the *Pastourelle,*" *Reading Medieval Studies* 9 (1983): 16–33.

hopes for a pun on *amores* with the *liber sine titulo*). He has no *mores* to which she cares to be converted.

As a lover in Andreas' *de Amore* is told, the *amicus* labors in vain ("In vanum ergo laboras," 88). What love can be undertaken against the desires of the heart? ("Praeterea qualis posset esse amor contra cordis voluntatem praesumptus?" 120). Nothing a lover gets is pleasing unless she gives it of her own free will ("Nota etiam, quod amans nihil sapidum ab amante consequitur nisi ex illius voluntate procedat," 9). The deflation of the conventional lover is almost comical. Like the *desultor Amoris,* the Ripoll *amicus* follows the advice of the *magister* and ends up alone. One can hear Marcabru's *toza* and her mockery of the wayward knight in "L'autrier jost' una sebissa": "bada, fols, bada" [Gape, fool; gape].[45]

4. Bernart de Ventadorn

Both Guillaume and the Ripoll poet ingest, subvert, and medievalize the *desultor Amoris* for their own purposes: the former reanimates Ovid; the latter domesticates him. In many respects, the troubadour who had the audacity to claim that he sang better than any other, "Non es meravelha s'eu chan / melhs de nul autre" (21.1–2), shows us how Ovid and his troubadour imitators can be ingested completely.[46] As Frederick Goldin says of Bernart, "What began to take shape in the songs of Guillaume IX is now completely developed."[47] What Goldin means is that Bernart is the heir and synthesizer of the conventions of the earlier troubadours, much as Bach serves as a watershed to Renaissance and Baroque music.

Bernart expands the imitation of the erotic Ovid. This is readily apparent in what Goldin calls Bernart's "dialectical technique," in which his voices and moods are adapted to different audiences.[48] He is Protean like Ovid's *desultor* and Guillaume's *ieu soi.* Yet Bernart, unlike Guillaume, is no pioneer; the latter has, as it were, established a colony to which the former has immigrated. Eminent medievalists in the earlier twentieth century,

---

45. The text and translation are from Goldin, *Troubadours,* 74.
46. The text and translations of Bernart are from Goldin, *Troubadours,* 108–59. Arabic numerals indicate poems and line numbers. Two recent works on the later troubadours: Linda Paterson, *Troubadours and Eloquence* (Oxford: Clarendon Press, 1975); Sarah Kay, *Subjectivity in Troubadour Poetry* (Cambridge: Cambridge University Press, 1990).
47. *Troubadours,* 108.
48. Ibid., 117.

such as Alfred Jeanroy and A.J. Denomy,[49] see Bernart as a type of break-
away figure—more sincere, idealistic, "romantic," courtly—based on such
passages such as the following, which features a much disputed and
sought-for phrase:

> fin' amors m'asegura
> de la freja biza.

(22.15–16)

[*fin' amors* protects me from the cold north wind.]

Still, much of Bernart's poetry derives from Guillaume's, even if the stress
on *con* is not quite so blatant. Perhaps Bernart is even more Ovidian: he
will change stances, give contradictory information, and allow the *pellis,*
or mask, to slip, just like the *desultor* does. Yet there is no acknowledgment
of the debt, nor is there an accompanying blatant subversion.

When one reads enough troubadour lyrics, one forgets that what is conventional in the *cansos* was cliché even to the neoteric elegists, albeit in
more cynical form. To Bernart (and everyone else), love is suffering:

> tan l'am eu, per que i ai dan

(21.20)

[I love her so much, and I suffer for it.]

Ovid's *desultor* makes the same point repeatedly: "quid me . . . laedis[?]"
[why do you hurt me so much?] (*Am.* 2.9a.3–4). Captivity occasions love's
suffering, as Ovid allegorizes in the *Amores* (1.2), in which Conscience and
Modesty are led in triumphal chains. Similarly, Bernart writes,

> no.m posc partir un dorn,
> aissi.m te pres s'amors e m'aliama.

(23.13–14)

---

49. Jeanroy, *La Poésie Lyrique des Troubadours,* 2 vols. (Toulouse: Privat, 1934), 2:13–33.
Father Denomy's work stresses what he considers to be the asexuality of later troubadour
lyrics in seven articles with such titles as "Fin Amors: The Pure Love of the Troubadours, Its
Amorality and Possible Source," *Medieval Studies* 7 (1945): 139–207. Donald Frank takes
issue with him on a number of grounds in "On the Troubadour *Fin' Amors,*" *Romance Notes*
7 (1966): 209–17.

[I can't move away the width of a hand, that's how her love holds me captive, puts me in chains.]

Bernart demonstrates his medieval aesthetics. Like Guillaume, he finds the parts of a poem and puts them together, perhaps more chastely than his Provençal predecessors, whom, he intimates, cannot touch him for artistry. Love is a pleasantly unpleasant experience.

Bernart's lover is as Protean as the *desultor*. He cannot be satisfied with one woman. Amid a cloying protestation of fidelity, he effects a bold and comic reversal:

> Totz tems volrai sa onor e sos bes
> e.lh serai om et amics e servire,
> e l'amarai, be li plass' o be.lh pes,
> c'om no pot cor destrenher ses aucire.
> No sai domna, volgues o no volgues,
> si.m volia, c'amar no la pogues.
>
> (23.22–27)

[I shall always desire her honor and her good, and I shall be her man, and her lover, and her servant, and I shall love her whether it pleases her or grieves her, for no one can constrain a heart without killing it. I don't know one woman that I could not love, if I wanted to, whether she wanted it or not.]

This is the voice of the *magister*. Likewise, after reams and reams of elegiac couplets in which the *desultor* laments his constrained heart and pledges unswerving fidelity, he admits, quite simply, that he wants them all: "noster in has omnes ambitiosus amor" (*Am.* 2.4.48).

Much of the *Amores* distinguishes between private and public behavior in love. Part of Ovid's joke is that a man is capable of only so many reversals before he forgets what he has pledged to whom. *Amores* 1.4 is the notorious set of directions for infidelity to Corinna at a banquet at which her husband is present: "Veneris lasciuia nostrae" (21). Bernart simply crystallizes the directive:

> Domna, a prezen amat
> autrui, e me a celat,
> si qu'eu n'aya tot lo pro
> et el la bela razo.
>
> (25.57–60)

[Lady, in public love the other one, and me in private, so that I get all the good of it, and he the edifying conversation.]

In mocking the "razo," or talk, as extraneous, Bernart delivers the actual *razo* (or theme) of Ovid's amoral love sequence. For Bernart's persona is also changeable and self-loathing, and he cannot keep himself from loving: "eu d'amar no.m posc tener" (26.11). Thanks to this infirmity of the will and self-absorption, he cannot understand the woman whom he claims to love:

> no vol so c'om voler,
> e so c'om li deveda, fai.

(26.35–36)

[she does not want what one ought to want, and what is forbidden to do, she does.]

Amores 3.4.4 can be put alongside these passages: "quae, quia non liceat, non facit, illa facit" [she who does not do because she may not, does (it anyway)].

As the *Amores* end, Ovid's *desultor,* true to his psychology, does not say things that one might expect him to say; he stops short. He does not admit his stupidity but instead confides that "non ego sum stultus, ut ante fui" (3.11a.32). He also cannot admit that he is at pains to love; instead he informs us that he will love unwillingly, despite his "hate": "odero, si potero; si non, inuitus amabo" (3.11b.35). Bernart's lover will have none of this:

> Dreihz es que.m sofranha
> totz jois, qu'eu eis lo.m tolh.

(27.71–72)

[It is right that I lack every joy, for I alone deprive myself of every joy.][50]

---

50. Compare this line from the twelfth-century French poem *Narcisus:* "Jou meïsmes me fas languir" (916). For a discussion of the poem and the issue, see Goldin, *The Mirror of Narcissus in the Courtly Love Lyric* (Ithaca: Cornell University Press, 1967), 37.

If we think of Bernart's lyrics as a Provençal *liber sine titulo*, a twelfth-century *Amores*, he imitates and revises Ovid by stating something unspoken but present in the erotica, something that needed to be said. This is the closest the medieval poet gets to subverting his classical model. His broad statement of self-defeat is as much a rebellion against the *auctor* as Guillaume's foulmouthed use of *con* can be perceived to be. Although T.S. Eliot's comments on "tradition" and the "individual talent" are not often cited anymore, they seem applicable to Bernart, Guillaume, and Ovid: "To conform would be for the new work not really to conform at all; it would not be new, and would therefore not be a work of art."[51] To paraphrase a fairly commonplace medieval idea, Bernart stands on the shoulders of a giant so that he may see further.[52]

Ovid's *desultor,* gargoyle or saint, is doubtless a palpable presence in troubadour poetry. Most often he surfaces in the Protean, mocking male voices of the troubadours; sometimes we find him submerged in the voices of women, such as the *trobairitz* and the Ripoll *amica.* In some respects, these imitations are subversive, just as most twelfth-century cannibalism of the entire Ovidian corpus is subversive. This was not lost on Dante. Through his reading of these troubadours, he too imbibes this pan-European *desultor* and learns to write love poetry that is heavily indebted to the amorous Ovid, even as he scrambles to distance his own erotic persona, the *io son,* from the ancient poet. This will lead us to ask: how "new" is the *Vita nuova*? How *fine* can his *amore* for Beatrice be?

---

51. Eliot, *Selected Essays* (New York: Harcourt Brace, 1950), 5.

52. Pierre de Blois (d. 1200) puts forth this idea: "Nos, quasi nani super gigantum humeros sumus, quorum beneficio longius, quam ipsi, speculamur." Cited in Greene, *The Light in Troy,* 84.

CHAPTER 4

"Io non lo 'nvidio": Dante's *Vita nuova* and the *desultor Amoris*

Barbara Nolan argues that the *Vita nuova* "has no predecessor or successor in medieval literature."[1] Her use of the adjective *medieval* is an important qualification, because the *Vita* certainly has its successors in the Renaissance. Petrarch, Ronsard, Du Bellay, Spenser, Sidney, and Shakespeare all create narrative sequences of poems incidentally concerned with composition. Dante's most evident variation on the paradigm is the prose commentary, the "severely arid analysis"[2] that accompanies his *canzoni* and *sonetti*. Yet, except for the use of the vernacular for criticism, the mixing of prose and verse (*prosimetron*) is also derivative. Martianus Capella's *de Nuptiis Philologiae et Mercurii* (fifth century), Boethius' *Consolatio* (sixth century), the *sequentia cum prosa* of the Mass (initiated in the eighth century), and Bernard Silvestris' *de Universitate Mundi* (twelfth century) are all works Dante knew. Also, Dante has one particularly important classical predecessor for the poetic sequence: Ovid and his *Amores,* which exercise a truly formative influence on the *Vita nuova.*

Although it has been said that "Ovid is one of the poets Dante most uses, but . . . least acknowledges,"[3] he mentions Ovid extensively in his works as a learned authority. In the *Convivio* (4.27), Dante describes him as a teacher of prudence, justice, generosity, and affability.[4] He gives his *auctor* "human" dimension in *Inferno* 4, the canto in which his persona,

---

1. "The *Vita nuova:* Dante's Book of Revelation," *Dante Studies* 88 (1970): 51.
2. See Dante Alighieri, *La Vita nuova,* trans. Barbara Reynolds (New York: Penguin, 1969), 18.
3. Teodolinda Berolini, *Dante's Poets: Textuality and Truth in the "Comedy"* (Princeton: Princeton University Press, 1984), 196.
4. See Robert S. Haller, ed. and trans., *Literary Criticism of Dante Alighieri* (Lincoln: University of Nebraska Press, 1973), 128.

the *io son,* manifests his humble egotism by allowing Ovid, Homer, Virgil, Horace, and Lucan to include him in their assembly to make a sixth among these lofty poetic minds: "sì ch' io fui sesto tra cotanto senno" (102).[5] However, in *Inferno* 25, Dante may be distancing himself from Ovid by means of a pun. When his narrator says that he does not envy the author of the *Metamorphoses* for his story of Cadmus and Arethusa because his own tangle of serpents and Florentines is far worse, using the words "io non lo 'nvidio" (99), he may also be saying, "io non Ovidio" [I am not Ovid].[6] If this is indeed a pun, it is doubly disingenuous. Dante raids the Ovidian corpus extensively, suggesting a type of appreciative envy.

Recent studies of Dante's debt to Ovid are beginning to complement earlier scholarship that documents Virgil's pervasive influence.[7] Since the *Metamorphoses* was the most widely perused Ovidian text in the Middle Ages, scholars naturally hear its echoes in the *Commedia.* Leonard Barkan demonstrates Dante's medieval appropriation of Ovid's classical, Protean poetics: "the great pagan vision of metamorphosis is to be respected, confronted, saved, and recast in an original form."[8] Similarly, in the *Vita nuova,* Dante confronts, saves, and recasts Ovid's erotic poetry. He

---

5. All citations and translations from the *Commedia* are from Dante Alighieri, *The Divine Comedy,* 6 vols., ed. and trans. Charles S. Singleton (Princeton: Princeton University Press, 1970–75). Jean de Meun anticipates Dante by including himself in a group of poets with Ovid (*Roman* 10522–30), albeit in a satrical manner. Peter Allen argues that Jean is "deprecatory" toward Ovid and "kicks him out of the way" (*The Art of Love,* 80–81). Ernst Robert Curtius reminds us that the *Roman* was well known in Italy in Dante's time (*European Literature,* 34). It appears that Dante inherits this topos, resuscitates Ovid, and kicks Jean out of the way. For a study linking Dante and the *Roman,* see Luigi Vanossi, *Dante e il "Roman de la Rose" saggio sul "Fiore"* (Firenze: Olschki, 1979). Chaucer's variation on the topos of including oneself in the academy reads: "kis the steppes, where as thow seest pace / Virgile, Ovide, Omer, Lucan, and Stace" (*Troilus* 5.1792–93).

Other articles on the subject include Leslie Cahoon, "Raping the Rose: Jean de Meun's Reading of Ovid's *Amores," Classical and Modern Literature* 6 (1985): 261–85; John V. Fleming, "Jean de Meun and the Ancient Poets," in *Rethinking the "Romance of the Rose": Text, Image, Reception,* ed. Kevin Brownlee and Sylvia Huot (Philadelphia: University of Pennsylvania Press, 1987), 81–100.

6. Peter S. Hawkins, "The Metamorphosis of Ovid," in *Dante and Ovid: Essays in Intertextuality,* ed. Madison U. Sowell (Binghamton: State University of New York Press, 1991), 19. See also Curtius on the relationship of this passage to what he calls "outdoing" (*European Literature,* 162–65).

7. Two recent collections of essays are Sowell, *Dante and Ovid;* Rachel Jacoff and Jeffrey T. Schnapp, eds., *The Poetry of Allusion: Virgil and Ovid in Dante's "Commedia"* (Palo Alto: Stanford University Press, 1991).

8. *The Gods Made Flesh,* 140. He is anticipated in the conception of Dante in competition with Ovid by Curtius (*European Literature,* 18).

rewrites the *Amores* for the thirteenth century in the "dolce stil novo" (*Purgatorio* 24.57) of the *stilnovisti*, whose troubadour-derived poetics owe much to the *magister* and *desultor Amoris*.

Both the *Vita* and the *Amores* are devoted to the progress of poet-lover personae who are fashioned after Dante and Ovid, respectively. Therefore, both poets can create "an explicit framework of fictionality" by establishing a distance between "speaking maker" (author) and "fictive speaker" (voice or character).[9] However, while Ovid repeats his own name at conspicuous intervals in the *Amores,* Dante is calculatedly content to be a "nameless" *io son* in the *Vita*. For Dante to refrain from self-advertisement reduces the ironic distance between author and persona, thereby creating the illusion that he and the *io son* are a composite, a humble and sincere pilgrim seeking love.[10] So the *Amores* serve as a paradigmatic point of departure.

At the end of the thirteenth century, Dante confronts at least two forms of medieval Ovidianism: the refined vernacular, nonreligious eroticism of the troubadours, and the Christianized Latin Ovid exemplified by such works as *de Vetula.* The *Vita nuova* reflects this tension. It is the first sustained work of the Middle Ages to attempt the exorcism of the *desultor Amoris* and to revise troubadour erotics, and it is fueled by the tenets of medieval Christianity. Beatrice is Madonna as well as *midons,* as Dante suggests in line 29 of "Donne ch'avete intelletto d'amore," the canzone to *Vita nuova* 19.[11]

Although Dante attempts to shift the focus of the sequence from the speaker to the creation of a poetics that transcends the self, he is only partially successful. Despite occasional triumphs, he finds it difficult indeed to idealize beyond the sensual a woman for whom he feels a powerful physical attraction. Though Dante makes no mention of the *Amores* in the *Vita,* the psychology of the anguished *io son* as he meditates on Beatrice is a variation on the dynamic of Ovid and *fin' Amors*—on lust, guilt, self-

---

9. See Bond, "Composing Yourself," 86.

10. Ovid names himself in the *Amores* in the following locations: Epigramma 1, 1.11.27, 2.1.2, 2.13.25. Another, simpler reason for Dante not to name himself is that he wrote for a coterie audience. As Barbara Reynolds reminds us, the *Vita* "was written for fellow poets and friends, many of them women, who shared the sensibility and thoughts of poets" (Dante, *La Vita nuova,* trans. Barbara Reynolds, 13).

11. My Italian text of the *Vita* is *La Vita nuova,* Edoardo Sanguineti and Alfonso Berardinelli, eds. (Milan: Garzanti, 1988). My translations are based on those in *Dante's "Vita nuova,"* ed. and trans. Mark Musa (Bloomington: Indiana University Press, 1973). Page numbers in parentheses following Dante's Italian and the English translations correspond to page numbers in these texts, respectively.

loathing, the obsession with fame, *midons,* and the *ars poetica.* Often the eroticism Dante so deeply sublimates belies its own sublimation by its very intensity. For this reason, he may fulfill Ovid's prophecy at the end of the *Ars amatoria:* he is one of the *iuuenes* who proclaims "NASO MAGIS-TER ERAT" (3.812).

1

Before turning to the dialectical imitation of the *Amores* in the *Vita nuova,* it will be useful to discuss the troubadours who filter Ovid's conventions for Dante. It was once a commonplace of criticism that Dante eventually "divests himself" of troubadour poetics and its Ovidian subtext, especially in the "Paolo and Francesca" episode of *Inferno* 5.[12] In his earlier writings, Charles Singleton implies that Dante ultimately rejects *fin' Amors,* but in a later essay, Singleton argues as proof of the existence of "courtly love" that the *Vita* begins "exactly *within* [its] cult."[13] Beatrice

is a creature of courtly love. She would never have existed . . . had there not been a tradition of courtly love: she was a *madonna* among

---

12. The Paolo and Francesca episode is ferociously contested by critics. As tempting as it is to discuss it fully in the context of Dante's Ovidianism, I restrain myself here. The two opposing schools of thought argue that Dante uses the doomed lovers either to reject *fin' Amors* or to endorse it tacitly and subversively. Commentaries in English include Charles S. Singleton, *An Essay on the "Vita nuova"* (Cambridge: Harvard University Press, 1949); Renato Poggioli, "Tragedy or Romance? A Reading of the Paolo and Francesca Episode in Dante's *Inferno,*" *PMLA* 72 (1957): 313–58; Colin Hardie, "Dante and the Tradition of Courtly Love," in *Patterns of Love and Courtesy: Essays in Memory of C.S. Lewis,* ed. John Lawlor (Evanston: Northwestern University Press, 1966), 26–44; Anna Hatcher and Mark Musa, "The Kiss: *Inferno V* and the Old French Prose *Lancelot,*" *Comparative Literature* 20 (1968): 97–109; Joan Ferrante and George D. Econoumou, eds. *In Pursuit of Perfection: Courtly Love in Medieval Literature* (London: Kennikat Press, 1975), introduction, esp. 12; Peter Dronke, "Francesca and Heloise," *Comparative Literature* 27 (1975): 113–35; John Scott, "Dante's Francesca and the Poet's Attitude towards Courtly Literature," *Reading Medieval Studies* 5 (1979): 4–20; Susan Noakes, "The Double Misreading of Paolo and Francesca," *Philological Quarterly* 62 (1983): 221–39; Christopher Kleinhenz, "Dante as Reader and Critic of Courtly Literature," in *Courtly Literature: Culture and Context,* ed. Keith Busby and Erik Kooper (Amsterdam: Benjamins, 1990), esp. 385–86. Dronke's comment is most instructive: "Dante simply does not show that moral indignation which some twentieth-century moralists . . . would like him to have shown" ("Francesca and Heloise," 126). He also notes the recurrence of rhyme words from *Vita nuova* 39 (*martiri, sospiri, desiri*) in Francesca's speech (126).

13. See Singleton, *Essay,* 32, and "Dante: Within Courtly Love and Beyond," in *The Meaning of Courtly Love,* ed. F.X. Newman (Albany: State University of New York Press, 1968), 46, respectively.

madonne, sung in the manner of *amoris accensio,* as that convention had come out of Provençe.[14]

The phrase *amoris accensio* (which Singleton appropriates from *de Vulgare Eloquentia*) has multiplex meanings. It signifies the flame, access, ascent, even the "very ecstasy of love" that Polonius (mistakenly) finds in Hamlet's letter to Ophelia. Yet *amoris accensio* is not just a phenomenon of the *Vita;* it stays with Dante into the *Commedia.* Even the ethereal and "chaste" *Paradiso* suggests that he is in no hurry to lose step with the *olde daunce.* In some respects, just as the gathering of poets in *Inferno* 4 obliterates Jean de Meun's desecration of the academy in the *Roman,* Dante's "rosa sempiterna" that "dilata ed ingrada" [dilates and rises] at *Paradiso* 30.124–25 revises Jean's "rose vermeille" in *Le roman de la rose* (21779), one that the Amant stimulates and causes to enlarge and expand in quite a different way: "fis eslargir et estendre" (21730). Yet such parody would be impossible without its source, to which Dante owes so very much. If he rejects courtly copulation, he cannot afford to "divest himself" of the Ovidian *fin' Amors* that sets it rocking in motion.

The Dante of criticism who wrote the *Convivio* also wrote *de Vulgare Eloquentia,* that Latin treatise that champions the use of the vernacular in poetry. In *de Vulgare Eloquentia* 2.2, he uses the Scholastic-Horatian formula of the *accessus* that his schoolmaster predecessors had established a century and a half earlier, demonstrating his concern with *utile* and *virtutem*[15] and the best subjects for poetry:

> hec tria, salus videlicet, venus et virtus, apparent esse illa magnalia que sint maxime pertractanda, hoc est ea que maxime sunt ad ista, ut armorum probitas, amoris accensio et directio voluntatis. (152)

> [these three (that is, self-preservation, the enjoyment of love, and virtue) are certainly those "splendidly great things" which should be written about using the best available means; or rather, the things which to the greatest extent tend toward them, which are prowess in arms, the flames of love, and direction of the will.] (35)

---

14. Singleton, "Dante," 52–53.

15. See Dante Alighieri, *Opera Minori,* ed. Pier Vincenzo Mengaldo, 2 vols. (Milan: Ricciardi, 1979), 2:150, 152. All further Latin references to the *de Vulgari* are from this source and are cited by page numbers in parentheses. Translations are based on those in Haller, *Dante Alighieri,* and are also indicated by page numbers in parentheses.

The term *venus,* or "the enjoyment of love," as it is chastely translated, refers to physical love, connected by analogy to the aforementioned "amoris accensio," the flame of love. The "directio voluntatis" is also invoked, the will that Shakespeare's Will, without a shred of virtue, will have in overplus as he pursues his dark lady (Sonnet 135). As Dante champions the use of the poetic vernacular in Latin prose, he also legitimizes its love language, its "jargon," if you will. Ovid and the troubadours certainly understood what Dante means by "amoris accensio," since he inherits the concept from them.

Throughout his career, Dante never "divests himself" of this Ovidian terminology. In the *ballata* to *Vita* 12, he uses the phrase "ben servidore" (19), a translation of the Provençal good servant-slave to *midons: bon servidor.* Dante also knew the term *fin' Amors,* since he cites it in a line by the trouvère Thibault de Champagne that he quotes in *de Vulgare* 1.9: "De fin amor si vient sen et bonté."[16] From *fin' Amors* comes true understanding and magnaminity. In *Vita* 3, Dante describes Beatrice as "cortesissima" (4), in his only use of the superlative form of the adjective *cortese.* As Christopher Kleinhenz states, this term "represents the consummate courtly lady of the earlier literary tradition, becoming . . . the supreme embodiment of the traits and attitudes characteristic of the courtly tradition."[17] Ultimately, it even fuels "l'amor che move il sole e l'altre stelle" [the Love that moves the sun and other stars] in the last line of the *Paradiso* (33.145).

Therefore, Dante's debt to his Ovidian troubadours cannot be overstated. His very poetics is founded on theirs—the tormented and changeable lover and his equally capricious lady, the (barely) sublimated eroticism, the "love language," the use of the vernacular, and the array of stanzaic forms and rhyme schemes, chief among them the canzone, which is basically an "Italianization" of the Provençal *canso.* Also, Guillaume IX and Bernart de Ventadorn kept the dynamic of the *Amores* in mind when they wrote, which the later troubadours and *stilnovisti* whom Dante admires, such as Sordello, Arnaut Daniel, and Guido Guinizelli, inherit. Dante, in turn, inherits and refines the same dynamic.

The Dante of the *Commedia* pays tribute to some of these troubadours

---

16. Haller, *Dante Alighieri,* 41.
17. "Dante as Reader," 386.

and their Ovidian legacy.[18] His academies of poets in the *Inferno* and *Purgatorio* show his line of descent: Homer, Virgil, Horace, Lucan, Ovid, Sordello, Arnaut Daniel, Guido Guinizelli, Dante. Although Sordello, Guinizelli, and Arnaut are mired in the *Purgatorio,* the honor and dignity that they are accorded is unmatched. Sordello embraces Virgil in a gesture of brotherly supplication: "abbracciòl là 've 'l minor s'appiglia" (7.15). Dante praises Guinizelli for his sweet lines: "Li dolce detti vostri" (26.112). Guinizelli then compliments Arnaut as the "miglior fabbro del parlar materno" (26.117), who is then allowed to identify himself in his mother tongue, Provençal: "Ieu sui Arnaut" (26.142).

Arnaut's disappearance at the end of the canto is particularly moving, rivaling Ser Brunetto's triumphant exit at the end of *Inferno* 15. The imagery symbolically imitates Dante's appropriation of his predecessors: "Poi s'ascose nel foco che li affina" (26.148). Just as Arnaut hides himself in the fire that refines them all, Dante conceals his troubadour legacy in the "foco che li affina." Yet there is no real division; this is no auto-da-fé. To take a line from Arnaut's most famous sestina, "Lo ferm voler," Dante and his Ovidian troubadours are as close as "lo detz de l'ongla," the finger to the nail. After all, Dante's shadow touches the flames of purgatory as well and makes them quiver: "io facea con l'ombra più rovente / parer la fiamma" (26.7–8). It is of the same substance as *amoris accensio,* the very flame of love from which Francesca speaks to the *io son* in *Inferno* 5.

2

In the *Vita nuova,* it is hardly surprising that Dante does not mention the *Amores,* a text that he is simultaneously imitating and attempting to exorcise. As the magister says, "si latet, ars prodest" (*AA* 2.313). Yet Dante cannot resist alluding to the *Remedia amoris* in *Vita* 25, citing the pagan *magister Amoris* (not Virgil, as one might expect) as precedent to defend personification and allegory. "Per Ovidio parla Amore, sì come se fosse persona humana" [through Ovid, Love speaks as though it were a human

---

18. In "Poets of Love and Exile," Janet Marie Smarr intimates that Dante "evokes his predecessors only to distance himself from them" (*Dante and Ovid: Essays in Intertextuality,* ed. Madison U. Sowell [Binghamton: State University of New York Press, 1991], 147). I argue that Dante emphasizes his *differences; distance* is not possible for him.

being] (50).[19] This is a way of paying a debt. Also, Dante is writing in the age of the *Remedia* Ovid, and it is not unusual that he should mention this work. As the sardonic Dante da Maiano writes to Dante in their literary correspondence,

D'Ovidio ciò mi son miso a provare
che disse per lo mal d'Amor guarire,
e ciò ver me non val mai che mentire;
per ch'eo mi rendo a sol merzé chiamare.

[I have set myself to test what Ovid prescribed as remedy for lovesickness; but so far as I'm concerned it is simply a lie: hence I resign myself to begging for pity.][20]

Thirteenth-century writers know that Ovid can be the master of mendacity, yet they rely on the *Remedia* as a medical text, moralize it to curb lasciviousness, or imitate it in its original satiric context: love is so foolish that it needs to be cured. Such divergent uses suggest the turbulence a "profane" and subversive pagan author can cause in a Christian society that must justify his utility. As Theodulf of Orleans had written in the eighth century of "Naso loquax" and others, "Plurima sub falso tegmine vera latent" [many truths lie under the cover of falsehood].[21] The Ovidian corpus becomes a template on which to burn variations, like acid on copper. Other writers, such as John of Garland, Jean de Meun, Richard de Fournival, and the anonymous makers of *de Vetula* and *La clef d'amors,* imitate, explicate, and subvert the master's voice.[22] All of these authorial currents propel Dante as he writes the *Vita.*

---

19. Robert Hollander praises this section as "one of the most brilliant passages of literary criticism written between the time of Servius and Macrobius and the close of the thirteenth century" ("*Vita nuova:* Dante's Perceptions of Beatrice," *Dante Studies* 92 [1974]: 6); Hardie dismisses it as "inadequate to his whole story," even "destructive of it" ("Dante," 32).

20. In Dante Alighieri, *Dante's Lyric Poetry,* ed. and trans. K. Foster and P. Boyd, 2 vols. (Oxford: Oxford University Press, 1967), 1:10–11.

21. "Namque ego suetus eram hos libros legisse frequenter," lines 18 and 20, in Godman, *Poetry of the Carolingian Renaissance,* 169. John of Salisbury paraphrases Theodulf's line in his twelfth-century *Entheticus:* "sub verborum tegmine vera latent" (*Metalogicon,* 206).

22. de Meun's subversion has already been discussed. John of Garland's *Integumenta Ovidii* is a learned and distilled moralization of the *Metamorphoses.* The text is from *Integumenta Ovidii,* ed. Fausto Ghisalberti (Milan: Casa Editrice Giuseppe Principato, 1933). For an analysis of the pervasive use of *integumentum* by medieval poets, see D.W. Robertson, *A Preface to Chaucer,* 19, 90, 316, 345–46, 359–60. The anonymous *La clef d'amors* is what

Of these texts, the one that Dante probably read and was most influenced by was *de Vetula,* a poem in three books of 2,357 Latin hexameter lines that exists in an astounding thirty-two manuscripts. It combines the *desultor* and *magister Amoris* in the person of Ovid himself, who is reconstituted according to Christian principles. Purported to be by Ovid (and sometimes attributed to Richard de Fourneval), it recounts his last love affair and his eventual conversion to Christianity.[23] Dante may have known it either in Latin or in Richard Lefèvre's enormous translation into French, *La Vielle, ou les dernières amours d'Ovide.*[24] The poem is full of Ovidian loci, which the author cleverly revises as he writes, so that a reader can observe the metamorphosis of Ovid's conversion. In two lines, he recants the whole of *Ars amatoria* 3:

Sunt alii ludi parvi, quos scire puellas
esse decens dixi, sed parva monere pudebat.

                                                          (1.636–37)

Thomas Greene would call a "contaminative" imitation of the *Ars amatoria,* translated into French. The text is from Auguste Doutrepont, ed., *La clef d'amors,* Bibliotheca Normannica 5 (Halle: Niemeyer, 1890). The *Consaus d'amours* of Richard de Fournival is another Ovidian treatise that explicates and justifies the principles of the *magister.* See William H. McLeod, ed., "The *Consaus D'Amours* of Richard de Fournival," *Studies in Philology* 32 (1935): 1–18. See also Reginald Hyatte, "Ovidius, Doctor Amoris: The Changing Attitudes towards Ovid's Eroticism in the Middle Ages as Seen in the Three Old French Adaptations of the *Remedia Amoris,*" *Florilegium* 4 (1982): 123–36. Some of the texts discussed here are most accessible in Norman Shapiro, trans., and James B. Wadsworth, ed., *The Comedy of Eros: Medieval French Guides to the Art of Love* (Urbana: University of Illinois Press, 1970).

    23. Paul Klopsch, ed., *Pseudo-Ovidius "de Vetula"* (Leiden: Brill, 1967), 160–74. All citations from the poem refer to this edition. Klopsch's introduction is unsurpassed. For an English language commentary on the manuscript tradition, see Dorothy M. Robathan, "An Introduction to the Pseudo-Ovidian *de Vetula,*" *TAPA* 87 (1957): 197–207. Dante's description of *amoris accensio* is suspiciously like Richard de Fourneval's in the *Consaus* (which he attributes to John of Garland):

    Amours est une foursenerie de pensée, fus sans estaindre, fains sans soeler, cous mals, boine douchours, plaisans folie, travaus sans repos, et repos sans travel. (McLeod, "The *Consaus D'Amours,*" 9)

    [Love is a folly of thought, a fire without quenching, a hunger without solace, a sweet illness, a profound sweetness, a pleasant folly, a labor without repose and a repose without labor] (my translation).

    24. See Sowell, *Dante and Ovid,* 7. Robathan mentions that Dante's son Piero quotes the *de Vetula* twice in his commentary on the *Commedia* ("The Pseudo-Ovidian *de Vetula,*" 199).

[There are other little games that I said it was fitting for girls to know, but it is shameful to recommend such base things.]

The last love affair is occasioned by his lust for a "virginei floris decor et decus" (2.203) whom he wishes to woo through an intermediary, the *vetula,* an old woman who is the granddaughter of the hag Dipsas in *Amores* 1.8, and who is the mother of La Vielle in the *Roman,* as well as Chaucer's Wyf of Bath. After the assignation is arranged and completed, Ovid discovers to his horror that he has slept with the *vetula,* not the *puella:*

> Credere quis posset, quod virgo quator implens
> . . . adeo cito consenuisset.
>
> (2.493–94)

[Who would believe that a virgin satisfied four times . . . would grow old so quickly.]

The *puella* sends the *vetula* in her stead to teach the wicked poet a wicked lesson indeed. As "Ovid" recounts this "metamorphosis," he paraphrases the opening of his most famous text (*Met.* 1.1f), which shows the subtlety of *de Vetula.* The *auctor* repudiates his own Protean poetics as he uses them:

> In nova formas
> corpora mutatas cecini, mirabiliorque
> non reperitur ibi mutatio quam fuit ista,
> scilicet, ut fuerit tam parvo tempore talis
> taliter in talem vetulam mutata puella.
>
> (2.495–99)

[I had sung of forms changed into new bodies, and there could hardly have been a greater mutation than that one there, so that in such a short time a girl could have been transfigured into such an old woman.]

Once shaken by this catastrophe, Ovid discovers philosophy and converts to Christianity, and he ends *de Vetula* with a hymn to the Blessed Virgin: "O virgo felix, o virgo significata / per stellas" (3.772–73).

Even in the thirteenth century, strong doubt existed as to whether or not Ovid wrote this poem, despite such authoritative proponents for its authenticity as Roger Bacon. One epigram slyly insinuates that Pseudo-Ovidius wrote the poem to "save" Ovid: "cupis Ovidium salvare per hec tua scripta." Another writer confesses that the idea of Ovid as prophet appeals to him: "Nempe placet michi non modicum, quod Naso propheta / sic fuerit Christi."[25] *De Vetula*, then, is the ultimate *remedia*, *clef*, and *integumentum*. The author resuscitates Ovid and reconfigures him for the thirteenth century by making him say everything that one would want him to say. Dante attempts a variation of the same trick in the *Vita nuova* by attempting to exorcise the amoral Protean *desultor* and to recast him in his guilt-ridden Christian *io son*. This exemplifies Thomas Greene's observation concerning the "dynamic and continuous interplay between the reader [such as Dante] and the distant voice whose very accent and idiom he sought to catch."[26]

Sometimes, Dante seems to be another medieval poet counting coup on Ovid, as the adjective in the first section of the *Vita* suggests: *Incipit vita nova.* He sets out to create a voice that differs from those of his forebears and contemporaries, even from that of his own semierotic *Rime petrose.*[27] Although Jerome Mazzaro goes so far as to suggest that *Vita* 31 and 32 constitute Dante's own "cure" for love,[28] Dante prescribes no such thing, only how one loves rightly. He attempts to do this by standing on Ovid's shoulders:

> Mens Bona ducetur manibus post terga retortis
>   et Pudor et castris quicquid Amoris obest.
>
> (Ovid Am. 1.2.31–32)

[Let Conscience be led with her arms tied behind her back, and Modesty and everyone else who marches on the field of Love.]

In *Vita* 24, Dante echoes and subverts these lines in the voice of Amor by excising Ovid's humor. "Pensa di benedicere lo dì che io ti presi, però che tu lo dei fare" (46) [See that you bless the day that I took you captive; it is

---

25. See Klopsch's appendices B and C, in *Pseudo-Ovidius "de Vetula,"* 286–87.

26. *The Light in Troy*, 93.

27. For the eroticism of the *Rime*, see Robert M. Durling and Ronald L. Martinez, *Time and the Crystal: Studies in Dante's "Rime Petrose"* (Berkeley: University of California Press, 1990), 83, 102–4, 126–27, 169–70, 188–89, 191–96, 381.

28. *The Figure of Dante: An Essay on the "Vita nuova"* (Princeton: Princeton University Press, 1981), 44. See *Remedia amoris*, 135–58.

your duty to do so] (51). Even earlier, in *Vita* 16, love attacks him so subversively that life nearly abandons him: "Amor m'assale subitanamente, /
si che la vita quasi m'abbandona" (27). Although the treatise-like nature
of the *Vita* is reminiscent of the *Remedia,* its self-reflection and kaleido-
scope of emotional turmoil mirror the *Amores* more fully. Dante's *io son*
seeks no cures for love.

3

The densely textured and problematic third section of the *Vita nuova*
reflects Dante's struggle to form a new poetics by showing his difference
from Ovid and the troubadours while building on their legacy. Like Guillaume IX and Bernart de Ventadorn, he cannibalizes, internalizes, and
subverts Ovid's *desultor;* unlike his Provençal predecessors, his medium is
Christianity. This imitative dualism demonstrates "a deliberate balancing
or blending of sacred and profane."[29] Yet *Vita* 3 also demonstrates how
difficult it was for Dante to refine his troubadours and to exorcise the
Ovidian subtext.

Dante's dream vision is one of the more horrifying in medieval literature, revealing the lover's corrosive guilt over his desires as he struggles to
repress them. Exactly nine years after the first sighting of Beatrice, Dante's
speaker beholds her in "vestita di colore bianchissimo" (3), the whitest
vestments of purity. After she greets him, he is overcome with bliss and
desire like a drunk, "come inebriato" (4), then he goes home and falls into
an ambiguous sleep or trance that he describes as "una maravigliosa
visione" (4). He then sees Amor, "uno segnore di pauroso aspetto" [that
Lord of Terrible Aspect] (4), who appears in a cloud of fire like an Old Testament prophet, inspiring terror and joy. Although Amor says many
things, the *io son* can only understand a few, one of which is:

"Ego dominus tuus." Ne le sue braccia mi parea vedere una persona
dormire nuda, salvo che involta mi parea in uno drappo sanguigno leg-
geramente; la quale io riguardando molto intentivamente, conobbi
ch'era la donna de la salute, la quale m'avea lo giorno dinanzi degnato
di salutare. E ne l'una de le mani mi parea che questi tenesse una cosa la
quale ardesse tutta, e pareami che mi dicesse queste parole: "Vide cor
tuum." E quando elli era stato alquanto, pareami che disvegliasse
questa che dormia; e tanto si sforzava per suo ingegno, che le facea

_____

29. Mazzaro, *The Figure of Dante,* xv.

mangiare questa cosa che in mano li ardea, la quale ella mangiava dubitosamente. Appresso ciò poco dimorava che la sua letizia si convertia in amarissimo pianto; e così piangendo, si ricogliea questa donna ne le sue braccia, e con essa mi parea che si ne gisse verso lo cielo.

(4–5)

["I am your lord." I seemed to see in his arms a sleeping figure, naked but lightly wrapped in a crimson cloth; looking intently at this figure, I recognized the lady of the greeting, the lady who earlier in the day had deigned to greet me. In one hand he seemed to be holding something that was all in flames, and it seemed to me that he said these words: "Behold your heart." And after some time had passed, he seemed to awaken the one who slept, and he forced her cunningly to eat of that burning object in his hand; she ate of it timidly. A short time after this, his happiness gave way to bitterest weeping, and weeping, he folded his arms around this lady, and together they seemed to ascend toward the heavens.]

(5–6)

Dante's speaker sees what a troubadour would want to see more than anything else: his beautiful lady practically naked, enticingly draped in a red mantle. Yet there is no hint of potential erotic congress. Instead, Beatrice eats his heart at the behest of Amor and dies. The lover's horror is total: "essenza membrar mi dà orrore" (6).

The few who have attempted a sustained analysis of the "maravigliosa visione" naturally interpret it in Christian terms. Barbara Nolan notes Dante's fluid use of Biblical and mystical parallels. The iconography of Amor and Beatrice is the Pietà, which could have been taken from Giotto. The lord in fire is reminiscent of Ezekiel 1.4 and Apocalypse 14.14. Furthermore, Beatrice's eating of the heart may be a conflation of two images from the writings of the twelfth-century mystic Richard of St. Victor: the ingestion of the Word, and the heart burning for Christ. Hence, in an attack on *fin' Amors,* Dante makes certain that "with humble passivity, Beatrice as Christ draws the narrator's burning heart into herself. She accepts his all-too-human courtly love (hence her distaste) by eating his heart . . . at the hand of her lord, Love."[30] This analysis accords well with

---

30. Barbara Nolan, "The *Vita nuova* and Richard of St. Victor's Phenomenology of Vision," *Dante Studies* 92 (1974): 40–44. She suggests the iconography of the Pietà from Giotto and the Nerezi Pietà (c. 1164).

a certain image of Dante that is familiar and somehow comforting: the stern moralist, the archetypal medieval Christian.

Beatrice may be draped in the crimson mantle of *caritas,*[31] but her nakedness still possesses a residue of eroticism. The heart she "eats" may certainly have something to do with twelfth-century mysticism, but Richard of St. Victor knew the *Ars amatoria* as well.[32] Besides, the climax of the vision has a locus in the very literature that Dante champions as the necessary precedent to his own writing. The author of the *vida* of Guillem de Cabestanh recounts that troubadour's murder by the cuckolded husband of his *enamorata,* Na Seremonda. To spite his wife further, the *mari jaloux* serves Guillem's heart to the unwitting Seremonda. When she is informed of the origin of her ghastly meal, her last words before committing suicide are

Seingner, ben m'avez dat si bon manjar que ja mais non manjarai d'autre.[33]

[Lord, you have given me such a good thing to eat that I shall never eat again.]

Sordello equates heart-eating with the acquisition of *corage;* Boccaccio implements the incident from the *vida* into the *Decameron* in the next century. To these Italian poets, there could be no greater symbolic manifestation of bravery, fidelity, and even the *religio Amoris.*[34] In Dante's transference of the image, he preserves some of these elements. Guillem's Seremonda ingests his heart unwittingly, and after her terrible discovery,

---

31. According to Musa, in *Dante's "Vita nuova,"* 103.

32. In his commentary on Psalm 90, Richard cites *Ars* 1.475. See Manitius, *Beiträge zur Geschichte des Ovidius,* 744.

33. Jean Boutière and A.H. Schutz, eds., *Biographies des troubadours* (Toulouse: Privat, 1950), 155.

34. In the fourteenth century, Boccaccio (*Decameron* 4.9) intensifies the grotesquerie of the same incident:

Ma unque a Dio non piaccia che sopra a così nobil vivanda, come è stata quella del cuore d'un così valoroso e così cortese cavaliere come messer Guiglielmo Guardustagno fu, mai altra vivanda vada.

[But God forbid that any other nourishment should pass my lips after such noble food as that of the heart of so worthy and courtly a knight as Sir Guiglielmo Guardustagno (was, but instead may I leave this life).]

she underscores the act as a symbolic affirmation of her fidelity to their love and then makes the ultimate sacrifice. Beatrice's act follows this rough outline. The most significant difference is that she is no cuckolder, knows what she eats, and makes the sacrifice on Love's prompting, which moves the god himself. The most visceral element of the "visione" is that Dante watches the event. What better way to steel the mind toward a fidelity that the *desultor Amoris* could never imagine?

Furthermore, what better way to burden oneself with guilt? The half-naked dream girl bravely endures a kind of torture for the sake of the *io son*. Worse, his loss of her and her ensuing ascension are caused not by something that he has actually done but by something he has not even dared to think about: his worldly, physical feelings. Beatrice "dies" to save him in this pietà for his lust.

The Pompeii beneath this twelfth-century residue is oddly Ovidian. (Perhaps the locus classicus for the eaten heart is Procne's terrible revenge on Tereus in *Metamorphoses* 6.655: "intus habes, quem poscis.") In the *Amores,* the *desultor* has a dream or vision of Corinna in a state of casual undress ("uenit tunica uelata recincta," 1.5.9), which foretells the consummation of the relationship (2.12). Later, she appears in a quasi-allegorical configuration that augurs her infidelity (3.5), a poem known to the Middle Ages as *somnium Ovidii* and preserved, studied, and imitated because of its congeniality to medieval poetics—to dream vision, allegory, and prophecy. The *desultor* is a (horned) bull, the old woman recommending the infidelity is a crow (cf. Dipsas, the Vielle, the *vetula*), and Corinna is a

---

The text is from *Decameron,* ed. Vittore Branca (Firenze: Presso L'Accademia Della Crusca, 1976), 317. The translation is from *The Decameron,* ed. Mark Musa and Peter Bondanella (New York: Norton, 1982), 300.

The image of heart eating as a manifestation of acquiring bravery is used by the Italian troubadour Sordello (who appears in *Purgatorio* 6 and 7) in his *planh* on the death of his Provençal lord En Blacatz:

tant es mortals lo dans, qu'ieu noy ai sospeisso
que jamais si revenha, s'en aital guiza no,
qu'om li traga lo cor, e qu'en manjo.l baro
que vivon descorat, pueys auran de cor pro.

[I have no hope this loss will ever be restored, it is so terrible, unless they draw his great heart out of him and give the barons, who have no heart, to eat of it. Then they will have heart once more.]

The text and translation are from Goldin, *Troubadours,* 312–13. In *Medieval French Literature,* Jessie Crossland cites Konrad von Würzburg's thirteenth-century romance *Das Herzmaere* as an example of the eaten heart.

"candida vacca" (10), a heifer whose hide is as white as the gown Beatrice wears in the incident that occasions the vision of the *io son* in *Vita* 3. Throughout both visions, the *desultor* remains true to his self-absorbed character. In the second vision (as in Dante's), the speaker's terror is complete: "terruerunt animum talia uisa meum" (3.5.2).

Along with the sacrifice of Na Seremonda, Dante conflates Ovid's visions and reconfigures them into his speaker's glorious nightmare of prophecy, nakedness, terror, allegory, and the subjective perception of events. Beatrice's nakedness is not erotic in the voyeuristic way that one might expect in the manner of Jean de Meun. It is a manifestation of her function as *nuda veritas* that emanates purity, fidelity, and sacrifice. Since she symbolizes abstract qualities, she cannot partake of ordinary fleshly beauty, which is why her appearance is generally not described (in *Vita* 19, we learn she has "Color de perle"). If Dante were to describe her in the manner of his predecessors, he would degrade her, just as the *desultor* unconsciously degrades Corinna in *Amores* 1.5, leaving only the *mons Veneris* to the imagination, or as the pseudo-Ovid of *de Vetula* does as he breathlessly pauses over every petal of his *flos virginitatis:* "O utinam nudam videam" (2.331).[35] Dante attempts to create a new erotics, fomented in part by the anti-Ovidian concept of fidelity. His *io son* also remains true to his character.

However, Dante's contemporaries were not fooled. In the last decade of the thirteenth century, before he had completed the *Vita,* he circulated the Guinizellian sonnet that would later accompany the prose vision, "A chiascun'alma presa e gentil core" [To every captive soul and gentle heart], to Guido Cavalcanti, Cino da Pistoia, and Dante da Maiano. Their replies offer no Christian hermeneutics. Guido's sonnet does not suggest that Beatrice was purging Dante of *fin' Amors* but that Amor viewed the lover's heart as sustenance for Beatrice instead (cf. Na Seremonda) and, fearing her death, gave it to her to eat: "nodrilla dello cor, di ciò temendo."[36] Cino's riposte is equally divergent from modern criticism:

---

35. See Goldin's explanation of a lyric of Guiraut de Calanso's: "As an emblem of the courtly class, [the lady] is characterized by the impersonality and repose that attend perfection; for any individualizing quality would diminish her stature"; such a lady "cannot be the light of the world and at the same time yield to personal preferences" (*The Mirror of Narcissus,* 76). The implications for Dante's Beatrice are fairly obvious.

36. The quotations from Cino, Guido, and de Maiano, as well as the translations, are from *Dante's Lyric Poetry,* 1:14–17.

e l'amorosa pena conoscendo
che ne la donna conceputo avea,
per pietà di lei pianse partendo.

[and Love wept as he went away, out of pity for her, knowing the pain
of love he had brought about in her.]

Since Dante generally places himself beneath Beatrice, it is difficult to
think of her as vulnerable in any way to him, or as earthly enough to
exhibit *Krankheitssymptomen.* Yet Cino's lines argue for mutuality
between the lovers. The most penetrating analysis of the dream—that of
Dante da Maiano, who, like the *Vita* Dante, is an avid reader of Ovid—is
usually dismissed as too coarse to be taken seriously. "If you are not
insane," Dante de Maiano counsels,

lavi la tua coglia largamente,
a ciò che stinga e passi lo vapore
lo qual ti fa favoleggiar loquendo

[give your testicles a good wash, so that the vapours that make you talk
nonsense be extinguished and dispersed]

This is not only sound medical advice but a useful warning against taking
oneself too seriously. Ovidian Dante da Maiano also rightly addresses the
underlying sexuality of *Vita* 3, the lust, guilt, and frustration that fuel the
"maravigliosa visione" of Beatrice, all shadows of the *desultor Amoris* that
Dante will try (and fail) to purge from his *Vita.*

4

In the manner of his troubadour masters, Dante's tacit imitation of the
Amores is often dialectical. However, where Guillaume or Arnaut canni-
balize the *desultor* and attempt to outdo or refine him, Dante's *io son* seems
to be a correction of the classical paradigm. This is most readily apparent
in the attempted reworking of the psychology of Ovid's persona: the Protean consciousness that creates a pose and violates it, his twisted logic as
normative, his misogynous ambition to be sexually predatory, and his
capacity for unwitting self-revelation. For example, in response to the terrible vision of *Vita* 3, Dante depicts love as an inherently reasonable and

therefore noble entity, thanks to Beatrice: "per lo volontade d'Amore, io quale mi comandava secondo lo consiglio de la ragione" (4.6–7). This concept that bears its fullest fruit in the canzone of *Vita* 19: "Donne ch' avete intelletto d'amore" (30). Yet to the *desultor,* love is inherently unreasonable and chaotic, which forces the lover into competition, battles, and captivity (*Am.* 1.2, 1.9, passim). His metaphor of a ship tossing on the waves ("auferor, ut rapida concita puppis aqua," 2.4.8), inherited by his troubadour imitators, corresponds to the contemporary notion of being "swept away." Hence the *desultor* absolves himself of responsibility for virtually any action. The most unique part of the *vita nova* for Dante's *amator novus* is that if love is reasonable, the new lover should seek responsibility and even accountability, all *nefas* to the *desultor.*

Therefore, as the *io son* becomes more enamored, he seeks to become more reasonable, an effort that truly diverges from convention. Dante symbolizes this process by attempting to fuse his "reasoning" *io son* with Amor so that they are indistinguishable, in *Vita* 9 and 11: "E chi avesse voluto conoscere Amore, fare lo potea mirando lo tremare de li occhi miei" (14) [and if anyone had wished to know Love, he might have done so by looking at my glistening eyes] (16–17). In *Vita* 24, Amor's last appearance in the sequence, the god then fuses himself with Beatrice because she so closely resembles him: "per molta simiglianza che ha meco" (47). To parrot Dante's phrasing, "anyone of subtle discernment" can see a trinity forming. Such reasonable fusion is again a response to the *Amores,* in this case the irreconcilable thirds of the triad always in dynamic conflict: *desultor,* Amor, Corinna. Ovid is at war with the quiver-bearing love god, whom he wishes to dismiss: "abeas pharetrate Cupido" (2.5.1). He is also at war with the grudge-bearing mistress, who attempts to control him by delusion: "si qua uolet regnare diu, deludat amantem" (2.19.33). Since Corinna has very little to do with Amor, the dynamic retains its tripartite nature.

Still, one must question Dante's trinity and whether it is unified at all. Amor cannot be both the *io son* and Beatrice if the former is in a completely subordinate position to the latter. They are simply not equal, which Dante stresses somewhat monotonously in the sections after *Vita* 24, climaxing in the encomium of the final section, 42:

E poi piaccia a colui che è sire de la cortesia, che la mia anima se ne possa gire a vedere la gloria de la sua donna, cioè di quella benedetta

Beatrice, la quale gloriosamente mira ne la faccia di colui *qui est per omnia secula benedictus.*

(74)

[And then may it please the One who is the Lord of graciousness that my soul ascend to behold the glory of its lady, that is, of the blessed Beatrice, who in glory contemplates the countenance of the One who is through all ages blessed.]

(86)

Besides his attempt to create a reasoning love, this is Dante's most radical effort to revise the Ovidian-troubadour erotic. Its blasphemy is astounding. First, to describe the Lord of Hosts as the "sire de la cortesia" is much more than "un senso alto e complesso, come valore e bene spirituale."[37] Without question, "cortesia" is a buzzword that nearly every troubadour, trouvère, and *stilnovisto* poet appropriates in its corresponding linguistic forms to describe a secular ethic irrevocably associated with a *fin' Amors* modified from Ovid. To Dante, the Lord of Hosts is also the Lord of *fin' Amors.* Second, replacing the Blessed Mother with Beatrice as the one eternally contemplating the face of God is also a radical breach, which Dante learned from Guinizelli. "Al cor gentil" ends with God rebuking the lover for preferring to see his lady in heaven before Himself or the Virgin and with the lover's insouciant reply that it was not a fault in him to love her: "Non me fu fallo, s'in lei posi amanza."[38]

Therefore, in exalting Beatrice to impossible levels of adoration, Dante stresses her singularity. The first of four conclusions that the *io son* reaches in *Vita* 13 is that the lady for whom Love makes one suffer is like none other: "la donna per cui Amore ti stringe così, non è come l'altre donne" (20). In fact, in the previous section, *Vita* 12, Beatrice is simply too pure to address directly, and in the ensuing episode, *Vita* 14, the *io son* is careful to use the honorific *voi.* Such humorless respect (or groveling) represents a sharp diversion from the manner in which Guillaume IX discusses his women, which is symbolized by that troubadour's synecdochic use of *con.*

Dante's superidealization of Beatrice is also an exorcism of Ovid's *desultor* and his physical and psychological abuse of Corinna, a woman

---

37. See Dante Alighieri, *La Vita nuova,* ed. Sanguineti and Berardinelli, 74 n. 7.
38. For the text of Guinizelli's lyric, see O'Donoghue, *The Courtly Love Tradition,* 60.

whom he beats ("mihi quam profitibar amare / laesa est," *Am.* 1.7.33–34),
and whom he rebukes for imperfect hair-dyeing (1.10), botched abortions
(2.13, 2.14), and infidelities so hurtful to him that he complains that she
prostitutes his art: "ingenio prostitit illa meo" (3.12.8). Dante's pseudo-
asexual veneration of his *domina* is just as radical in its apparent anti-
Ovidianism as the opposite literary trend, such as the use of the erotica to
teach schoolboys their Latin or the effort to make Ovid like an Evangelist,
as in these often-cited lines from the twelfth-century *Concilium Romarici:*

> Intromissis omnibus virginum agminibus,
> Lecta sunt in medium, quasi evangelium,
> Precepta Ovidii, doctoris egregii.[39]

[in the middle of the entire gathering of virgins, the precepts of Ovid,
that excellent doctor, were read in place of the Evangelists.]

Yet Dante cannot maintain his radicalism, nor does he particularly wish to
do so. Like most other medieval Ovidians, he maintains a medium position, because he cannot afford to repudiate completely an author to whom
he is so heavily indebted. From first to last in the *Amores,* love is suffering
("uror," 1.1.26; "mortuus esse uelim," 3.14.40). Likewise, for Dante in
Vita 7, it is the host and home of every torment: "io son d'ogni tormento
ostale e chiave" (8). In *Vita* 16, the sufferer enumerates the symptoms of
his lovesickness: confusion, alienation, pallor, and heart tremors (27). He
even wanders in a maze of love in *Vita* 13 ("così mi trovo in amorosa
erranza!" 21), which is a variation on the Ovidian-troubadour metaphor
of the ship on the waves in *Amores* 2.4.

One might counter that the inner turmoil of the devoted *io son* is terri-
bly chaste in comparison with the "tormentis secubitu" that the faithless
desultor laments as he lies abed without female companionship (3.10.16).
Yet the sexuality that Dante da Maiano observes in the sonnet to *Vita* 3 is
something that the *io son* never really expunges from his *coglia.* This is best
exemplified in the sections of the *Vita* concerned with the *schermo,* the lady
that Dante uses as a screen for his affections because lusting after Beatrice
would simply be too impure. When he admits, in section 38, that he thinks
of the *schermo* too much ("pensava di lei così," 68), he is also admitting to

---

39. "Concile de Remiremont," 23–25. The text is from Charles Oulmont, ed., *Les débats
du clerc et du chevalier dans la littérature poétique du Moyen-Age* (Paris: Champion, 1911), 94.
The translation is mine.

the torments of *secubitus*. But for whom? When, in the psychomachia of *Vita* 38, one thought assures the *io son* that his lust for the *schermo* is "uno spiramento d'Amore," which in turn emanates from "li occhi de la donna che tanto pietosa ci s'hae mostrata" (68) [the eyes of the lady who has shown us so much compassion] (78), it seems painfully apparent that the *io son* does not lust for his screen lady at all; rather he lusts for Beatrice. *Vide cor tuum*, Amor said of his flaming heart; *lavi la tua coglia largamente*, said Dante de Maiano.

An indication of the bond between the *io son* and the *desultor* can be discerned in *Vita* 18, a section that criticism usually identifies as the turning point of the entire work. The most poorly kept secret in Florence is Dante's love for Beatrice, even though he makes a great show of secrecy. (Like the *desultor*, he truly loathes himself; unlike his Ovidian great-grandfather, his self-loathing is bound up with his idealization for a woman who snubs him.) Every encounter he has with his peers simply underscores his "crush."

His climactic social interaction is with a group of women who are understandably puzzled by a man who loves someone whose presence he cannot endure: "Dilloci chè certo lo fine di cotale amore conviene che sia novissimo" (28) [Tell us, for surely the goal of such a love must be strange indeed] (31). The *io son* replies that Beatrice has snubbed him, and, as a result, he will put all of his bliss ("tutta la mia beatitudine," 28) into something infallible. Further amused, the ladies ask where his "beatitudine" resides at present. He replies, "In quelle parole che lodano la donna mia" (29) [In those words that praise my lady] (31). Trapped by the truth, the *io son* must now listen to what he has dreaded to hear. The ladies hint that his words were written "con altro intendimento" (29), with some other intent than to praise Beatrice. This is his epiphany, his anagnorisis. He has been writing not to praise Beatrice (whom he has just admitted that he does not think infallible) but to please himself, to gain fame.

Proven a liar twice over, the *io son* takes a vow of sincerity. However, this is the great trick of the *Vita nuova*. Who, after all, is Beatrice? Like Corinna, she is an authorial construct, a fulcrum for the poet's own praise. Although the *io son* seems subordinate to Beatrice, this is actually quite a difficult thing for him to swallow, as if it were a live scorpion. If the *Vita nuova* were really concerned with Beatrice, it would have been an anonymous production. Yet it is not, despite the persona's "humble" namelessness. In *Vita* 28, the speaker refuses to discuss Beatrice's death because it would entail praising himself as someone worthy of her intercession and because complimenting oneself is most reprehensible: "la quale cosa è al postutto biasimevole a chi lo fae" (55). Yet Beatrice intercedes for the *io son* throughout the *Vita,* as well as the *Commedia*—so he praises himself.

Dante learns this dubiety from Ovid. If the persona says what he is not, he might be believed. Yet if he is not believed, it allows for useful ironic distance between fictive speaker and speaking maker. Even before the *desultor* finishes the simple kernel sentence, "non sum desultor amoris" (*Am.* 1.3.15), we know that he is precisely what he claims he is not. Just as Dante disdains the notion of self-advertisement, the notion of the *Vita nuova* as a testament to himself as a poet becomes painfully obvious. Beatrice, the purported focus of the sequence, is almost as ancillary to it as Corinna is to the *Amores.*

Ovid and his personae concern themselves constantly with poetic fame. The epic poet begins the last section of the *Metamorphoses* with "Iamque opus exegi" (15.871), a deliberate echo of Horace's declaration that he has built a monument ("Exegi monumentum," *Odes* 3.30.1). The *desultor* concludes books 1 and 3 of the *Amores* with similar bravura: "uiuam, parsque mei multa superstes erit" [I will live, and the better part of me will live forever] (1.15.42); "post mea mansurum fata superstes opus" [(unheroic elegies,) you will survive after my passing, posthumous work] (3.15.20).

The Dante of the *de Vulgari,* brother to the *io son* of the *Vita,* is somewhat subtler in self-advertisement but no less eager for fame. Several passages in the treatise (e.g., 2.2) foretell the poetic academy of *Inferno* 4, such as the groupings of troubadour and *stilnovisti* poetry into which Dante inserts his own verse (anonymously), so that he effectively makes the better part of himself live forever with Bertran de Born, Arnaut, Girault de Borneilh, and Cino. This Ovidian lust for fame is another inheritance from the twelfth century. The troubadours were really the first poets after antiquity who consistently named themselves and thus advertised themselves. When Dante admits "cantiones magis deferunt suis conditoribus quam ballate,"[40] that he writes canzones instead of *ballate* because the former inspire greater honor, he places himself firmly in the same tradition. He too is attempting to build a monument.

If one thinks of the *Vita nuova* as a chapel (or a small cathedral), the figure of Ovid, who seems to have been intended to be a gargoyle on the outer facade, instead has been moved to the inside, with his grotesque little head atop a pair of shoulders that were intended to represent a saint

---

40. *De Vulgari,* 158.

or an Evangelist. With his flair for self-promotion and his adherence to the conventions of *fin' Amors* and to the triangular dynamic of the *Amores,* Dante's *io son* is at root an Ovidian creation. Despite the attempted exorcism of the *desultor* and the Christianization of troubadour erotics, Dante creates a persona who is equally unreliable in his narration—who is, again, one of the *iuuenes* who proclaims, "NASO MAGISTER ERAT."

CHAPTER 5

"La dolce vista": Petrarch's Exorcism of the *desultor*

Quod amare solebam, iam non amo; mentior: amo, sed parcius; iterum ecce mentitus sum: amo, sed verecundius, sed tristius; iantandem verum dixi. Sic est enim; amo, sed quod non amare amem, quod odisse cupiam; amo tamen, sed invitus, sed coactus, sed mestus et lugens. Et in me ipso versiculi illius famosissimi sententiam miser experior: "Odero, si potero; si non, invitus amabo." (*Familiarum rerum libri* 4.1)[1]

[What I was accustomed to love I love no more: I am a liar: I love, but more sparingly; behold, I am again a liar; I love, but more chastely, more unhappily; finally I have spoken the truth. This is what I mean to say: I love, but I should not love what I love, I desire what I hate; still I love, but against my will, coerced, fearful and mourning. And, miserable, I experience in myself the proof of this most famous little verse: "I will hate, if I am able; if not, I will love against my will."]

Throughout his Latin prose, Petrarch cites Ovid as a learned authority, a great genius ("magni vir ingenii") who cannot be equaled: "puto nullum aequari posse Naso poetae."[2] In two of his dialogues, the *Secretum,* an imaginary conversation with Augustine, and *de Remediis Utriusque Fortune,* a debate between Gaudium and Ratio, the combatants fire lines from the *Ars amatoria, Amores,* and *Remedia amoris* at each other. Ratio and

---

1. *Francesco Petrarca: Prose,* ed. G. Martellotti et al. (Milan: Ricciardi, 1955), 838. Unless otherwise specified, all references to Petrarch's Latin works are to this edition, and all translations from these texts are my own, unless otherwise specified.

2. For "magni vir ingenii," see *de Vita Solitaria* 2 (*Prose,* 532); for "puto nullum . . . poetae," see Dorothy M. Robathan, "Ovid in the Middle Ages," in *Ovid,* ed. J.W. Binns (London: Routledge, 1973), 205.

(*mirabile dictu*) Augustine raid the profane author's corpus without apology. So it may be inevitable that Petrarch shows his debt to the *desultor* of the *Amores* by quoting him in his most famous *epistola* from the *Familiarum rerum libri*, "The Ascent of Mount Ventoux" (4.1), a document that Jacob Burckhardt and Ernst Robert Curtius enshrine as a foundation of Renaissance humanism.[3] In an even greater tribute, Petrarch bases the dynamic of his vernacular sequence—the *Rime sparse,* or *Canzoniere*—on the Apollo and Daphne myth in the *Metamorphoses.*

Yet other passages from the prose suggest that Petrarch considers Ovid to be "lascivissimus," or immoral:

Ille michi quidem magni vir ingenii videtur, sed lascivi et lubrici et prorsus mulierosi animi fuisse, quem conventus feminei delectarent usque adeo, ut in illis felicitatis sue apicem summamque reponeret. Itaque *Amatoriam artem* scribens, insanum opus et meritam (nisi fallor) exilii sui causam. (*de Vita Solitaria* 2)[4]

[He seems to me to have been a man of great genius, but of a lascivious and deceitful sort and given entirely to the pursuit of women, a man whom sexual encounters with women delighted above all, so that his greatest happiness lay in such small pleasures. And so writing the *Ars amatoria,* an insane work (unless I am greatly mistaken), merited the cause of his exile.]

So it may also be inevitable that Petrarch must attempt to expunge the spirit of the *desultor* almost completely from the *Rime,* an exorcism that he performs in the aforementioned letter even as he pays tribute to Ovid. The line on which Petrarch works his variations with such virtuosity, "odero si potero; si non, inuitus amabo" (*Am.* 3.11b.34), epitomizes the erotic tangle of *puellae* in which the *desultor* finds himself. Petrarch appropriates it to explain his agonized self-reflection at the inception of his reborn spiritual and intellectual life, just before he opens his personal copy of the *Confessions* (8.12) to foretell his fate—precisely as Augustine opened another book (Rom. 13.13) to foretell his own, in imitation of Roman emperors who had performed the same feat with the *Iliad.* In some ways, Petrarch's

---

3. For Burckhardt, see *The Civilization of the Renaissance in Italy,* trans. S.G.C. Middlemore, 2 vols. (New York: Harper, 1960), 2:294–97. For Curtius, see *European Literature,* 143–44.

4. For "lascivissimus poetarum Naso," see *Senilium rerum libri* 2.1 (to Boccaccio), in *Prose,* 1050; for *de Vita Solitaria,* see *Prose,* 532.

commentary on the *versiculus* resembles a "moralization" of Ovid (i.e., preservation through reconfiguration), in the fourteenth-century manner of his friend Pierre Bersuire's prose *Ovidius moralizatus.*[5] At the same time, it suggests that Petrarch will succeed in casting out from his poetry the pagan paradigm of the *desultor* that Dante's *io son* cannot remove from the *Vita nuova.*

1

In the *Rime,* the persona moralizes its Ovidian model and then exorcises it. Accordingly, Thomas M. Greene reminds us that Petrarch chose "to write verse that could itself be subread and demanded to be subread, verse bearing within it the latent presence of an ancient author."[6] If one "subreads" the *Rime* for the *desultor* and notes the outline of his form, one finds a new man inside it. His speaker establishes his credibility and sincerity by confessing throughout the sequence rather than in retrospect, by invoking the demons that torment him, and by upbraiding himself—all admissions that the *desultor* and the Dantean *io son* make only when they discover that they have been lying to themselves. Petrarch's forced, painful honesty is deliberately intended to prevent us from calling him a liar.

---

5. Bersuire, a Benedictine monk, took the Latin name Petrus Berchorius. His *Ovidius moralizatus* comprises the fifteenth chapter of his *Reductiorum morale,* which ought not to be confused with the anonymous vernacular poem, the *Ovide moralisé* (although some commentators ascribe the poem to Bersuire or suggest that he drew on it for his Latin prose commentary). There were several early sixteenth-century printed editions of the *Ovidius moralizatus* under the name of Thomas Walleys: 1509, 1511, 1515, 1521. The title page of the 1509 edition reads: "Metamorphosis Ouidia / na Moraliter a Magistro Thoma Walleys Anglico de profes / sione praedicatorum sub sanctissimo patre Dominico: explanata / Venundatur in aedibus Ascensianis / & sub pelicano in vico sancti Iacobi / Parisiis." See Petrus Berchorius, *Reductorium morale, liber XV, cap. ii–xv: "Ovidius moralizatus,"* ed. J. Engels (Utrecht: Instituut voor Laat Latijn der Rijksuniversiteit, 1962).

On the Bersuire-Petrarch friendship, see Barkan, *The Gods Made Flesh,* 185, and Petrarch, *Lord Morley's "Tryumphes of Fraunces Petrarcke": The First English Translation of the "Trionfi,"* ed. D.D. Carnicelli (Cambridge: Harvard University Press, 1971), passim. On Petrarch's originality, see Sara Sturm-Maddox, *Petrarch's Metamorphoses: Text and Subtext in the "Rime Sparse,"* (Columbia: University of Missouri Press, 1985), 13: "What *is* new in Petrarch's version is the introduction of a classical paradigm for this frustrated passion, this hopeless yet perpetual pursuit."

6. *The Light in Troy,* 95. Greene cites Petrarch's *Familiarum rerum libri* 23.19 on imitation. Petrarch argues that one should avoid mere reproduction, because dissimilarity is also important. In fact, "idipsum simile lateat, nec deprehendi possit, nisi tacita mentis indagine, ut intelligi simile queat potius quam dici" [The similarity should be planted so deep that it can only be extricated by quiet meditation. The quality is to be felt rather than defined] (Greene's translation, 95–96).

Since Petrarch designs the *Rime* to seem confessional, it is tempting to
eliminate the idea of persona. Yet the danger of such elimination is to misread the sequence as Wordsworthian autobiography. Still, such monikers
as *ieu soi* or *desultor* seem misplaced in describing Petrarch's voice, which
is designed to convey the importance of being an earnest poet. So the more
neutral *persona* or *speaker* would be better names for the narrator of the
Rime, although Petrarch sought to forge the image of himself *as* himself
for public dissemination.

Petrarch cultivates the idea of sincerity in both his private poetic persona and his more public, epistolary voice, and he often strives to join the
two, which can create confusion. Beneath the banter of a letter to Gia-
como Colonna lies a defensive anxiety about his credibility:

> Quid ergo ais? finxisse me michi speciosum Lauree nomen, ut esset et de
> qua ego loquerer et propter quam de me multi loquerentur? . . . In hoc
> uno vere utinam iocareris; simulatio esset utinam et non furor! Sed,
> crede michi, nemo sine magno labore diu simulat; laborare autem
> gratis, ut insanus videaris, insania summa est.
>
> > *(Familiarum rerum libri* 2.9)[7]

> [What are you saying? I invented the dazzling name of Laura, so that I
> might have something to say and so that many men would talk about
> me? . . . About this you joke constantly, that it is all simulation and not
> madness. But believe me, no one can simulate long without great labor;
> to labor uselessly to seem mad is the ultimate madness.]

Yet Laura *is* a fiction, a fulcrum for a poet's praise, as the etymology of her
name suggests (i.e., *laurus;* she crowns the speaker laureate in *Rime*
119.103–5). Petrarch strongly believed that the genesis of poetry is *imitatio,* a kind of simulation, and that the effort expended in composition is

---

7. *Prose,* 824. Some commentators believe that Petrarch's letters are no more trustworthy
than the vernacular poetry for narrative reliability, since they were carefully revised throughout his career. See Giuseppe Billanovich, "Petrarca e il Ventuso," *Italia medioevale e umanistica* 9 (1966): 389–401, and Francisco Rico, *Vida u obra de Petrarca,* North Carolina Studies
in Romance Literature and Language 33 (Chapel Hill: University of North Carolina Press,
1974). Lyell Asher writes concerning "Mount Ventoux": "Though I think it is believable that
Petrarch fabricated this event and others in the letter to suit his extrareligious designs, it is
indeed unlikely that he would have done so readily or lightly. In fact, *Familiares* 4.1 seems to
be immeasurably gnarled and enriched by precisely the tension produced when reverent
forms are used to advance irreverent aims" ("Petrarch at the Peak of Fame," *PMLA* 108
[1993]: 1051).

Herculean in any case. Therefore, it is tempting to misread his explication of his own poetry as worthy of Ovid himself. But one ought not to confuse the letter writer with the vernacular poet or the "Franciscus" of the Latin prose works, as much as these voices seem to harmonize. Ultimately, the Petrarch of the *Rime* is a critique of the *desultor*.

The repudiation of the tradition to which Petrarch owes so much begins in the first poem of the sequence. He establishes his credibility by apologizing immediately for his shortcomings as man and poet. This strategy may disarm the reader who expects a more conventional boast or invocation, and it may invite the reader to apprehend the speaker on his own terms. Therefore, Petrarch needs no agonized moment of anagnorisis or epiphany at midsequence, no blundering into a group of ladies who remind the speaker that he is selfish, no sublimation of longing, no stage whisper of the lover's unworthiness in this the real *Vita nuova*, in which one must navigate without a prose commentary.[8] This honesty also helps establish Petrarch's worth and originality as a vernacular poet in whom, a critic reminds us, the concept of poet as *vates*, seer, and prophet is revivified,[9] a concept that Ovid had helped to denigrate in his erotic poetry.

2

Petrarch's sophisticated reconfiguration of the *desultor* in his lyric poetry owes much to the tradition established in the previous century, one that produced the *Integumenta Ovidii* and *de Vetula*. This reconfiguration is also informed by the practices of his contemporaries, who mock, moralize, or imitate Ovid. For example, Boccaccio sees a number of correspondences between himself and the *magister,* and he even refers to the text of the first three days of the *Decameron* as "senza titulo," which, as Robert M. Hollander usefully explains, is a shortened Italian translation of the familiar medieval name for the *Amores, Ovidius sine titulo.*[10] Those who moralize Ovid do this as a means of preservation, using exegetical

---

8. Robert M. Durling maintains "there is no mediation between poems," and "the reader must supply the narrative and psychological inferences." See Petrarch, *Petrarch's Lyric Poems,* ed. and trans. Robert M. Durling (Cambridge: Harvard University Press, 1976), 10. Similarly, Sturm-Maddox observes that the reader must connect the "blank spaces between the formally independent components" to identify "a temporally linear account of events in the life of a single speaker" (*Petrarch's Metamorphoses,* 1).

9. Marjorie O'Rourke Boyle, *Petrarch's Genius: Pentimento and Prophecy* (Berkeley: University of California Press, 1991), 46.

10. See Hollander, *Boccaccio's Two Venuses* (New York: Columbia University Press, 1977), 112–16.

commentary. For example, in his erotic poetry, Ovid constantly returns to
the myth of Jupiter and Danae because it illustrates his own attitudes
about the predatory male, the recalcitrant female, and money. However,
the anonymous author of the *Ovide moralisé* reinterprets the story typologically. The randy Roman god is "Dieu, nostres aidierres" (4.5578).[11]
And of the hapless maiden in the tower, he says, "Par Dané puet estre
entendue / Virginitez de Dieu amee" (4.5583–84). Perseus, created in the
golden shower of this Annunciation, is Christ. Acrisius,

> qui Persea
> Deboute et chace et congea,
> Puet signifier Judaïme,
> Qui Jhesu, son niez et son prime,
> Refuse et dechace et deboute.

> (4.5620–24)

[whom Perseus rejects and chases and freezes, signifies Judaism, which
Jesus, his kinsman and originator, refuses and chases and dispossesses.]

Petrarch's friend Pierre Bersuire confirms this anti-Semitic interpretation
in the Latin prose of the *Ovidius moralizatus*. Acrisius represents the "populus iudaicus ipsam cum filio suo repudiauit,"[12] forcing the Flight into

---

11. For the text, see "*Ovide moralisé*": *Poème du commencement du quatorzième siècle*, ed.
C. De Boer, 5 vols. (Amsterdam: Muller, 1915–38), 2:125–28. Some rough translations of the
two shorter passages I have cited in the text from French follow: "God, our helper"; "By
'Danae,' one is meant to understand 'the Virgin beloved of God.'" Here Bersuire seems to
confuse or conflate the rejected, hunted, and frozen Phineus (*Met.* 5.210–11) with Acrisius,
who suffers no such indignities at the hands of Perseus, and who is actually restored to his
throne by his grandson (5.237–38). However, since Danae's father at first refused to admit
that Jove conceived Perseus in a golden shower, the conflation of events is understandable,
and it is useful for the moralizer's purpose:

mox tamen Acrisium—tanta est praesentia veri—
tam violasse deum quam non agnosse nepotem paenitet . . .

(*Met.* 4.612–14)

[However, Acrisius soon repents that he did not acknowledge his grandson and that he
rejected the god—so great is the efficacy of truth]

12. In fuller quotation this passage reads, "Pater igitur istius puellae: id est populus
iudaicus ipsam cum filio suo repudiauit: fidemque ipsius refutauit." The beginning may be
translated, "The father of this girl represents the Jewish people [who] repudiated [Mary] and
her son." The grammar of the last clause is ambiguous: "he [Jesu] refuted their [Jewish]
faith," or, "[the Jewish people] refuted [Jesu's] faith." See Berchorius, "*Ovidius moralizatus*,"
83.

Egypt by Danae-Mary. Although Rabelais taught his age (and ours) to
view Pierre Bersuire and the *Moralisé* poet as bigoted imbeciles who, like
the author of *de Vetula,* fallaciously impose Christianity on the *Metamorphoses,*[13] moralization ought to be seen in context. Its excesses underscore
the efforts of fourteenth-century writers to justify the use of this important
pagan author in a Christian society. And this technique was enormously
influential on Petrarch.

Although Petrarch's intellect towers over Bersuire's workaday Latin
prose and the octosyllabic couplets of the *Ovide moralisé,* he adapts their
concept of moralization into the Renaissance. He also subverts it.
Although Petrarch equates Apollo and Christ because both are, in their
respective universes, the sun and light of the world, the former a type of
the latter (*Rime* 3),[14] he sometimes repudiates such correspondences by
personalizing them:

> i' non fu' mai quel nuvol d'oro
> che poi discese in prezioza pioggia
> sì che 'l foco di Giove in parte spense
>
> (23.161–63)[15]

[I was never the cloud of gold that once descended in a precious rain so
that it partly quenched the fire of Jove]

Several readings are possible. The speaker is not the stuff of Ovidian myth
(cf. *Met.* 4.611, passim) but a human being. He has not been permitted the
ultimate sensual gratification that he seeks. His situation does not correspond to the typological reading of the Jupiter-Danae-Perseus story that

---

13. In the prologue to *Gargantua,* Rabelais says: "Si le croiez, vous n'approchez ne de
pieds ne de mains à mon opinion, qui decrete icelles aussi peu avoir esté songées d'Homere
que d'Ovide en ses *Metamorphoses* de l'Evangile, lesquelz un Frere Lubin, vray croque lar-
don, s'est efforcé demonstrer, si d'adventure il rencontroit gens aussi folz que luy, et (comme
dict le proverbe) couvercle digne du chaudron." The text is from Rabelais, *La vie tres
horrificque du grand Gargantua,* ed. V.L. Saulnier and Jean-Yves Pouilloux (Paris: Garnier-
Flammarion, 1968), 45. I translate the passage as follows: "If you think [that Homer meant
to allegorize as Plutarch and others believe], you are not within a hand or a foot of my opinion; I think that these [allegories] were as little dreamed of by Homer as the Gospel was by
Ovid in his *Metamorphoses,* as a certain Friar Lubin, a true bacon-stealer, has tried to show,
so that by chance he may find men as crazy as he, and (as the proverb goes) a lid to cover his
pot."

14. Boyle, *Petrarch's Genius,* 33.

15. My text of the *Rime* follows Petrarch, *Petrarch's Lyric Poems,* ed. Durling. All English translations are Durling's, unless otherwise noted.

Bersuire advances. Still, the underlying concept of moralization usefully complicates the allusion and unifies a diversity of readings. And the technique suggests another reading: Petrarch is no *desultor Amoris.*

Sometimes Ovid is invoked only to be revoked. One critic argues that Petrarch's use of the *Metamorphoses* "allows the introduction of sexual content otherwise forbidden by the unalterable distance between the lover and the inaccessible object of his desire."[16] So when his speaker congratulates Pygmalion (*Met.* 10.243–44), he vents his lust for Laura vicariously: "se mille volte / n'avesti quel ch' i' sol una vorrei!" [since you received a thousand times what I yearn to have just once] (*Rime* 78.13–14). Here, "unalterable distance" is unfathomably erotic, as is the speaker's masochism: "mille piacer non vaglion un tormento" [a thousand of their pleasures are not worth one of my torments] (*Rime* 231.4). Again, the idea of sincerity is crucial. The part of the *desultor* that Petrarch exorcises is precisely that which Dante could not—the duplicitous, Protean sexual predator.

3

Petrarch's repudiation of the *desultor Amoris* necessarily engages a revision of Dante and his fellows: a new persona living the *vita nova.* Although he dutifully alludes to the "cor gentile" and "gentil core" (*Rime* 67.10, 158.6) of Guinizelli's famous poem and Francesca's speech in the *Inferno* (5.100), he aspires to be a "cortesi amanti" (*Rime* 72.75) instead of the Dantean *io son* who laments, "mio primo giovenile errore" (*Vita nuova* 1.3).[17] Furthermore, Petrarch usurps and fragments Dante's puzzling figure in *Vita* 3 of a naked Beatrice who eats the flaming heart of the *io son* and ascends to heaven in the arms of Amor. He also describes Laura as "viva et bella et nuda" (*Rime* 278.5), but in *Rime* 23, her nakedness, compared to Beatrice's, seems sensual and feral despite the allusion to Diana: "quella fera bella et cruda / in una fonte ignuda" [that lovely wild creature was in a spring naked] (149–50). Earlier, Laura

> m' aperse il petto el' cor prese con mano,
> dicendo a me: "Di ciò non far parola."

(73–74)

---

16. Sturm-Maddox, *Petrarch's Metamorphoses,* 19.

17. Boyle explains that Petrarch's use of the Apollo and Daphne fable in the *Rime* "entails the revision of the stilnovist model," since both paradigms focus on "profane" love, loss, and immortality (*Petrarch's Genius,* 127).

[opened my breast and took my heart with her hand, saying to me, "Make no word of this."]

In *Rime* 199, Petrarch apostrophizes to the beautiful hand that grasps his heart: "O bella man che mi destringi 'l cor" (199.1). Here, in contrast to the passive Beatrice to whom Cupid feeds the *cor*, Laura, albeit hyperbolically, serves as the aggressor. Petrarch's heart, like that of the *io son*, is engulfed in flames. He knows it is impossible that "mesuratamente il mio cor arda," that his heart burn moderately. Yet there is no Pietàn iconography:

Così più volte à 'l cor racceso et spento,
i 'l so che 'l sento et spesso me n'adiro.

(135.74–75)

[Thus often she has relit and extinguished my heart: I know it who feel it, and often I am angered by it.]

Just as Beatrice eats Dante's heart, Petrarch eats Dante's *maravigliosa visione* in *Vita* 3. In *Rime* 360, he compares himself to gold refined by fire: "com' oro che nel foco affina" (5). This is almost a word-for-word rendition of Dante's great tribute to the *miglior fabbro* Arnaut Daniel in the *Purgatorio,* who hides himself in the fire that refines them all: "Poi s'ascose nel foco che li affina" (26.148). However, whereas Dante explains his *differences* from his Ovidian troubadours through his imagery, Petrarch's allusion exemplifies his *distance* from Ovid, his Provençal imitators, and Dante. His fire does not purify the dialect of the tribe; it refines him. Instead of Dante's nightmarish Cupid commanding him, "Vide cor tuum," Petrarch commands us as readers, "Vide cor meum."

It could be said that Petrarch's passionate sensuality seems reminiscent of the *desultor* Ovid. However, in the manner of a lyrical, vernacular, and talented Bersuire, Petrarch tempers the eroticism that follows. Unlike his fourteenth-century colleagues Chaucer and Boccaccio, Petrarch *begins* his great vernacular work with an apology, hoping to find pity as well as pardon: "spero trovar pietà, non che perdono" (1.8). In this, he seems to douse the flames that one usually associates with his poetry and its imitators:

et del mio vaneggiar vergogna è 'l frutto,
e 'l pentersi, e 'l conoscer chiaramente

che quanto piace al mondo è breve sogno.

(1.12–14)

[and of my raving, shame is the fruit, and repentance, and the clear knowledge that whatever pleases in the world is a brief dream.]

Dante's *io son* does not invalidate the whole of his little book at the outset; Ovid's *desultor* mocks the very concept of shame.

Yet Petrarch's speaker nearly repudiates everything that will ensue in the *Rime*. He makes the reader conscious of the absurdity of the protesting lyric voice, a very different activity from the *desultor*-ish comic distancing of self from the elegiac tradition in *Amores* 1.1. Petrarch's speaker agonizes over the passions that have separated body and soul, and Love upbraids him:

rispondemi Amor: "Non ti rimembra
che questo è privilegio degli amanti,
sciolti da tutte qualitati umane?"

(15.12–14)

[Love replies to me: "Do you not remember that this is a privilege of lovers, released from all human qualities?"]

Amor denies the lover his humanity despite his protestations, reminding his charge of his privileged position, one that he had asserted in *Rime* 3, in which he compares his situation to the Crucifixion, and, by analogy, himself to Christ. Petrarch's speaker elevates his passion by equating it with the Passion, since he first sees Laura on 6 April 1327, Good Friday: "miei guai / nel commune dolor s'incominciaro" [my misfortunes began in the midst of universal woe] (3.7–8). Later, the lover recalls and appropriates the Fifth Wound by describing Laura as "chi m'à 'l fianco ferito et chi 'l risalda" [she who has wounded my side and heals it] (105.87). In *Rime* 61, the anaphoric "benedetto" [blessed be] echoes the rhetoric of the Beatitudes (Matt. 5.3–12). Although Petrarch's speaker would seem to profane the spirit of Christ's words by privileging Laura over any of those less fortunate who deserve to be blessed, perhaps this echoing of Scripture helps heal the lover's spirit and justifies him as he creates a new context for a new love. It is another way of moralizing and exorcising the pagan *desultor*, who would never think of sacrificing himself for anything.

4

However, Petrarch's lover does not pretend to sainthood. He knows that the Ovidian pattern is etched into all men, of which he is one. One poetical part of this pattern is the familiar idea that a writer is a self-centered creature who unconsciously subordinates everything to the pursuit of his own greatness. Such Ovidian phrases as "a me retorni et di me stesso pensi" [I return to myself and think of myself] (71.90) frequently recur. In contrast to the Dantean *io son,* the speaker alludes to the *Amores* and confesses to *desultor*-ish emotions, thus demonstrating the need for exorcising them.

Certainly some Ovidian aspects are more difficult to reprocess than others, such as the dual desire for a woman and for poetical fame. The Apollo-Daphne paradigm of frustrated pursuit is clearly manifest in the *Rime,* and Petrarch refashions it as a form of self-advertisement:

> ei duo mi trasformaro in quel ch' i' sono,
> facendomi d'uom vivo un lauro verde
> che per fredda stagion foglia non perde
>
> (23.38–40)

[those two (love and Laura) transformed me into what I am, making me of a living man a green laurel that loses no leaf for all the cold season]

Eternal Laura is herself the agent of the poet's transcendent transformation. She whom Petrarch immortalizes makes him immortal as well, despite his protests to the contrary:

> Et certo ogni mio studio in quel tempo era
> pur di sfogare il doloroso core
> in qualche modo, non d'acquistar fama.
>
> (*Rime* 293.9–11)

[And certainly all my effort in that time was only to give vent to my sorrowing heart in some fashion, not to gain fame.]

Yet Petrarch cannot discuss Laura's transcendence without reference to *fama:* "il viso che laudato / sarà, s' io vivo, in più di mille carte" [that face . . . which shall be praised, if I live, on more than a thousand pages] (43.10–11). He knows not only that he will "live" but also that the life of his work is all that will preserve Laura. In this "profanely literary act of self-exhibition,"[18] he would appear to differ very little from the *io son* of the *Vita nuova* or from the Ovidian *desultor*.

Surely Laura differs from Corinna and the Dantean *schermo*. Criticism generally stresses her centrality to the *Rime* and hence to the spirit of the sequence: she is a *nova figura* in the manner of Martianus Capella's Philologia or Boethius' Philosophia. Yet, as Robert Durling rightly explains, "Laura herself is not the central focus of the poetry. Her psychology remains transcendent, mysterious."[19] I would go even further and suggest that Petrarch does not mean for Laura to possess a psychology, because he does not tell us enough about her for us to assume that she has one. Like all other sonnet ladies who make up her train, she exists, contrary to Petrarch's assertions, merely as a reflector for the persona, just as Corinna does for the *desultor*. The speaker's lust for Laura and the poetic immortality she provides are his most implacably Ovidian characteristics.

Yet Petrarch reprocesses these demonic aspects in subtle ways, such as by rewriting minor conventions from the *Amores*. He describes Desire taking the "fren," or bit (6.9), which is inevitably harsh or hard ("duro fren," 147.2; "sì duro 'l freno," 173.8). Similarly, Ovid writes,

---

18. Asher, "Petrarch," 1059.

19. For Durling's comment on "psychology," see Petrarch, *Lyric Poems,* 7. Aldo S. Bernardo makes an interesting case for Martianus Capella's Philologia as an inspiration for Laura. See his parallels in "Laura as a 'Nova figura,'" in *Francesco Petrarca: Citizen of the World* (Albany: State University of New York Press, 1980), 182. Martianus' initial description of Philologia in *de Nuptiis Philologiae et Mercurii* is worth reading:

> Est igitur prisci generis doctissima virgo conscia Parnasso, cui fulgent sidera coetu, cui nec Tartareos claustra occultare recessus nec lavis arbitrium rutilantia fulmina possunt, fluctigena spectans qualis sub gurgite Nereus quaeque tuos norit fratrum per regna recursus, pervigil immodico penetrans arcana labore, quae possit docta totum praevertere cura, quod superis praescire datum.

> [There is a maiden of ancient lineage, highly educated and well acquainted with Parnassus; upon her the constellations shone in close proximity; no hidden region can conceal from her the movements of the stars through Tartarus, nor can thunderbolts hide from her the will of Jove: she beholds under the sea the nature of wave-borne Nereus. She knows your circuits through the several kingdoms of your brothers: secrets of knowledge so that with her patient learning she can anticipate all that it is given to gods to foreknow.]

The text is from *Martianus Capella,* 16. The translation is from *Martianus Capella and the Seven Liberal Arts,* ed. and trans. W.H. Stahl and R. Johnson, 2 vols. (New York: Columbia University Press, 1969), 2:14.

ut rapit in praeceps dominum spumantia frustra
frena retentantem durior oris equus.

(*Am.* 2.9b.29–30)

[So a horse, hard of mouth, seizes the foaming bit while the rider labors
uselessly to restrain him.]

More often, Petrarch reins in these Ovidian commonplaces and twists
them. The bull who does not love the yoke in the *Amores* ("nec iuga taurus
amat," 3.11b.36) finds his Petrarchan burden more agreeable ("dolce
giogo," *Rime* 197.3). When the lover explains Laura's capture of him—
"Così caddi a la rete" [Thus I fell into the net] (181.12). Petrarch reverses
one of Ovid's more notorious images from the *Ars amatoria,* the predatory
male lover as *venator* extending the net for any *puellae* who may happen
into it: "scit bene uenator, ceruis ubi retia tendat" (1.45). At the beginning
of the *Rime,* Amor's revenge on the conventionally scoffing lover is "leg-
giadra," or graceful (2.1), in studied contrast to the stumbling *desultor,*
who complains about Love's sharp arrows: "me miserum! certas habuit
puer ille sagittas" (*Am.* 1.1.25).

These scraps and soundings are an important part of Petrarch's attempt
to transcend the physical limitations of earthly love by confessing his sexual feelings constantly. He refers repeatedly to the beautiful garment of
Laura's earthly limbs: "la bella vesta / . . . de le terrene membra" (8.1–2).
And these "terrene membra" are not merely agents of philosophical spec-
ulation for the speaker or aspects of God's creation. They inspire simple,
animal lust:

Amor che dentro a l'anima bolliva
per rimembranza de le treccie bionde

(67.5–6)

[Love, which boiled within my breast for memory of her blonde tresses]

The speaker finds himself compelled to discuss Laura's face, hair, and eyes
("dir del viso et de le chiome / et de' begli occhi ond' io sempre ragiono,"
74.5–6), characteristics that he is indeed always talking about. When
Laura dies, Petrarch devotes *Rime* 299, a litany of grief, to her physical
qualities and to how much his eyes have lost: "quanto manca / agli occhi
miei" (13–14). Desire (*desio*), as foolish (*folle*) as it might be, never leaves

him (see 6.1, 17.6, 19.5, 47.14, 211.1); it is immortalized along with Laura and strangely purified.

In the familiar Ovidian pattern, Petrarch's speaker becomes angry at Laura's indifference—"voi non cale" [you don't care] (133.4)—and at his own inability to overcome his lust:

> Non credo che pascesse mai per selva
> sì aspra fera, o di notte o di giorno,
> come costei ch' i' piango a l'ombra e al sole
>
> (22.19–21)

[I do not believe that there ever grazed in any wood so cruel a beast, either by night or by day, as she whom I weep for in the shadow and in the sun]

Dante applies such Ovidian invective only to the recalcitrant lady of the *Rime petrose,* never to Beatrice. Yet the Petrarchan conception of Laura as a sweet and bitter enemy is not isolated but frequent: "dolce et acerba mia nemica" (23.69; see also 73.29, 118.5). This too is Ovidian. The famous dictum of the *desultor* may come to mind: "dulce puella malum est" (*Am.* 2.9b.26). Petrarch's interesting twist on the convention is that Laura is somewhat enamored of herself; her mirror is his "adversario" (*Rime* 45.1) and one of many murderous mirrors that she has exhausted with self-love: "micidiali specchi / che 'n vagheggiar voi stessa avete stanchi" (46.7–8). Shakespeare's Will takes this up with his fair youth: accused of being "contracted to thine owne bright eyes," the youth is commanded to "Looke in thy glasse" (Sonnets 1.5, 3.1). The vanity of the beloved is almost as eternal as the speaker's.

Again, however, the lover's *desultor*-like behavior is sporadic. And Petrarch must illustrate the need for exorcism, especially from sexual torment. So the persona's anti-Ovidian solution—the acceptance and praise of Laura's virginity in a Christian context—is one that is strangely familiar to us because our own Petrarchan poets have made us accustomed to it. Amor joins himself with chastity in her: "Amor s'è in lei con onestate aggiunto" (*Rime* 215.9). Petrarch wisely allows Laura to reinforce the concept, and he endorses it without irony. She teaches her own mother, who does not understand her daughter's chastity: "'e' non fur, madre mia, / senza onestà mai cose belle o care'" [there never were, mother, things lovely or dear without virtue] (262.3–4). Laura becomes both mother and lover, Honesty and Beauty (285.9; 297.1–2). At the end of the *Rime,* Petrarch's speaker concludes that virtue is a subtle art, not something granted by chance: "non a caso è vertute, anzi è bell'arte" (355.14). These concepts regarding chastity address the cynical libertinism of the *Amores* directly. Petrarch makes other comments about the Ovidian persona by implication. Corinna and Dipsas denigrate the *desultor* (*Am.* 1.8); Laura does nothing of the kind. Although the *desultor* intends such conversations to reflect badly on the women, Ovid makes certain that the speeches undercut his speaker. Petrarch does not wish to undercut anyone, especially his persona.

Petrarch exorcises Ovid not only in his vernacular poetry but in his prose works, and he does so in an analogous fashion. In the prose works, Petrarch replaces Ovid's profane authority with one of impeccable sanctity, Augustine, with his paradigm of renunciation and conversion. The love of God must supersede the love of earthly creatures. The *Confessions* dramatize the discipline needed to subordinate and expunge the tormenting delights of the flesh that ought not fasten themselves to the soul with the glue of love: "anima mea . . . non eis infigatur glutine amore per sensus corporis."[20] Petrarch uses the saint's artistic and moral example to re-create this struggle in the *Rime.*

Petrarch's Augustine knows the erotica surprisingly well and frequently uses a line from it as a negative example. In *Secretum* 3,[21] Augustine teaches Franciscus to substitute divine for earthly love, citing Ovid's well-known tag from the *Remedia amoris:* "successore nouo uincitur omnis amor" [every love is conquered by a new one] (462). Although Ovid is merely satirizing Virgil's adage from the *Eclogues,* "omnia vincit amor" (10.69), Augustine appropriates it for his own Christian didactic purposes, appealing to his pupil's profane knowledge and demonstrating how it can be put to sacred use.

Sometimes Petrarch's Augustine is more direct in his exorcism. Once, when Franciscus quotes Ovid, Augustine dismisses the *desultor* as foolish: "Has ineptias amplius audire non valeo" (*Secretum* 3).[22] Earlier in the conversation, Augustine himself quotes Ovid:

---

20. *Confessions* 1.174.

21. *Prose,* 162.

22. Translated, "I don't want to hear any more about such foolish things" (*Prose,* 140).

A: An non succurrit illud Ovidii: "velle parum est; cupias, ut re
     potiaris, oportet."
F: Intelligo, sed et desiderasse putabam.
A: Fallebaris.

                                                              (*Secretum* 1)[23]

[A: Perhaps this line from Ovid comes to mind: "it's a small thing to
      wish; it's much grander to possess what you desire." (*EP* 3.1.35)
F: I understand, and I have known what it is to desire.
A: You have been deceived.]

Here Augustine explains that Franciscus has been deceived not only by his
desires, but by his justification of them by Ovidian authority. So when
Petrarch reconfigures the *versiculus* from the *Amores* (3.11b.34) during his
epiphany on Mount Ventoux, he demonstrates that he has learned from
the Saint's teachings and that he can moralize or repudiate Ovid in his own
way. The same process occurs in the *Rime* as well:

     Ché mortal cosa amar con tanta fede
     quanto a Dio sol per debito convensi
     più disdice a chi più pregio brama.

                                                              (264.99–101)

[For the more one desires honor, the more one is forbidden to love a
mortal thing with the faith that belongs to God alone.]

Profane authority, such as Ovid's, is itself mortal—not only subject to
mortality, but death-dealing. Perhaps this is why there is no proud
"Iamque opus exegi" (*Met.* 15.871) in the *Rime,* as devoted as Petrarch
may seem to the pursuit of his own fame. However, there are other, more
surprising, repudiations.

     Ultimately happy that Laura resists his desire ("veggio ch' ella /per lo
migliore al mio desir contese" 289.5–6), the speaker later confides,

     I' vo piangendo i miei passati tempi
     i quai posi in amar cosa mortale
     senza levarmi a volo

                                                              (365.1–3)

_____

23. *Prose,* 44.

[I go weeping for my past time, which I spent in loving a mortal thing without lifting myself in flight]

Laura herself must be repudiated. In the manner of the thirteenth-century *de Vetula,* the *Rime* ends with an invocation to the Virgin (366). It confirms the attitude of sincerity that Petrarch has taken such pains to develop elsewhere: "chi m'inganna / altri ch' io stesso e 'l desiar soverchio?" [who deceives me but myself and my excessive desire?] (70.31–32). Just as the desire for fame and female flesh is his most Ovidian trait, his consistent self-awareness is his most anti-Ovidian characteristic, his *nosce teipsum.*

Ultimately, Petrarch's speaker repudiates the conventional rhetorical postures for which he would be known. He does not believe that one can die of grief: "né credo ch' uom di dolor mora" (271.4). He has, after all, outlived Laura considerably. He asks Love what he can do to him now that she is dead: "ormai che puoi tu farme?" (270.75). As foretold from *Rime* 1, even Laura is dust, and she has been for decades, which her spirit confirms at the end: "'quel che tu cerchi è terra già molt'anni'" (359.61). Petrarch's persona is a bewildering voice that deconstructs itself, but without the self-destruction of the *desultor.*

Yet a successful imitation of this voice eluded the writers of the early sixteenth century. Some of Petrarch's Italian poetry was translated into English and French by enthusiastic yet inexperienced poets in the 1530s and 1540s. As they stood on the shoulders of a giant (so the phrase goes), they invented the sonnet form for their own languages. Yet Thomas Wyatt, the Earl of Surrey, and Joachim Du Bellay (as well as the very young Edmund Spenser) could not reproduce the master's progressively undulating inner turmoil and feeling, because they did not render the entire *Rime sparse* into French and English. Accordingly, their compatriots did not often read Petrarch, even though the Italian texts were accessible. They read uneven translations of great and effusively emotional lyrics that, removed from their sequential order, seemed to exhibit characteristics that could be easily misunderstood as maudlin, that the lesser poets of midcentury slavishly imitated, and that the greater makers parodied unrelentingly. The result of such imitation and parody is Petrarchism, created by "les Petrarquizers," as Joachim Du Bellay, himself a former Petrarchist, later named them in his moment of renunciation.[24] Petrarch's

---

24. Du Bellay's Petrarchan sonnet sequence is *L'Olive* (1549). His renunciation of the tradition appears in "Contre les Petrarquistes" in *Jeux rustiques* (1558). See Floyd Gray, ed., *Anthologie de la poesie Française du XVIe siècle* (New York: Irvington, 1978), 202–7.

complex persona is sometimes reduced to a stock of clichés set to uneven meter and slant rhyme.

However, Petrarch's exorcism of the Ovidian voice is an aberration in literary history, even in the Renaissance itself. The moment that the *desultor* disappears, English and French poets attempt to bring him back in their anti-Petrarchist mode. The satirical strain in Sir Philip Sidney, Pierre de Ronsard, and Shakespeare is really the reintroduction of the mocking male Ovidian voice, the *desultor* whom Petrarch took such pains to exorcise. In this way, Shakespeare's Sonnets are part of the long Ovidian tradition in which Petrarchism is an aberration: they demonstrate how Will loves against his will.

CHAPTER 6

"After that I loathe, I runne": Shakespeare's Sonnets 127–54 and Marlowe's *All Ovids Elegies*

odero, si potero; si non, inuitus amabo.

(Ovid *Am.* 3.11b.35)

Ile hate, if I can; if not, love gainst my will.

(Marlowe *All Ovids Elegies* 3.10.35)

Who taught thee how to make me love thee more,
The more I heare and see just cause of hate?

(Shakespeare Sonnet 150.9–10)

Oviddius Naso was the man. And why in deed *Naso,* but for smelling out the odoriferous flowers of fauncy? the jerkes of invention[?] imitarie is nothing. (Shakespeare *Love's Labour's Lost* 4.2)[1]

In his definitive work on Shakespeare and Ovid, Jonathan Bate demonstrates the inadequacy of the word *source* to describe the playwright's debt to his classical *auctor.* He prefers *affinity, precedent,* and, more contemporaneous with Shakespeare, *paradigma* (paradigm), which is culled from the

---

1. All quotations from Shakespeare's Sonnets are taken from the 1609 Quarto in *Shakespeare's Sonnets,* ed. Stephen Booth (New Haven: Yale University Press, 1977)—with *u, v, i, j,* and long *s* modernized—and are referenced with the abbreviation *SS.* All other Shakespearean references are taken from Helge Kökeritz, ed., *Mr. William Shakespeares Comedies, Histories, and Tragedies,* (New Haven: Yale University Press, 1954), a facsimile of the First Folio of 1623. Quotations from Marlowe's *All Ovids Elegies,* referenced with the abbreviation *AOE,* are from *The Complete Works of Christopher Marlowe,* ed. Roma Gill, 3 vols. projected (Oxford: Oxford University Press, 1987–), 1:2–84.

Elizabethan rhetorician George Puttenham (1589).[2] The term *paradigma* approximates the type of Renaissance *imitatio* that Thomas Greene classifies as "dialectical" or competitive.[3] Just as Ovid before him, Shakespeare knew that the jerks of invention are simply impossible without predecessors to refashion and reanimate. Therefore, in *Love's Labour's Lost*, Holofernes the pedant is quite wrong: *imitari* is everything.

Bate clarifies a small but vexed critical issue: the idea that Arthur Golding's rendering of the *Metamorphoses* into fourteeners in 1567, rather than the *auctor* himself, fomented Shakespeare's Ovidianism. In response to those who cannot imagine that Shakespeare would have needed English translations to help him navigate Latin literary culture, Bate proves that Golding's Ovid was indeed a trove of images for the Sonnets (and the plays), particularly those concerned with transformation and mutability. Yet he does not argue strongly for other Elizabethan translations as intermediating Ovidian *paradigmata*—besides Thomas Heywood's rendering of the *Ars amatoria* into English (c. 1600–13)—preferring to cast his lot with Golding. Elsewhere, he refers cursorily to the importance of Ovid's Corinna to Petrarch and Sidney, and he suggests that neoteric elegies could have functioned as exempla for makers of sonnets.[4] I argue that the *Amores* served as a formative intertext or *paradigma* for Sonnets 127–54 and that one means of transmission must have been Christopher Marlowe's translations, *All Ovids Elegies* (written in the 1580s and published between 1595 and 1600). I also argue that what some have labeled anti-Petrarchism is a variety of proto-Ovidianism, instead.[5] Marlowe's Ovid

---

2. "if ye will draw the judgements precedent and authorized by antiquitie as veritable, and peradventure fayned and imagined for some purpose, into similitude or dissimilitude with our present actions and affaires, it is called resemblance by example" (*The Arte of English Poesie* [London: Richard Field, 1589; reprint, Menston, England: Scolar Press, 1968], 205).

3. See *The Light in Troy,* 43–48.

4. For Bate on Ovid and the Sonnets, see "Ovid and the Sonnets; Or, Did Shakespeare Feel the Anxiety of Influence?" *Shakespeare Survey* 42 (1990): 65–76. See also Bate, *Shakespeare and Ovid* (Oxford: Clarendon Press, 1993), 3–4, 42–46, 83–84, 87. Bate makes a particularly useful comment for my purposes: "the most profound affinities may be the least demonstrable precisely because they go deeper than the explicit local parallel. The problem with affinities is that if you're looking for them they're easy to find, but if you're not they cease to exist" (*Shakespeare and Ovid,* 190).

5. Although it is immensely tempting to discuss the first 126 sonnets ostensibly addressed to the fair youth and to analyze, as one colleague of mine put it so memorably to me, "how . . . this idealistic, anguished, and homoerotic love alters the reader's understanding of the heterosexual duplicities of the final [dark lady] sonnets," I demur, except when the sonnets to the young man concern the dark lady directly (as do, for example, 40, 41, 42, 135, &c). Unfortunately, this subject is beyond the bounds of this chapter and this book. The sonnets

helped complicate Shakespeare's response not only to Petrarch but to Petrarchism.

Shakespeare's "dark lady" sonnets (1599 and 1609) reanimate the *desultor* whom Petrarch had taken such pains to exorcise from lyric poetry. Actually, Shakespeare's Ovidian persona in these poems, Will, owes a great deal to Marlowe's version of this voice from antiquity, which exists in two versions: *Certaine of Ovids Elegies* (ten translations from the *Amores,* published in 1599), and *All Ovids Elegies* (a relatively complete rendering of Ovid's three books).[6] The redacted *Elegies* were notorious and were considered subversive enough to be burned by ecclesiastical

---

to the young man have been discussed as a group—endlessly, I might add—by many distinguished commentators over nearly four centuries. Although a thorough study of them is essential to the discussion of Shakespeare's response to Petrarchism—another subject ably and endlessly discussed in criticism—these (homoerotic) poems are simply not informed by the Ovid of the *Amores* in the way that the (heterocentric) sonnets to the dark lady are. Furthermore, Sonnets 127–54 have received relatively little attention as a group—hence I attend to them in this chapter. The most widely praised recent studies of the homoerotic elements in Sonnets 1–126 are Joseph Pequigney, *Such Is My Love: A Study of Shakespeare's Sonnets* (Chicago: University of Chicago Press, 1985); Bruce R. Smith, *Homosexual Desire in Shakespeare's England: A Cultural Poetics* (Chicago: University of Chicago Press, 1994), 225–270.

6. Both texts of Marlowe's translations are subject to immense scholarly controversy. The ten *Certaine* elegies are, in this order, 1.1, 1.3, 1.5, 3.13, 1.15, 1.13, 2.4, 2.10, 3.6, and 1.2. See Lee Pearcy, *The Mediated Muse: English Translations of Ovid, 1560–1700* (Hamden, Conn.: Archon, 1984). They were published with forty-eight of Sir John Davies'*Epigrams*. The fuller version of the translation, *All Ovids Elegies,* has no date of publication, although some postulate a date in the early seventeenth century (Gill, in Marlowe, *The Complete Works* [1987–], 1:8). Stephen Orgel suggests c. 1600 in *Christopher Marlowe: The Complete Poems and Translations,* ed. Stephen Orgel (Harmondsworth: Penguin, 1971), 10. In a prefatory note to his facsimile edition of the Bindley text, *All Ovids Elegies: 3. Bookes. By C.M. Epigrams by J.D.* (London: Scolar Press, 1973), A.J. Smith posits 1595–96 and suggests that the later *Certaine* text was excerpted from the nearly complete *All* text. Marlowe did not translate *Amores* 3.5, a poem known to the Middle Ages as *somnium Ovidii,* perhaps because it was not included in his editon of the poems. Even now, Kenney is reluctant to attribute it to Ovid (see Ovid, *P. Ovidii Nasonis Amores,* x–xii).

The dates of publication for *All Ovids Elegies* and the Sonnets are of no help in ascertaining influence. Marlowe's translations are often (if not always) considered juvenilia, perhaps a relic of his Cambridge days (he took his M.A. in 1587), while many Shakespeare scholars date the Sonnets around 1593, the year that the theaters were closed because of the plague, and the year that Marlowe died (29 May). Two "dark lady" sonnets were published in 1599 in *A Passionate Pilgrim* (those numbered 138 and 144 in the 1609 Quarto), the same year in which *Certaine of Ovids Elegies* was burned, but a year after Francis Meres makes reference to Shakespeare's circulation of "sugared sonnets among his private friends" in the *Palladis Tamia* (1598). Since *Shake-speares Sonnets* was passed around in manuscript, it is possible that *All Ovids Elegies* was also circulated at an earlier date, and that Shakespeare read it. (It is a curious fact that Davies' epigrams survive in manuscript form while *All Ovids Elegies* does not.)

order; this is probably why *All Ovids Elegies* had to be published across the Channel at Middleburgh in Holland. Ben Jonson thought one poem (1.15) worthy of parody in *The Poetaster* (c. 1602), a play in which Ovid is a (somewhat disreputable) character.[7] Sir John Harington wrote what seems to be a competing version of *Amores* 2.4 in quatrains, "Ovids Confession," for the esteemed military commander Sir John Norris around 1593.[8] Along with such notoriety, if one considers Shakespeare's familiarity with Marlowe and virtual adoration of Ovid, it would have been unusual if he had not read the translated material in partial or intact form, printed or in manuscript. At least one phrase from *All Ovids Elegies*, "The Moone sleepes with *Endymion*" (1.13.43), surfaces in the plays (*The Merchant of Venice* 5.1).[9]

However, there are better reasons for suspecting that Shakespeare used Marlowe's uneven translations to transfuse Ovid into the body of his sonnets. As Stephen Orgel remarks, "this is Marlowe's sonnet sequence, the psychomachia of a poet-lover whose love is both his creation and his ultimate monomania, frustration, and despair."[10] If the *Elegies* resemble such a sequence, they would naturally appeal to a writer attempting to depict the psyche of a troubled lover. Also, the two texts possess a number of similarities, both integral and superficial. At times, Shakespeare's use of *All Ovids Elegies* resembles his usual appropriation of Marlowe, which often constitutes "a process of imitative re-creation merging into critical parody."[11] Therefore, it is likely that Marlowe served as transmitter, although

---

7. For a study of Jonson's use of Marlowe, see James A. Riddell, "Ben Jonson and 'Marlowe's Mighty Line,'" in "*A Poet and Filthy Play-Maker*": *New Essays on Christopher Marlowe,* ed. Kenneth Friedenreich, Roma Gill, and Constance Kuriyama (New York: AMS Press, 1988), 37–49. One might also want to read Shakespeare's famous Sonnet 55 on this same theme. For the circumstances of the Dutch publication of Marlowe's translations, see Marlowe, *The Complete Poems and Translations,* 10. Concerning the notoriety of *All Ovids Elegies,* Fredson Bowers writes: "The record in the Stationers' Register of the ecclesiastical order of 1 June 1599 to call in and burn 'Davys Epigrams, with Marlowes Elegys' probably refers to O2 [*Certaine of Ovids Elegies*]" (Marlowe, *Christopher Marlowe: The Complete Works,* ed. Fredson Bowers, 2 vols. (Cambridge: Cambridge University Press, 1973), 2:311.

8. Harington's translation was later handsomely copied out for Prince Henry in 1605. See Ruth Hughey, ed., *The Arundel Harington Manuscript of Tudor Poetry,* 2 vols. (Columbus: Ohio State University Press, 1960), text: 1:253–54;. commentary: 2:352–54.

9. Gill makes no specific case for Shakespeare reading Marlowe's translations, but she notes this parallel nonetheless (Marlowe, *The Complete Works* [1987–], 1:229). The lines belong to Portia, who has just vanquished Shylock and is preparing to do the same to Bassanio: "Peace, how the Moone sleepes with *Endimion* / And would not be awak'd."

10. Marlowe, *The Complete Poems and Translations,* 233.

11. Nicholas Brooke, "Marlowe as Provocative Agent in Shakespeare's Early Plays," *Shakespeare Survey* 14 (1961): 44.

Shakespeare knew the *Amores* well enough to affix "uilia miretur uulgus" (1.15.35) to the title page of *Venus and Adonis* (1593).

1

O Poet carelesse of thy argument

—*AOE* 3.1.16

Most critics scornfully grant Marlowe a certain cleverness in the *Elegies,* as if they had no idea how ferociously difficult translation can be.[12] To imitate the Protean poetics of Ovid can defy the skills of even the most seasoned *traducteur.* Yet when sex is the subject, the young Marlowe is sometimes quite deft. His *desultor* suggests to Corinna that when they encounter each other in a crowd,

_____

12. Criticism of *All Ovids Elegies* is scanty and often scornful, but the textual scholarship is thorough and oddly appreciative. Marlowe's translations are lovingly documented yet are dismissed altogether as poetry. This paradox is best demonstrated in the work of Roma Gill, the most recent editor of *All Ovids Elegies.* Gill's most recent essays on *All Ovids Elegies* are the aforementioned introduction to her edition of *The Complete Works* (1987–), and "Marlowe and the Art of Translation," in *"A Poet and Filthy Play-Maker": New Essays on Christopher Marlowe,* ed. Kenneth Friedenreich, Roma Gill, and Constance Kuriyama (New York: AMS Press, 1988), 327–42. In the latter, she explains that Marlowe's technique of *metaphrasis* and his lack of knowledge about Roman amatory customs made him inadequate for his task (330). Gill's earliest essay on the subject—"'Snakes Leape by Verse,'" in *Christopher Marlowe,* ed. Brian Morris (New York: Hill and Wang, 1968), 133–50—deserves special attention because of its virulence. In that essay, Gill is, I think, overcritical of Marlowe, spanking him for mistranslations and slapping his wrists for his habit of changing the meaning to fit the rhyme. She says that Marlowe's Latin and English "are often those of the schoolboy, careless or ignorant of idiom and too lazy to check his guesses with a dictionary" (135). She adds, "One begins to question the efficacy of the Elizabethan education system when an Archbishop Parker scholar can make such elementary mistakes" (137). On his translations of the hair-dyeing and abortion poems (1.14, 2.13, 2.14) Gill writes: "Marlowe is unable to simulate the necessary mixture of anger and anxiety. His is a narrower range of feeling where emotions are deeper and more personal" (138). His range of feeling aside, I would argue that not only his youth but his ignorance of elegiac conventions—and their vibrant heterosexuality—ought to be considered when attempting to assess Marlowe's familiarity with his material.

Gill proposes that Marlowe used no discernible commentary on the *Amores* to help him in translation. She posits Philip Plantin's edition of the *Opera* (Antwerp, 1575) and implies that any "incompetence" is Marlowe's fault (*The Complete Works,* 1:6). The detective work of Lee Pearcy serves as counterpoint. He argues that Marlowe's Ovid was certainly taken from the *Ennaratio* of Dominicus Niger (Basle, 1549), a text that includes a commentary that would have forced Marlowe to mistranslate. See Pearcy's "Marlowe, Dominicus Niger, and Ovid's *Amores,*" *Notes and Queries* 27 (1980): 315–18. See also Pearcy, *The Mediated Muse,* 19.

There will I finde thee, or be found by thee,
There touch whatever thou canst touch of mee.

(AOE 1.4.57–58)

Verbs shift appropriately from active to passive, buffeted by internal and
end rhyme. Furthermore, the translator demonstrates some prosodic subtlety; the metrical turbulence of the reversed feet and extra (or elided) syl-
lable underscores the risibility of the wittily indefinite diction. Marlowe is
most successful in Englishing his Ovid when punning on male tumescence
and detumescence. Men often write well about this physiological transformation peculiar to their gender:

When in this workes first verse I trod aloft,
Love slackt my Muse, and made my numbers soft.

(1.1.22)

As one might expect, Marlowe equates poetry with potency, but he makes
an unexpected parallel between love and impotence. He sometimes
reverses these equations tactfully: "Sooth Lovers . . . rise up in swelling
armes" (1.9.25–26). In other instances, he is quite tasteless about the matter: "seeing thee, I thinke my thing will swell" (2.15.25). Yet Marlowe possesses an awareness of his special effects. The mimesis of the "aloft"/"soft"
rhyme is priapic. The couplet may be the closest one can get to the rising
hexameter and falling pentameter of the Latin elegiac couplet, which Ovid
used to imitate his favorite metamorphosis throughout his erotic poetry.

Shakespeare uses this metrical-erectile pun to imitate the same metamorphosis, one to which he alludes in his works only slightly less than the
sprouting *cornua* of cuckolds, who may, as Lavatch reminds us, "joule
horns together like any Deare i'th Herd" (*All's Well That Ends Well* 1.3):

No want of conscience hold it that I call,
Her love, for whose deare love I rise and fall.

(SS 151.13–14)

The couplet summarizes the swelling and shrinking that the enjambed and
end-stopped lines have been imitating in their balanced alternation.[13] Per-

---

13. In *A New Variorum Edition of Shakespeare: The Sonnets,* ed. Hyder Rollins, 2 vols.
(Philadelphia: Lippincott, 1944), a bemused Rollins, well aware of the metrical sex puns, cites
the indignantly puzzled T.G. Tucker on Sonnet 151: "This composition is one which, from

haps Shakespeare learned more from Marlowe than the ability to bombast out a blank verse; perhaps he learned the utility of the epigrammatic couplet in imitating male sexuality.

J.B. Steane, who tentatively praises the *Elegies* as "underread and underrated poems," notes deeper, thematic "affinities" between Marlowe and Ovid:

> violence and scorn, independence and impudence, a sharp undeceived sophistication, shrewd amatory Machiavellianism, hard brilliance, and youthful energy[14]

With the exception of "youthful energy," he could just as easily be describing the desiccated Will, a reincarnation and revision of Marlowe's naive young blade and Ovid's *desultor Amoris.* Although Shakespeare excises the incidental conventions of neoteric elegy (writing in wine on the table, groveling before the eunuch who guards the lady's door, and fornicating with her maid), he heightens the nasty dynamic of the relationship between the lover and lady by aging the former and removing all sense of morality from the latter. Shakespeare also does not emphasize the *vir,* or cuckolded husband, of the married dark lady. Instead, Will becomes a kind of cuckold as the dark lady steals the "lovely Boy" (*SS* 126.1) he did not dare to touch. Furthermore, Will exhibits a type of self-loathing even more intense than what Shakespeare found in his classical model. Unlike Ovid's young *desultor,* Will knows that he is old enough to know better.

---

the nature of its contents, might well be let die. We must not on that account deny its authorship, but it may be noted that the breaks and runnings-on of the lines (8, 10, and especially the latter) produce an effect of jerkiness strange to an ear accustomed to the usual movement in the sonnets" (1:387).

In "The Inception of the Closed Heroic Couplet," *Modern Philology* 66 (1969): 306–21, W.B. Piper is quite generous to Marlowe: "the lack of inflection in English forced him to simplify Ovid's rhetorical patterns and . . . he found the cue for these simplifications in Ovid himself" (316). Piper implies that the heavily end-stopped lines and medial caesuras that one might criticize in *All Ovids Elegies* were actually conventional for Latin poetry, since Ovid's couplets are closed and the caesura occurs after the third long vowel almost 90 percent of the time (311). So Marlowe adheres strictly to his model, metrically speaking, regarding balance, inversion, and parallelism (313) in his "remarkable duplication" of *Amores* 1.15 (315), the very poem that Jonson parodies in *The Poetaster.*

14. *Marlowe: A Critical Study* (Cambridge: Cambridge University Press, 1964), 280, 296. Steane's defense of *All Ovids Elegies* is in response to his early twentieth-century predecessors, but it also anticipates Gill: "Charges of incompetence and immaturity have so crabbed the approach that one feels a frowning countenance to be expected of the discriminating reader throughout. For myself, I find it impossible to maintain beyond a few lines" (285). Simply put, these are unrelievedly jocular, male-oriented poems.

2

le belzza è il vero trofeo della vittoria dell'anima, quando essa con la virtù divina
signoreggia la natura materiale e col suo lume vince le tenebre del corpo. Non è
adunque da dir che la bellezza faccia le donne superbe o crudeli . . . né ancor si
debbono imputare alle donne belle quelle inimicizie, morti, destrucioni, di che son
causa gli appetiti immoderati degli omini.

         —Castiglione *Il libro del cortegiano* 4.59

Beawtie is the true monument and spoile of the victorye of the soule, whan she
with heavenlye influence beareth rule over materiall and grosse nature, and with
her light overcommeth the darknesse of the bodye. It is not . . . to bee spoken that
beauty maketh women proude or cruel . . . Neither yet ought beautifull women to
beare the blame of that hatred, mortalitie, and destruction, which the unbridled
appetites of men are the cause of.

         —Sir Thomas Hoby's translation (1551)[15]

One can hear Shakespeare reanimating *All Ovids Elegies* in his sonnets and
reprocessing their conventions. For example, the facetious question that
the *desultor* asks the husband who knows that he is being cuckolded,
"Shall I *poore soule* be never interdicted?" (*AOE* 2.19.53), is revised into
the vocative in sublime Shakespearean form: "*Poore soule* the center of my
sinfull earth" (*SS* 146.1; my emphasis). This excruciatingly penitential sonnet represents a kind of answer to Marlowe's prosaic Ovidian query. Will,
a man who used to ask such facetious questions and who knows that his
better part really is poor, would like nothing better than interdiction, since
excess has made his soul "pine within and suffer dearth" (*SS* 146.3). Similarly, the hint of sexual frustration in "My mistris hath her wish, my wish
remaine" (*AOE* 3.2.81) is refined into a rich network of puns: "Who ever
hath her wish, thou hast thy *Will*" (*SS* 135.1). "Will" comes to represent
the dark lady's lust and husband, as well as Will himself, forever wishing
that his will be (un)done. Certain habits of thought transmigrate as well.
The Marlovian *desultor,* fond of epigrams, devotes some to physical desire:
"Wee skorne things lawfull, stolne sweetes we affect" (*AOE* 2.19.3). Shakespeare, more subtle in his use of maxims, crystallizes Marlowe's idea in his
notorious diatribe against lust: "Had, having, and in quest, to have
extreame" (*SS* 129.10). In the progression of tenses from past to future

---

15. Castiglione, *Opere di Baldassare Castiglione, Giovanni della Casa, Benvenuto Cellini,*
ed. Carlo Cordié (Milan: Ricciardi, 1960), 346; Hoby, *The Book of the Courtier,* ed. W.H.D.
Rouse and Drayton Henderson (London: Dent, 1928; reprint, 1948), 311.

and in the metrical space allotted therein, Shakespeare, like Ovid, analyzes the foolishness of a desire that prefers the chase and its stolen sweets ("in quest, to have") to things one may take for granted ("Had").

Like Petrarch before him, Shakespeare finds in Ovid the paradigm of the lover who strives for his own hurt with an inability to prevent it that is deliciously maddening to him. But Shakespeare, unlike his Italian predecessor, has no wish to exorcise the *desultor;* instead, he ages, Anglicizes, and hardens him. In this, the Marlovian incarnation of Ovid's speaker seems to have been a particularly important aid. When he confesses to Amor, "I am thy captive I" who is "manacled and bound" (*AOE* 1.2.19, 30), he foretells his speaker's masochistic plea to Corinna that she lie about her infidelity:

> let me erre, and thinke I am right,
> And like a Wittall think thee voide of slight.
>
> (3.13.29–30)

Marlowe reproduces moderately well Ovid's concept of self-imposed psychological captivity, a state of mind to which Shakespeare devotes Sonnet 133: "Prison my heart in thy steele bosomes warde" (9). Will, a more seasoned brother in masochism, also prefers mendacity: "Simply I credit her false speaking tongue" (*SS* 138.7). He too is manacled and bound, his "Mistrisse thrall" (154.12), a slave and "captive I."

In both sequences, Marlowe and Shakespeare make their personae obsessed with the beautiful yet deadly eyes of their mistresses. They inherit this hoary, courtly convention from Petrarch and his sixteenth-century imitators. Laura's eyes are repositories of truth, *viae sacrae.* Marlowe, disdainful of Petrarchism, stresses Ovid's insistence that Corinna's eyes are portals of infidelity that painfully occlude the lover's sight:

> Sharpe eyes she had: radiant like starres they be,
> By which she perjurd oft hath lyed to me.
>
> . . . .
>
> By her eyes I remember late she swore,
> And by mine eys, and mine were pained sore.
>
> (*AOE* 3.3.9–10, 13–14)

Since Ovid continually characterizes his lover as *perfidus,* a liar, the reader may be left to infer that this pain is richly deserved. The accusations of

Marlowe's speaker that Corinna has "perjurd" herself redound somewhat spectacularly on him, in much the same way that they do on Ovid's *desultor:* "mentita est perfida saepe mihi" (*Am.* 3.3.10).

Will, *perfidus* or *perfidiosus,* uses Marlowe's legal term with a small but significant variation. He admits that his own eyes lie because he has falsely praised the dark lady as fair: "more perjurde eye, / To swere against the truth so foule a lie" (*SS* 152.13–14). Yet, despite Will's intended insult, the author intimates his narrator's blindness, one whose eyes "behold and see not what they see" (137.2). Again, Corinna's eyes can inflict pain—"in mine eyes good wench no paine transfuse" (*AOE* 3.3.48)—yet Shakespeare makes this phenomenon more pronounced in the dark lady. Will begs her, "Wound me not with thine eye" (*SS* 139.3); he admonishes her, "in my sight / . . . forbeare to glance thine eye aside" (5–6); and then he confides to us, "Her prettie lookes have beene mine enemies" (10). Shakespeare's most original improvisation on Petrarch and the Marlovian Ovid may be his cuckold's cursed balm, Will's self-imposed blindness to infidelity: "Those that can see thou lov'st, and I am blind" (149.14).

In both sequences, the woman's dark complexion and sexuality occasion the lover's compulsion. Although this idea is meant to oppose the convention of blonde chastity, an enticingly swarthy lady was not particularly new in the sonnet sequences of the sixteenth century. Ronsard's Marie (1556) and Daniel's Delia (1601) are brunettes. Ovid, who may have served as classical precedent on this matter, sometimes equates dark hair with sexual proclivity, an idea that Marlowe dutifully passes along. Cypassis, Corinna's maid with whom the *desultor* consorts, is "browne" (*AOE* 2.8.22). Furthermore,

> A white wench thralls me, so doth golden yellowe
> And nut-browne girls in doing have no fellowe.
> If her white necke be shadoed with blacke haire
> Why so was *Ledas,* yet was *Leda* faire.
>
> (2.4.39–42)

Granted, Marlowe's Corinna was not necessarily the precedent for this sexual-cosmetic equation, though some hirsute passages from the *Elegies* may echo in the later Sonnets. When Will says (fleeringly) of the dark lady, "If haires be wiers, black wiers grow on her head" (*SS* 130.4), it is possible to be reminded of the *desultor,* who derides Corinna for her unsuccessful attempts at hair care:

How patiently hot irons they did take
In crooked trammells crispy curles to make.

(AOE 1.14.25–26)

Shakespeare's variation on convention is to equate physical darkness with moral turpitude. Will is so entranced with the dark lady's eyes of "Raven blacke" (SS 127.9) that to him, "blacke is fairest in my judgements place" (131.12), and "beauty her selfe is blacke" (132.13). At the same time, she is "blacke" in her "deeds" (131.13) and "as black as hell, as darke as night" (147.14). Will condemns his mistress and himself by the means of what attracts him to her.

3

la satieté engendre le dégoust: c'est une passion mousse, hebetée, lasse et endormee: "Si qua volet regnare diu, contemnat amantem" (Am. 2.19.33).
—Montaigne Essais 2.15

Satiety begets distaste: It is a dull, blunt, weary, and drouzy passion: "If any list long to beare sway, / Scorne she her lover, ere she play."
—John Florio's translation (1603)[16]

The most significant kinship between the Sonnets and All Ovids Elegies is that both Shakespeare and Marlowe fashion speakers who feel themselves to be enmeshed in decadent sensuality.[17] One man is a middle-aged version

---

16. The text is from Montaigne, Essais, ed. A. Lhéritier, 3 vols. (Paris: Union Générale, 1964), 2:416. Florio's translation is from Montaigne, Essays, ed. L.C. Harmer, trans. John Florio, 3 vols. (London: Everyman, 1910; reprint, 1980), 2:336. In the tag from the Amores, many, including Kenney (Ovid, P. Ovidii Nasonis Amores, 65), read "deludat" for "contemnat."

17. Gill sees nothing distinctive about Ovid's finely crafted and complex persona in the Amores: "Instead of being cries—of pain or pleasure—from the heart of the individual lover they utter sentiments to which every amorous bosom can return on echo. . . .He experiences every mood of every lover, whether he is triumphant in his mistress' arms, jealous at a banquet, servile at her locked door, or even impotent in her bed. . . . The feelings of Naso may for the most part have been oft thought—and intentionally so—but the style of Ovid raises them above the commonplace" ("'Snakes Leape by Verse,'" 139).

Since Ovid competes with his elegiac predecessors Propertius and Tibullus as he writes his erotic poetry, it is unlikely that he wishes to depict "every mood of every lover" without a touch of satire. Furthermore, in reference to Marlowe and Shakespeare, the "bosom" that Gill describes so universally might be more profitably modified with the adjective Roman. The mood of the desultor and the infidelities and abortions he recounts might have seemed quite new and somewhat decadent to an Elizabethan as subjects for poetry. For Ovid as satirist of his predecessors, see Durling, "Ovid as Praeceptor."

of the other. Perhaps the youthful *desultor,* not given to reflection, declines into Will, a much older man who, steeping in his "bath and healthfull remedy" for venereal disease (*SS* 154.11), can do nothing else but reprocess his experiences. What is exciting, keen, new, and invigorating to the *desultor* and once was to Will is now a dull, blunt, weary, and drowsy passion to the latter.

Old or young, both personae are afflicted with judgment that might be described most kindly as poor. Each man finds himself becoming a dilapidated Apollo chasing a Daphne whom he wishes would turn into a tree: "What flies, I followe, what followes me I shunne" (*AOE* 2.19.36). Pursuit does not merely humiliate the pursuer because it wounds his vanity by illustrating his undesirability to the beloved. It also betrays his real weakness, compulsion:

> So runst thou after that which flies from thee,
> Whilst I thy babe chace thee a farre behind.
>
> (*SS* 143.9–10)

Shakespeare complicates the paradigm by making it a triangle, thereby augmenting his speaker's mortification. As Will chases his unwilling mistress, he must suffer the additional indignity of watching her chase his friend. He is further embarrassed by the knowledge that he cannot stop loving a woman who lacks the decency to be humiliated by her pursuit of this friend and who continues running after that which flies from her.

Occasionally, the Marlovian *desultor* and Will attempt to soothe their humiliation with misogyny, the real darkness in *All Ovids Elegies* and the Sonnets (aside from hair color). Ovid was of course labeled an antifeminist even in the Middle Ages (for which he was both applauded and criticized). Marlowe, "sacramental" in his imitation,[18] again reproduces his source:

> Only a Woman gets spoiles from a Man,
> Farmes out her-self on nights for what she can.
>
> (*AOE* 1.10.29–30)

The sentiment is unfortunately familiar: women are hypocritical sexual mercenaries whose voracious appetites compel them to seek recompense for favors that they are not supposed to enjoy bestowing. Yet as such ver-

---

18. See Greene, *The Light in Troy,* 38–39.

biage accrues in the *Amores,* it becomes clear that the *desultor* is the misogynist, since this character is so egotistically predatory; and Ovid elsewhere attempts sympathetic and detailed portraits of women's psychology (see especially his Medea in *Heroides* 12 and *Metamorphoses* 7). Whenever the *desultor* recounts a woman's conversation in the *Amores,* she is sure to say something that a woman-hater would expect her to say. For example, Corinna's nurse Dipsas advises her to fleece her adulterous suitors:

> "Dissemble so, as lov'd he may be thought,
> And take heed least he gets that love for nought.
> . . . .
> Let thy tongue flater, while thy minde harme-workes."
>
> (1.8.71–72, 103)

This advice is simply a projection of what the *desultor* believes that a woman thinks ("gets spoiles from a Man"), and it can hardly be taken at face value from a man who dissembles, who views love as a financial transaction, and whose own "minde harme-workes." So, by the time the *Amores* end, Ovid ensures that his *desultor* has virtually no credibility:

> Nor canst by watching keepe her minde from sinne,
> All being shut out, th'adulterer is within.
>
> (3.4.7–8)

The last line, meant to define Corinna as adulterous by nature, actually redounds on the *desultor,* an adulterer accustomed to being "shut out." Marlowe translates Ovid's *nequitia* as "sinne," which would seem to underscore his point that women are sexually sinful by nature: "a wench is a perpetuall evill" (2.5.4).

If Shakespeare's sympathetic and psychologically complex women characters—such as Rosalind, Cleopatra, or Portia—can be cited as evidence, it seems clear that he maintains his critical distance from Will concerning such "evil," just as Ovid does from his *desultor.* Marlowe may have served as intermediary, but Will's misogyny is simply more subtle, less declarative, and perhaps more nefarious. He dispraises women in his eagerness to praise his lovely boy. The youth possesses a "womans gentle hart," yet one

> not acquainted
> With shifting change as is false womens fashion;

An eye more bright than theirs, lesse false in rowling.

> (20.3–5)

This proves to be wishful thinking in at least two ways. The youth is unfaithful to Will; also, "th'adulterer" is surely "within," because Will proves himself to be "false," "shifting," and "rowling." In Sonnets 127–54, he reads the dark lady as all women in microcosm; her parts become synecdochic to him:

All this the world well knowes, yet none knowes well
To shun the heaven that leads men to this hell.

> (129.13–14)

The essence of biological femaleness is the epitome of "sinne," because "hell" is a slang term for "The Womans part" that Shakespeare's Posthumus invests with similarly diabolic significance in *Cymbeline* (2.5). Here Shakespeare condenses, intensifies, and reinterprets the tiresome and shopworn misogyny of his Marlovian *paradigma.* Will's objectification of the dark lady is sinister, pathological.

Yet masochistic compulsion prevents the break that a more self-possessed person would deem necessary. Both the *desultor* and Will are pathetic types who complain of faithlessness but who stand by for more cuckolding. In both sequences, the panacea is self-deception:

me let crafty damsells words deceive,
Great joyes by hope I inly shall conceive.
.   .   .   .
Ile think all true, though it be feigned matter.

> (*AOE* 2.9.43–44, 2.11.53)

Corinna's unfaithfulness is particularly troublesome to the *desultor* because he has now become the cuckold whom he has despised all along, a bachelor version of the husband whom he and Corinna trick at banquets or whom he insults to his face (1.4, 2.19, 3.4). There is no trust between them:

Ask'st why I chaunge? because thou crav'st reward:
This cause hath thee from pleasing me debard.

> (1.10.11–12)

Here, "thee" and "me" are grammatically interchangeable as the direct objects of "pleasing" and "debard," which relates the confusion, fickleness, and instability of the lovers. The *desultor* and Corinna are incapable of pleasing one another. The speaker blames his paramour; Marlowe, through a trick of grammar, blames the speaker.

Will demonstrates such anger and self-loathing throughout the Sonnets: "Made [mad] In pursut and in possession so" (*SS* 129.9). Yet, unlike the Ovidian *desultor,* he is capable of vacillating between polemic and wearied bemusement. In Sonnet 138, Will anatomizes his psychology, as well as the dark lady's:

On both sides thus is simple truth supprest.

. . . .

. . . I lye with her, and she with me,
And in our faults by lyes we flattered be.

(8, 13–14)

This is really the only sonnet to which one could apply the term *mutuality* concerning the relationship, although it is hardly healthy: "I do beleeve her though I know she lyes" (2). A third variation on the Ovidian paradigm, besides the odd touch of humor and the (very faint) glimmer of accord, is that the dark lady practices self-deception as well: "wherefore sayes she not she is unjust?" (9). If Will is to be believed, it would appear that she knows that she *is* "unjust." The lovers flatter one another with sex and lies about age and faithfulness. They know "loves best habit is in *seeming* trust" (11; my emphasis). Not every cause debars them from pleasure. Yet Will is incapable of maintaining such seeming trust. Like his Ovidian precursor, his ego is monstrous.

Even after the *desultor* admits his dubiety, he blames his female object for his own impulse to deceive, as if she had absorbed this by osmosis. Hence he undercuts his own condemnation of Corinna. "Couzend, I am the couzeners sacrifice" (*AOE* 3.3.22), whines the supreme cozener. Although he claims he will not "tell" Corinna's "vaine tongues filthy lyes" and "God-wronging perjuries" (3.10.21–22), this general enunciation serves as a telling of them. Throughout the *Amores,* Ovid masterfully repeats this ironic bifurcating pattern so that his *desultor* loses his credibility. As he inveighs against his mistress, he reveals his viciousness, a tendency that Marlowe reproduces:

Heere I display my lewd and loose behaviour.
I loathe, yet after that I loathe, I runne,
Oh how the burthen irkes, that we should shunne.
I cannot rule my selfe.

(2.4.4–7)

Yet as the young Marlowe strains for rhyme, he has no particular desire to reproduce the literal meaning of the Ovidian text, and he is perhaps more baldfaced. The classical *desultor* is slightly less forthcoming. He will confess his vices if that is useful: "confiteor, si quid prodest delicta fateri" (*Am.* 2.4.3). His explanation for his behavior rests in the ambiguous adjective "demens" (4), which ranges in meaning from "agitated" to "completely insane." So Marlowe amplifies, even exaggerates. The lack of subtlety creates a different character, whose Ovidian subtleties Shakespeare masterfully restores.

Sometimes it is a matter of diction. An important clue to the unreliability of the *desultor* and to the difference between Marlowe and Ovid is the translation of "nil ego, quod nullo tempore laedat, amo" (*Am.* 2.19.8): "Nothing I love, that at all times availes me" (*AOE* 2.19.8). What Ovid seems to mean is: "I cannot love something that never hurts me." However, Marlowe's reading is entirely possible. His important word is "Nothing," because of its function as a multiplex pun. It is distasteful slang for "the Womans part," in keeping with the speaker's negative attitude toward women and the tendency to reduce them by synecdoche (cf. Will's "hell," *SS* 129.14, previously quoted). Also, "Nothing" serves as the existential *nihil,* the abyss. Since the lover possesses no love or faith, he can only love nothing: "Ile hate, if I can; if not, love gainst my will" (*AOE* 3.10.35). Yet a surface reading of the line is perhaps the most instructive. "Nothing I love" explains what one might have inferred much earlier. The *desultor* is incapable of love, as Marlowe hints in an inexact rendering of the Ovidian "uror, et in uacuo pectore regnat Amor" (*Am.* 1.1.26): "I burne, love in my idle bosome sits" (*AOE* 1.1.30). Actually, *uacuo* means "empty," not "idle." Love, like nature, abhors a vacuum; or perhaps lust, unlike nature, requires a vacuum. It burns in empty bosoms.

Shakespeare, with Marlowe's assistance, imitates Ovid's ironic bifurcating pattern. Will's capacity for self-revelation similarly demolishes his credibility as a critic of his sexual object. Yet Shakespeare condenses Will's masochism and corrosive anger into the three dozen sonnets concerned with the dark lady. He more fully realizes what might be termed the "Ovidian spirit," because Will's psychology can truly be epitomized in "nil ego, quod nullo tempore laedat, amo" (*Am.* 2.19.8). He can only love what hurts him. This is true regarding the dark lady; this is also true concerning his love for his beautiful boy.

Three of the most accusatory sonnets, 142, 147, and 152, are also the most indicative of Will's unreliability. In the manner of his paradigm, his bitterness is palpable: "she that makes me sinne awards me paine" (*SS* 141.14); "I against my selfe with thee pertake" (149.2). Likewise, his histrionics betray him:

> those lips of thine,
> That have prophan'd their scarlet ornaments,
> And seald false bonds of love as oft as mine
>
> (142.5–7)

The rhyme words call attention to themselves, because Will cannot distinguish between "thine" and "mine." Also, "mine" is grammatically ambiguous. It functions as an alternative object of "seald" with "false bonds of love": the dark lady has been unfaithful to Will, a complaint one would expect from him. Yet "mine" can also serve as an appositive subject of "seald," which betrays Will's faithlessness to his much-maligned mistress as well.[19] Furthermore, it has not occurred to Will that he has been an agent of the dark lady's legal infidelity to her own husband. Here, like Marlowe, Shakespeare demonstrates the utility of dubious grammar.

In Sonnet 147, Shakespeare revises Marlowe by the exposition of a method. Like the *desultor,* Will admits his loose and lewd behavior (cf. *Am.* 2.4) by confessing that he runs after what he loathes. Yet Marlowe contents himself with general statements. Shakespeare's Will explains a process:

> My reason the Phisition to my love,
> Angry that his prescriptions are not kept
> Hath left me, and I desperate now approove,
> Desire is death, which Phisick did except.
> Past cure I am, now Reason is past care,
> And frantick madde with ever-more unrest.
> My thoughts and my discourse as mad mens are,
> At randon from the truth vainly exprest.
>
> (*SS* 147.5–12)

---

19. See Booth's reading of "as oft as mine" (*Shakespeare's Sonnets,* 492 n. 7).

Reason, personified as Will's physician, abandons him in frustration yet apparently finds himself afflicted by the same plague, as "frantick madde" as his besotted patient. Here, one might say that Shakespeare allows Will to explain what "I cannot rule my selfe" (*AOE* 2.4.7) *really* means. The root of Will's self-loathing is encapsulated in the idea that his "discourse" is "At randon from the truth": he is a liar. His self-abuse is most indicative in his self-description: "pent in thee" (*SS* 133.13); "morgag'd" (134.2); "neere slaine" (139.13); "vassall wretch" (141.12); "poore infant" (143.8); "blinde" (148.13); "tirant" (149.4); "poore drudge" (151.11); "perjurde" (152.13); "a sad distemperd guest" (153.12); and, redundantly, "my Mistrisse thrall" (154.12).

Since Will has no native Paelignus to claim him as "foster-childe" (*AOE* 3.14.3) or to which he can pay homage (*Am.* 3.15), he finds himself reduced to admitting in Sonnets 153 and 154 that, good for nothing else, he is at leisure to be wise. So Sonnet 152 provides an anticlimactic climax. Fully conscious of his histrionics, Will is nonetheless unconsciously self-revelatory:

> In loving thee thou know'st I am forsworne,
> But thou art twice forsworn to me love swearing;
> In act thy bed-vow broake and new faith torne,
> In vowing new hate after new love bearing.
>
> (1–4)

Although Will admits that he is unfaithful to someone in loving the dark lady, she is still at fault for occasioning his compulsion, for her infidelity to her husband, and for (sanely) swearing off Will. As the sonnet twists into its second quatrain, Will's logic becomes more skewed:

> But why of two othes breach doe I accuse thee,
> When I breake twenty: I am perjur'd most,
> For all my vowes are othes but to misuse thee.
> And all my honest faith in thee is lost.
>
> (5–8)

It would seem that Will finally admits the extent of his dubiety: "perjur'd most," his habit is to "misuse." Yet this too is somehow not his fault:

For I have sworne deepe o[t]hes of thy deepe kindenesse:
Othes of thy love, thy truth, thy constancie,

. . . .
For I have sworne thee faire: more perjurde eye,
To swere against the truth so foule a lie.

                                                    (9–10, 13–14)

If Will is more a liar than the dark lady, he explains, it is only because she
has refused to actualize his rhetoric, to become the poetic construct that he
had envisioned—much as Corinna fails the *desultor* by not appreciating
his poetic praise, which she is supposed to reciprocate by providing sexual
favors: "when I praise a pretty wenches face / Shee in requitall doth me oft
imbrace" (*AOE* 2.1.33–34). Of course, this is fallacious. Will never attests
to the dark lady's kindness, love, truth, or constancy. For that matter, she
is, to him, only "as rare, / As any she bel'd with false compare" (*SS*
130.13–14), a marginally better alternative to those women he derides for
"Fairing the foule with Arts faulse borrow'd face" (127.6). In Will, Shakespeare crystallizes the hypocrisy of the *desultor,* be it Ovid's or Marlowe's,
and outdoes them both.

   If the Catullan *odi et amo* can be applied to the *desultor* and Will, it is
obvious that they turn the *odi* on themselves; there is no *amo.* Since their
hearts are either idle or empty, only lust can reign there. It is therefore not
surprising that each man generally finds himself alone, with the exception
of a predictably indefatigable yet unreliable companion:

Now when he should not jette, he boults upright,
And craves his taske, and seekes to be at fight.
Lie downe with shame, and see thou stirre no more,
Seeing thou wouldst deceive me as before.

                                                    (*AOE* 3.6.67–70)

This is probably Ovid's most graphic (and appropriate) symbol of physical
love: its instability, fickleness, and odd propensity for making its devotees
think that it is the only thing on which they may maintain a firm grip. Marlowe Anglicizes the passage into his mimetic rising and falling couplets,
disyllabic words rhyming with the monosyllabic. As one might expect,
Shakespeare revises the concept into sonnet form:

    flesh staies no farther reason,
But rysing at thy name doth point out thee,
As his triumphant prize, proud of this pride,
He is contented thy poore drudge to be
To stand in thy affaires, fall by thy side.

(SS 151.8–12)

It would appear that Shakespeare is amusing himself with some male-oriented poetics, illustrating the idea of dialectical *imitatio* yet again. He shows the reader that he has more potency than Ovid or Marlowe, both poetically and priapically. At the same time, like the *desultor,* Will is aware that he is passion's slave. He does not bother to invoke the Ovidian "non ego sum stultus, ut ante fui" (*Am.* 3.11a.32), which Marlowe translates "I am not as I was before, unwise" (*AOE* 3.10.32), because he is old enough to know that he will always be "stultus." Besides, potency has its downfalls, as Will, steeping in his clap-curing bath, suggests in his final line: "Loves fire heates water, water cooles not love" (*SS* 154.14).

    Shakespeare's use of Marlowe and Ovid exemplifies the definition and functions of a "formative intertext." It is a text that, by its very existence, helps to form another; it invites, even encourages, the imitation and subversion of itself. The images of reproduction and renewal in the Sonnets encourage such definition making. For example, when Will admonishes his lovely boy that his "face should forme an other" (*SS* 3.2), it is ironic that Will himself forms many faces. So Ovid's *Amores,* with Marlowe's help, forms the faces of Will, the youth, the lady. And, for an anachronistic pun based on the terminology of gender and cultural criticism, both the youth and the lady serve as Other to Will.

    I have not endeavored to declare that Shakespeare worked on Sonnets 127–54 with *All Ovids Elegies* by his side, surreptitiously purchased from a Dutch agent, or with a charred copy of the *Certaine* text open before him, snatched from the censor's bonfire. Nor am I insisting that he was innocent of the Latin *Amores.* I argue instead that Shakespeare partakes of Marlowe's Ovidianism just as he partakes of Golding's. Will and his dark lady owe something to the Marlovian *desultor* and Corinna, who fulfill Puttenham's idea of *paradigma,* that "precedent . . . fayned and imagined . . . into similitude or dissimilitude with our present actions and affaires."[20]

---

20. See note 2 in this chapter.

So Shakespeare's "anti-Petrarchism" undoes Petrarch's exorcism of the *desultor Amoris* and restores this self-destructing, mocking male voice to its familiar place in lyric poetry. To Anglicize the Ovid of the *Amores* into all of his middle-aged, unhappy, and unreconstructed masculinity is something that Shakespeare, with Marlowe's help, certainly accomplishes— and with a vengeance.

Afterword

The *desultor Amoris* finds no terminus in Shakespeare's unfortunate Will. Seventeenth-century English authors are particularly interested in keeping the classical paradigm alive by reinventing it for their own era. In their poems and plays, the *desultor* is restored to youth; his nature is more hardened and much less self-reflective than Shakespeare's dilapidated persona. Perhaps because of the rise of neoclassicism and the corresponding decline of the sonnet sequence as a fashionable literary form, the reinvigorated, fully Anglicized *desultor* reaches his most concentrated incarnation in John Donne's *Elegies* (c. 1597); their pentameter rhyming couplets are the closest approximation of the quantitative elegiacs that the English could manage (as Marlowe had proven in *All Ovids Elegies*). Furthermore, Donne's baroque gallant, replete with the paradoxical, humorous, irritating voice familiar to those more acquainted with the *Songs and Sonets* (1633), recalls Ovid's own *desultor* in the *Amores* more accurately than any other speaker since antiquity: he is naive, insensitive, foulmouthed, and self-deconstructing.

I was tempted to include a chapter on Donne's *Elegies* and to trace the tradition into the seventeenth century. Like Maximianus, Guillaume IX, Dante, Petrarch, and Shakespeare, Donne masterfully reproduces and transforms the conventions he inherits into useful poetic matter for his own time. Like his predecessors, Donne makes Ovid new, repudiates him, yet shows his debt in unmistakable ways, all characteristic of the formative intertextuality to which this book is devoted.

However, this foray into Jacobean England would have entailed a fairly thorough investigation of English seventeenth-century Ovidianism in poetic and dramatic form. I believe this in itself would comprise a considerable (i.e., book length) study, which should certainly *begin* with Donne.

155

Once could then turn to prerevolutionary drama, because playwrights knew that the *desultor* is simply too good to keep offstage. I think of such plays as John Fletcher's The *Wild-Goose Chase* (1621) with its Mirabel, as well as Philip Massinger's *A New Way to Pay Old Debts* (c. 1625) with its Sir Giles Overreach: "Virgin me no virgins! / I must have you lose that name, or you lose me" (3.2). And the paradigm of the *desultor* informs narrative poetry and creeps into the English translations of other works in the Ovidian corpus: George Chapman's *Ovids Banquet of Sence* (1595), George Sandys' version of the *Metamorphoses* (1626), and, most intriguing to me, Thomas Heywood's rendition of the *Ars amatoria* (c. 1600–13), published and republished extensively in the revolutionary period and throughout the Restoration. I think also of the so-called Courtly Amorists (i.e., Richard Lovelace, Robert Herrick, Edmund Waller) whose politics and poetics John Milton despised. Their *desultor*-ish, carpe diem blandishments are indignantly satirized in the seductive speeches of Satan to Eve in *Paradise Lost* (1667, 1674), whose first utterance to his prey echoes the Amorists' lyrical wordplay: "Wonder not, sovran Mistress . . . who art sole Wonder" (*Paradise Lost* 9.532–33). Also, just as Shakespeare undoes the Petrarchan aberration, John Wilmot, Earl of Rochester (1647–80), answers Milton's criticism of carpe diem by outdoing its English adherents before Cromwell, in a voice surely modeled on the *Amores* or *Ars amatoria*: "I swive as well as others do, / I'm young, not yet deform'd" ("The Mock Song" 1–2).

Since this Ovidian poet was almost certainly the prototype for the great rakes of the Restoration stage, a writer analyzing the tradition would certainly want to account for the interplay between the playwrights, the classical *desultor*, and Rochester. Here the lines are more complicated, the variations on the *paradigma* more diffuse. Think of William Wycherley's Horner in *The Country Wife*: "I am a Machiavel in love, Madam" (4.3). Consider George Etheredge's Dorimant in *The Man of Mode; Or, Sir Fopling Flutter* (1676): "I have known many women make a difficulty of losing a maidenhead, who afterwards made none of making a cuckold" (1.1). Even William Congreve's reformed rake Mirabell (not to be confused with Fletcher's unreformed seducer whom all try to seduce) in the magnificent *The Way of the World* (1700) triggers any number of associations between himself, Ovid, Rochester, and his rakish Restoration peers whenever he speaks: "a woman who is not a fool can have but one reason for associating with a man who is one" (1.3). However, this figure becomes evil and tragic in Nicholas Rowe's sentimental *The Fair Penitent* (1703), whose rake, Lothario, has become metonymic for the way our culture has come to regard such a person.

One might also wish to discuss poems by women authors of the period, such as Lady Mary Wortley Montagu (1689–1762). More fluent in Latin literature than most men of her day, she wrote an (anonymous) four-hundred-line paraphrase of the *Ars* (1745), and she knew a *desultor* when she saw one: "I loathe the lewd rake, the dressed fopling despise"; she also appropriates Ovid to champion a woman's right to say no: "We harden like trees, and like rivers are cold" ("The Lover" 45, 48). In this, Montagu is part of that ancillary Ovidian tradition inculcated in the twelfth century, epitomized by the Ripoll *amica*, *les trobairitz*, and the women in Andreas' *de Amore*, all of whom attempt to teach their medieval "rake-hells" how not to be so rakish or hellish.

A scholar who sought to be truly inclusive could even extend the tradition to Byron's *Don Juan* (1823), whose narrator and hero owe much to the erotic Ovid. Those who think of film as literature might also recognize the tradition and character (if not a conscious use of the classical source) in *Alfie* (1966). Michael Caine's nuanced performance, replete with direct and *desultor*-ish addresses to the camera, may not only leave us wondering, as he does, "What's it all about?" but whether the director had enjoyed the *Amores* at some time in his life.

Again, however, this is a subject for a different book. Just as no scholar would want to resemble Nabokov's Charles Kinbote, no scholar would want his work to fulfill by analogy Dr. Johnson's savage comment on *Paradise Lost*: "None ever wished it longer than it is."

Bibliography

Abrams, M.H. "How to Do Things with Texts." In *Critical Theory since 1965*, ed. Hazard Adams and Leroy Searle, 436–51. Tallahassee: Florida State University Press, 1986.

Adams, Hazard, and Leroy Searle, eds. *Critical Theory since 1965*. Tallahassee: Florida State University Press, 1986.

Alighieri, Dante. *The Divine Comedy*. Ed. and trans. John D. Sinclair. 3 vols. Oxford: Oxford University Press, 1961.

———. *Dante's Lyric Poetry*. Ed. and trans. K. Foster and P. Boyd. 2 vols. Oxford: Oxford University Press, 1967.

———. *La Vita nuova*. Trans. Barbara Reynolds. New York: Penguin, 1969.

———. *The Divine Comedy*. Ed. and trans. Charles S. Singleton. 6 vols. Princeton: Princeton University Press, 1970–75.

———. *Dante's "Vita nuova."* Ed. and trans. Mark Musa. Bloomington: Indiana University Press, 1973.

———. *Dante Alighieri: Opera minori*. Ed. Pier Vincenzo Mengaldo. 2 vols. Milan: Ricciardi, 1979.

———. *La Vita nuova*. Ed. Edoardo Sanguineti and Alfonso Berardinelli. Milan: Garzanti, 1988.

Allen, Peter. *The Art of Love: Amatory Fiction from Ovid to the "Romance of the Rose."* Philadelphia: University of Pennsylvania Press, 1992.

Alton, E.H., and E.W. Wormell. "Ovid in the Mediaeval Schoolroom." *Hermathena* 94 (1960): 21–38; 95 (1961): 67–82.

Andreas Capellanus. *De amore*. Ed. E. Trojel. Munich: Eidos, 1964.

Aristotle. *The Rhetoric and Poetics of Aristotle*. Ed. Friedrich Solmsen. Trans. W. Rhys Roberts and Ingram Bywater. New York: Modern Library, 1954.

Asher, Lyell. "Petrarch at the Peak of Fame." *PMLA* 108 (1993): 1050–63.

Augustine. *St. Augustine's Confessions*. Trans. W. Watts. 2 vols. Cambridge: Harvard University Press, 1912. Reprint, 1989.

Baehrens, Emil. *Poetae Latini minores*. 5 vols. Leipzig: Teubner, 1883.

Bardolini, Teodolinda. *Dante's Poets: Textuality and Truth in the "Comedy."* Princeton: Princeton University Press, 1984.

Barkan, Leonard. *The Gods Made Flesh: Metamorphosis and the Pursuit of Paganism.* New Haven: Yale University Press, 1986.

Barsby, J.A. "*Desultor Amoris* in *Amores* 1.3." *Classical Philology* 70 (1975): 44–45.

Bate, Jonathan. "Ovid and the Sonnets; Or, Did Shakespeare Feel the Anxiety of Influence?" *Shakespeare Survey* 42 (1990): 65–76.

———. *Shakespeare and Ovid.* Oxford: Clarendon Press, 1993.

Bate, Keith. "Ovid, Medieval Latin, and the *Pastourelle.*" *Reading Medieval Studies* 9 (1983): 16–33.

Baudri of Bourgueil. *Baldricus Burgulianus Carmina.* Ed. Karlheinz Hilbert. Heidelberg: Carl Winter, 1979.

Bec, Pierre, ed. *Burlesque et obscénite chez les troubadours: Le contre-texte au Moyen Age.* Paris: Stock, 1984.

Benson, Robert L., and Giles Constable, eds. *Renaissance and Renewal in the Twelfth Century.* Cambridge: Harvard University Press, 1982.

Benton, John F. "Clio and Venus: An Historical View of Medieval Love." In *The Meaning of Courtly Love*, ed. F.X. Newman, 19–42. Albany: State University of New York Press, 1968.

———. "Consciousness of Self and Perceptions of Individuality." In *Renaissance and Renewal in the Twelfth Century*, ed. Robert L. Benson and Giles Constable, 263–95. Cambridge: Harvard University Press, 1982.

Berchorius, Petrus. *Reductium morale, liber xv, cap. ii–xv: "Ovidius moralizatus."* Ed. J. Engels. Utrecht: Instituut voor Laat Latijn der Rijksuniversiteit, 1962.

Bernardo, Aldo S. *Petrarch, Laura, and the "Triumphs."* Albany: State University of New York Press, 1974.

———. *Francesco Petrarca: Citizen of the World.* Albany: State University of New York Press, 1980.

Berolini, Teodolinda. *Dante's Poets: Textuality and Truth in the "Comedy."* Princeton: Princeton University Press, 1984.

Béroul. *Le roman de Tristan: Poème du XIIe siècle.* Ed. Ernest Muret and L.M. Defourques. 4th ed. Paris: Champion, 1982.

Billanovich, Giuseppe. "Petrarca e il Ventuso." *Italia medioevale e umanistica* 9 (1966): 389–401.

Binns, J.W., ed. *Ovid.* London: Routledge, 1973.

———. *Intellectual Culture in Elizabethan and Jacobean England: The Latin Writings of the Age.* Leeds: Francis Cairns, 1990.

Blodgett, E.D. "The Well-Wrought Void: Reflections on the *Ars amatoria.*" *Classical Journal* 68 (1973): 322–33.

Boase, Roger. *The Origin and Meaning of Courtly Love: A Critical Survey of European Scholarship.* Manchester: Manchester University Press, 1977.

Boccaccio, Giovanni. *Decameron.* Ed. Vittore Branca. Firenze: Presso L'Accademia Della Crusca, 1976.

———. *The Decameron.* Ed. Mark Musa and Peter Bondanella. New York: Norton, 1982.

Bogin, Meg, ed. and trans. *The Women Troubadours.* New York: Norton, 1980.

Bond, Gerald. "*Iocus amoris*: The Poetry of Baudri of Bourgueil and the Problem of Persona." *Traditio* 42 (1986): 143–93.

———. "Composing Yourself: Ovid's *Heroides*, Baudri of Bourgueil, and the Formation of the Ovidian Subculture." *Mediaevalia* 13 (1989 [1987]): 83–118.

Booth, Wayne C. *The Rhetoric of Fiction.* Chicago: University of Chicago Press, 1961.

Boswell, John. *Christianity, Social Tolerance, and Homosexuality: Gay People in Western Europe from the Beginning of the Christian Era to the Fourteenth Century.* Chicago: University of Chicago Press, 1981.

Boutière, Jean, and A.H. Schutz, eds. *Biographies des Troubadours.* Toulouse: Privat, 1950.

Boyle, Marjorie O'Rourke. *Petrarch's Genius: Pentimento and Prophecy.* Berkeley: University of California Press, 1991.

Briffault, Robert. *The Troubadours.* Bloomington: Indiana University Press, 1965.

Brooke, Nicholas. "Marlowe as Provocative Agent in Shakespeare's Early Plays." *Shakespeare Survey* 14 (1961): 34–44.

Bruns, Gerald R. "The Originality of Texts in a Manuscript Culture." *Comparative Literature* 32 (1980): 113–29.

Buecheler, F., and V. Riese, eds. *Carmina Latina Epigrapha: Anthologia Latina.* 3 vols. Leipzig: Teubner, 1895–1926.

Burck, E. "Ovid, *Amores* 1.3 im Rahmen der römischen Liebesdichtung." *Der altsprachliche Unterricht* 20 (1977): 463–81.

Burckhardt, Jacob. *The Civilization of the Renaissance in Italy.* Trans. S.G.C. Middlemore. 2 vols. New York: Harper, 1960.

Busby, Keith, and Erik Kooper, eds. *Courtly Literature: Culture and Context.* Amsterdam: Benjamins, 1990.

Bynum, Caroline Walker. *Jesus as Mother: Studies in the Spirituality of the High Middle Ages.* Berkeley: University of California Press, 1982.

Cadden, Joan. "Medieval Scientific and Medical Views of Sexuality: Questions of Propriety." *Medievalia et Humanistica*, n.s., 14 (1986): 157–71.

Cahoon, Leslie. "A Program for Betrayal: Ovidian *Nequitia* in *Amores* I.i, II.i, and III.i." *Helios*, n.s., 12 (1985): 29–40.

———. "Raping the Rose: Jean de Meun's Reading of Ovid's *Amores*." *Classical and Modern Literature* 6 (1985): 261–85.

———. "The Anxieties of Influence: Ovid's Reception by the Early Troubadours." *Mediaevalia* 13 (1989 [1987]): 119–56.

Cairns, Francis. "Ovidio, *Amores* 1.3: Dipendenza Letteraria vs. Independenza Intellettuale." *Cultura, Poesia, Ideologia nell' Opera di Ovidio*, ed. Italo Gallo and Luciano Nicastri, 27–40. Napoli: Edizioni Scientifiche Italiane, 1991.

Castiglione, Baldassare. *The Book of the Courtier.* Ed. W.H.D. Rouse and Drayton Henderson. Trans. Sir Thomas Hoby. London: Dent, 1948.

———. *Opere di Baldassare Castiglione, Giovanni della Casa, Benvenuto Cellini.* Ed. Carlo Cordié. Milan: Ricciardi, 1960.

Chaucer, Geoffrey. *The Riverside Chaucer.* Ed. Larry D. Benson. 3d ed. Boston: Houghton-Mifflin, 1987.

Chrétien de Troyes. *Le chevalier de la charrete*. Ed. Mario Roques. Paris: Champion, 1970.

Christine de Pizan. *Poems of Cupid, God of Love*. Ed. and trans. Thelma S. Fenster and Mary Carpenter Erler. Leiden: Brill, 1990.

Cicero. *Brutus and Orator*. Trans. G.L. Hendrickson and H.M. Hubbell. Cambridge: Harvard University Press, 1962.

———. *De oratore, De fato, Paradoxica Stoicorum, De partitione oratoria*. Trans. E.W. Sutton and H. Rackham. 3 vols. Cambridge: Harvard University Press, 1967.

[———]. *Ad Herennium*. Trans. Harry Caplan. Cambridge: Harvard University Press, 1981.

Crossland, Jessie. "Ovid's Contribution to the Conception of Love Known as '*L'amour courtois*.'" *Modern Language Review* 42 (1947): 199–206.

———. *Medieval French Literature*. Oxford: Blackwell, 1956.

Curran, Leo C. "*Desultores Amores*: Ovid's *Amores* 1.3." *Classical Philology* 6 (1966): 47–49.

Curtius, Ernst Robert. *European Literature and the Latin Middle Ages*. Trans. Willard R. Trask. Princeton: University Press, 1954.

Davidson, J.F. "Some Thoughts on Ovid *Amores* 1.3." *Collection Latomus* 168 (1980): 278–85.

Davis, John T. *Fictus Adulter: Poet as Actor in the "Amores."* Amsterdam: Gieben, 1989.

De Boer, C., ed. *"Ovide moralisé": Poème du commencement du quatorzième siècle*. 5 vols. Amsterdam: Muller, 1915–38.

de Lorris, Guillaume, and Jean de Meun. *Le roman de la rose*. Ed. Daniel Poirion. Paris: Garnier-Flammarion, 1974.

Denomy, A.J. "Fin Amors: The Pure Love of the Troubadours, Its Amorality and Possible Source." *Medieval Studies* 7 (1945): 139–207.

Desmond, Marilynn. "Introduction." *Mediaevalia* 13 (1989 [1987]): 1–8.

Donaldson, E. Talbot. *Speaking of Chaucer*. New York: Norton, 1970.

Donne, John. *The Complete English Poems of John Donne*. Ed. C.A. Patrides. London: Dent, 1985.

Doutrepont, Auguste, ed. *La clef d'amors*. Bibliotheca Normannica 5. Halle: Niemeyer, 1890.

Dronke, Peter. *Medieval Latin and the Rise of European Love-Lyric*. 2 vols. Oxford: Oxford University Press, 1965.

———. "Francesca and Heloise." *Comparative Literature* 27 (1975): 113–35.

———. "The Interpretation of the Ripoll Love Songs." *Romance Philology* 33 (1979): 14–42.

Du Quesnay, I.M. Le M. "The *Amores*." In *Ovid*, ed. J.W. Binns, 1–48. London: Routledge, 1973.

Durling, Robert. "Ovid as *Praeceptor Amoris*." *Classical Journal* 53 (1957): 157–67.

———. *The Figure of the Poet in Renaissance Epic*. Cambridge: Harvard University Press, 1965.

Durling, Robert, and Ronald L. Martinez. *Time and the Crystal: Studies in Dante's "Rime Petrose."* Berkeley: University of California Press, 1990.

Eliot, T.S. *Selected Essays.* New York: Harcourt Brace, 1950.

Elliot, Allison Goddard. "The Bedraggled Cupid: Ovidian Satire in *Carmina Burana* 105." *Traditio* 37 (1981): 426–37.

Elliot, Robert. *The Literary Persona.* Chicago: University of Chicago Press, 1982.

Fantazzi, Charles. "Marcabru's *Pastourelle*: Courtly Love Decoded." *Studies in Philology* 71 (1974): 385–403.

Faral, Edmond. "Ovide et quelques autres sources du roman d'Enéas." *Romania* 40 (1911): 161–234.

Fenster, Thelma S., and Mary Carpenter Erler, ed. and trans. *Poems of Cupid, God of Love.* Leiden: Brill, 1990.

Ferrante, Joan. "'Cortes Amor' in Medieval Texts." *Speculum* 55 (1980): 686–95.

Ferrante, Joan, and George D. Economou, eds. *In Pursuit of Perfection: Courtly Love in Medieval Literature.* London: Kennikat Press, 1975.

Fleming, John V. "Jean de Meun and the Ancient Poets." In *Rethinking "The Romance of the Rose": Text, Image, Reception,* ed. Kevin Brownlee and Sylvia Huot, 81–100. Philadelphia: University of Pennsylvania Press, 1987.

Frank, Donald. "On the Troubadour *Fin' Amors.*" *Romance Notes* 7 (1966): 209–17.

Frappier, Jean. "Sur un procès fait à l'amour courtois." *Romania* 93 (1972): 145–93.

———. *Amour courtois et Table Ronde.* Geneva: Droz, 1973.

Friedenreich, Kenneth, Roma Gill, and Constance Kuriyama, eds. *"A Poet and Filthy Play-Maker": New Essays on Christopher Marlowe.* New York: AMS Press, 1988.

Fyler, John M. "*Omnia Vincit Amor*: Incongruity and the Limitations of Structure in Ovid's Elegiac Poetry." *Classical Journal* 66 (1971): 196–203.

———. *Chaucer and Ovid.* New Haven: Yale University Press, 1979.

Gallo, Italo, and Luciano Nicastri, eds. *Cultura, Poesia, Ideologia nell' Opera di Ovidio.* Napoli: Edizioni Scientifiche Italiane, 1991.

Gamel, Mary-Kay. "'Non sine caede': Abortion Politics and Poetics in Ovid's *Amores.*" *Helios,* n.s., 16 (1989): 183–206.

Gauly, Bardo Maria. *Liebeserfahrungen: Zur Rolle das elegischen Ich in Ovids "Amores."* Frankfurt: Lang, 1990.

Gill, Roma. "'Snakes Leape by Verse.'" In *Christopher Marlowe,* ed. Brian Morris, 133–50. New York: Hill and Wang, 1968.

———. "Marlowe and the Art of Translation." In *"A Poet and Filthy Play-Maker": New Essays on Christopher Marlowe,* ed. Kenneth Friedenreich, Roma Gill, and Constance Kuriyama, 327–42. New York: AMS Press, 1988.

Godman, Peter, ed. and trans. *Poetry of the Carolingian Renaissance.* London: Duckworth, 1985.

Godman, Peter, and Oswyn Murray, eds. *Latin Poetry in the Classical Tradition: Essays in Medieval and Renaissance Literature.* Oxford: Clarendon Press, 1990.

Goldin, Frederick. *The Mirror of Narcissus in the Courtly Love Lyric.* Ithaca: Cornell University Press, 1967.

———, ed. and trans. *Lyrics of the Troubadours and Trouvères: An Anthology and a History*. New York: Anchor, 1973.

Gray, Floyd, ed. *Anthologie de la poesie Français du XVIe siècle*. New York: Irvington, 1978.

Green, Peter. *Essays in Classical Antiquity*. London: Murray, 1960.

———, ed. and trans. *Ovid: The Erotic Poems*. New York: Penguin, 1982.

Greene, Thomas M. *The Light in Troy: Imitation and Discovery in Renaissance Poetry*. New Haven: Yale University Press, 1982.

Gross, Nicholas P. "Rhetorical Wit and Amatory Persuasion in Ovid." *Classical Journal* 74 (1979): 305–18.

Guillaume IX. *The Poetry of William VII, Count of Poitiers, IX Duke of Aquitaine*. Ed. and trans. Gerald A. Bond. New York: Garland, 1982.

Haller, Robert S., ed. and trans. *Literary Criticism of Dante Alighieri*. Lincoln: University of Nebraska Press, 1973.

Hanning, Robert W. *The Individual in Twelfth-Century Romance*. New Haven: Yale University Press, 1977.

———. "Courtly Contexts for Urban *Cultus*: Responses to Ovid in Chrétien's *Cligès* and Marie's *Guigemar*." *Symposium* 35 (1981): 34–56.

Hardie, Colin. "Dante and the Tradition of Courtly Love." In *Patterns of Love and Courtesy: Essays in Memory of C.S. Lewis*, ed. John Lawlor, 26–44. Evanston: Northwestern University Press, 1966.

Hatcher, Anna, and Mark Musa. "The Kiss: *Inferno V* and the Old French Prose *Lancelot*." *Comparative Literature* 20 (1968): 97–109.

Hawkins, Peter S. "The Metamorphosis of Ovid." In *Dante and Ovid: Essays in Intertextuality*, ed. Madison U. Sowell, 17–34. Binghamton: State University of New York Press, 1991.

Heer, Fredrich. *The Medieval World*. Trans. Janet Sondheimer. New York: New American Library, 1962.

Hexter, Ralph. *Ovid and Medieval Schooling: Studies in Medieval School Commentaries on Ovid's "Ars amatoria," "Epistulae ex Ponto," and "Epistulae heroidum."* Munich: Arbeo-Gesellschaft, 1986.

Hoby, Thomas. *The Book of the Courtier*. Ed. W.H.D. Rouse and Drayton Henderson. London: Dent, 1928. Reprint, 1948.

Hollander, Robert. "*Vita nuova*: Dante's Perceptions of Beatrice." *Dante Studies* 92 (1974): 1–18.

———. *Boccaccio's Two Venuses*. New York: Columbia University Press, 1977.

Horace. *Q. Horati Flacci opera*. Ed. H.W. Garrod. Oxford: Clarendon Press, 1984.

Hughey, Ruth, ed. *The Arundel Harington Manuscript of Tudor Poetry*. 2 vols. Columbus: Ohio State University Press, 1960.

Huizinga, Johan. *Homo Ludens: A Study of the Play Element in Culture*. Trans. George Steiner. London: Paladin, 1970.

Huygens, R.B.C. *Accessus ad auctores*. Leiden: Brill, 1970.

Hyatte, Reginald. "Ovidius, Doctor Amoris: The Changing Attitudes towards Ovid's Eroticism in the Middle Ages as Seen in the Three Old French Adaptations of the *Remedia Amoris*." *Florilegium* 4 (1982): 123–36.

Isidore of Seville. *Isidore Hispalensis Episcopi Etymologiarum sive Originum Libri XX*. Ed. W.M. Lindsay. 2 vols. Oxford: Oxford University Press, 1911.

Jacoff, Rachel, and Jeffrey T. Schnapp, eds. *The Poetry of Allusion: Virgil and Ovid in Dante's "Commedia."* Palo Alto: Stanford University Press, 1991.

Jameson, Caroline. "Ovid in the Sixteenth Century." In *Ovid*, ed. J.W. Binns, 210–42, London: Routledge: 1973.

Javitch, Daniel. "Rescuing Ovid from the Allegorizers." *Comparative Literature* 30 (1978): 97–107.

Jeanroy, Alfred. *La Poésie Lyrique des Troubadours.* 2 vols. Toulouse: Privat, 1934.

———. *Historie sommaire de la poésie occitane.* Paris, 1945. Reprint, Geneva: Slatkine Reprints, 1973.

John of Garland. *Integumenta Ovidii.* Ed. Fausto Ghisalberti. Milan: Casa Editrice Giuseppe Principato, 1933.

———. *The "Parisiana Poetria" of John of Garland.* Ed. Traugott Lawlor. New Haven: Yale University Press, 1974.

John of Salisbury. *Metalogicon.* Ed. C.C.J. Webb. Oxford: Oxford University Press, 1929.

Johnson, W.R. "Ringing Down the Curtain on Love." *Helios,* n.s., 12 (1985): 21–28.

Kalstone, David. "Sir Philip Sidney and 'Poore *Petrarchs* Long Deceased Woes." *Journal of English and Germanic Philology* 63 (1964): 21–32.

Kay, Sarah. *Subjectivity in Troubadour Poetry.* Cambridge: Cambridge University Press, 1990.

Kelly, Douglas. *Medieval Imagination: Rhetoric and the Poetry of Courtly Love.* Madison: University of Wisconsin Press, 1978.

Keul, Meike. *Liebe im Widerstreit: Interpretationen zu Ovids "Amores" und ihrem literarischen Hintergrund.* Frankfurt: Lang, 1989.

Kleinhenz, Christopher. "Dante as Reader and Critic of Courtly Literature." In *Courtly Literature: Culture and Context*, ed. Keith Busby and Erik Kooper, 79–94, Amsterdam: Benjamins, 1990.

Klopsch, Paul, ed. *Pseudo-Ovidius "de Vetula."* Leiden: Brill, 1967.

Korten, Christine. *Ovid, Augustus und der Kult der Vestalinnen: Eine religionspolitische These zur Verbannung Ovids.* Frankfurt: Lang, 1992.

Latzke, Therese, ed. "Die carmina erotica der Ripollsammlung." *Mittellateinisches Jahrbuch* 10 (1974–75): 138–201.

Lawlor, John, ed. *Patterns of Love and Courtesy: Essays in Memory of C.S. Lewis.* Evanston: Northwestern University Press, 1966.

Lazar, Moshé. *Amour courtois et "fin' Amors" dans la littérature du XIIe siècle.* Paris: Klincksieck, 1964.

Leclercq, Jean. *The Love of Learning and the Desire for God.* Trans. C. Misrahi. New York: Fordham University Press, 1961.

Lemay, Helen Rodnite. *Women's Secrets: A Translation of Pseudo-Albertus Magnus' "De Secretis Mulierum" with Commentaries.* Albany: State University of New York Press, 1992.

Lewis, C.S. *The Allegory of Love: A Study in Medieval Tradition.* Oxford: Oxford University Press, 1936. Reprint, 1977.

Luck, George. *The Latin Love Elegy.* New York: Barnes and Noble, 1960.

Manitius, M. *Beiträge zur Geschichte des Ovidius und andrer römischer Schiftsteller im Mittelalter.* Leipzig: Weicher, 1900.

Marie de France. *Les lais de Marie de France.* Ed. Jean Rychner. Paris: Champion: 1983.

Marlowe, Christopher. *The Complete Poems and Translations.* Ed. Stephen Orgel. Harmondsworth: Penguin, 1971.

———. *All Ovids Elegies: 3. Bookes. By C.M. Epigrams by J.D.* Middlebourgh: [no date]. Reprint, with an introduction by A.J. Smith, London: Scolar Press, 1973.

———. *Christopher Marlowe: The Complete Works.* Ed. Fredson Bowers. 2 vols. Cambridge: Cambridge University Press, 1973.

———. *The Complete Works of Christopher Marlowe.* Ed. Roma Gill. 3 vols. to date. Oxford: Oxford University Press, 1987–.

Martianus Capella. *Martianus Capella.* Ed. Adolph Dick. Leipzig: Teubner, 1925.

———. *Martianus Capella and the Seven Liberal Arts.* Ed. and trans. W.H. Stahl and R. Johnson. New York: Columbia University Press, 1969.

Mazzaro, Jerome. *The Figure of Dante: An Essay on the "Vita nuova."* Princeton: Princeton University Press, 1981.

McGregor, James. "Ovid at School: From the Ninth to the Fifteenth Century." *Classical Folia* 15 (1961): 29–51.

McLeod, William H., ed. "The *Consaus D'Amours* of Richard de Fournival." *Studies in Philology* 32 (1935): 1–18.

Menocal, Maria Rosa. *The Arabic Role in Medieval Literary History: A Forgotten Heritage.* Philadelphia: University of Pennsylvania Press, 1987.

Miller, Paul Allen. "Sidney, Petrarch, and Ovid, or Imitation as Subversion." *English Literary History* 58 (1991): 499–522.

Minnis, A.J. *Medieval Theory of Authorship: Scholastic Literary Attitudes in the Later Middle Ages.* 2d ed. Philadelphia: University of Pennsylvania Press, 1988.

Minnis, A.J., and A.B. Scott, eds. *Medieval Literary Theory and Criticism, c. 1100–c. 1375: The Commentary Tradition.* Rev. ed. Oxford: Clarendon Press, 1991.

Minta, Stephen. *Petrarch and Petrarchism: The English and French Traditions.* Manchester: Manchester University Press, 1980.

Montaigne, Michel de. *Essais.* Ed. A. Lhéritier. 3 vols. Paris: Union Général, 1964.

———. *Essays.* Ed. L.C. Harmer. Trans. John Florio. 3 vols. London: Everyman, 1910. Reprint, 1980.

Morris, Brian, ed. *Christopher Marlowe.* New York: Hill and Wang, 1968.

Morris, Colin. *The Discovery of the Individual: 1050–1200.* Toronto: University of Toronto Press, 1972.

Muir, Lynette. *Literature and Society in Medieval France.* New York: St. Martin's, 1985.

Myerowitz, Molly. *Ovid's Games of Love.* Detroit: Wayne State University Press, 1985.

Nelli, René. *L'erotique des troubadours.* 2 vols. Paris: Union Générale, 1974.

Newman, F.X., ed. *The Meaning of Courtly Love.* Albany: State University of New York Press, 1968.

Noakes, Susan. "The Double Misreading of Paolo and Francesca." *Philological Quarterly* 62 (1983): 221–39.

Nolan, Barbara. "The *Vita nuova*: Dante's Book of Revelation." *Dante Studies* 88 (1970): 51–78.

———. "The *Vita nuova* and Richard of St. Victor's Phenomenology of Vision." *Dante Studies* 92 (1974): 35–54.

O'Donoghue, Bernard. *The Courtly Love Tradition*. Manchester: Manchester University Press, 1982.

Olson, Susan. "Immutable Love: Two Good Women in Marcabru." *Neophilologus* 60 (1976): 190–99.

Olstein, Katherine. "*Amores* 1.3 and Duplicity as a Way of Love." *TAPA* 105 (1975): 241–58.

Otis, Brooks. *Ovid as an Epic Poet*. Cambridge: Cambridge University Press, 1970.

Oulmont, Charles, ed. *Les débats du clerc et du chevalier dans la littérature poetique du Moyen-Age*. Paris: Champion, 1911.

Ovid. *P. Ovidi Nasonis Tristium libri quinque Ibis Ex Ponto libri quattor Halieutica Fragmenta*. Ed. S.G. Owen. Oxford: Clarendon Press, 1978.

———. *Heroides and Amores*. Trans. Grant Showerman. London: 1914. Rev. ed., ed. G.P. Goold. Cambridge: Harvard University Press, 1986.

———. *Ovid: Amores: Text, Prolegomena, and Commentary*. Ed. J.C. McKeown. 4 vols. to date. Wolfeboro, N.H.: Francis Cairns, 1987–

———. *Ovidius Metamorphoses*. Ed. W.S. Anderson. Leipzig: Teubner, 1993.

———. *P. Ovidii Nasonis Amores Medicamina faciei feminae Ars amatoria Remedia amoris*. Ed. E.J. Kenney. 2d. ed. Oxford: Clarendon Press, 1994.

Paris, Gaston. "Lais inédits." *Romania* 8 (1879): 29–72.

———. "Le Conte de Charrette." *Romania* 12 (1883): 459–534.

Parker, Douglass. "The Ovidian Coda." *Arion* 8 (1969): 80–97.

Paterson, Linda. *Troubadours and Eloquence*. Oxford: Clarendon Press, 1975.

Pearcy, Lee. "Marlowe, Dominicus Niger, and Ovid's *Amores*." *Notes and Queries* 27 (1980): 315–18.

———. *The Mediated Muse: English Translations of Ovid, 1560–1700*. Hamden, Conn.: Archon, 1984.

Pequigney, Joseph. *Such Is My Love: A Study of Shakespeare's Sonnets*. Chicago: University of Chicago Press, 1985.

Peradotto, J., and J.P. Sullivan, eds. *Women in the Ancient World*. Albany: State University of New York Press, 1984.

Petrarch. *Francesco Petrarca: Rime, Trionfi e Poesie Latine*. Ed. F. Neri et al. Milan: Ricciardi, 1951.

———. *Francesco Petrarca: Prose*. Ed. G. Martellotti et al. Milan: Ricciardi, 1955.

———. *Lord Morley's "Tryumphes of Fraunces Petrarcke": The First English Translation of the "Trionfi."* Ed. D.D. Carnicelli. Cambridge: Harvard University Press, 1971.

———. *Petrarch's Lyric Poems*. Ed. and trans. Robert M. Durling. Cambridge: Harvard University Press, 1976.

Piper, W.B. "The Inception of the Closed Heroic Couplet." *Modern Philology* 66 (1969): 306–21.

Plato. *Gorgias*. Ed. and trans. Walter Hamilton. Harmondsworth: Penguin, 1960.

Poggioli, Renato. "Tragedy or Romance? A Reading of the Paolo and Francesca Episode in Dante's *Inferno*." *PMLA* 72 (1957): 313–58.

Pomeroy, Sarah. *Goddesses, Whores, Wives, and Slaves: Women in Classical Antiquity*. New York: Schocken, 1975.

Propertius. *Sextii Propertii carmina*. Ed. E.A. Barber. Oxford: Clarendon Press, 1953.

Prudentius. *Prudentius*. Ed. and trans. H.J. Thomson. 2 vols. Cambridge: Harvard University Press, 1969.

Puttenham, George. *The Arte of English Poesie*. London: Richard Field, 1589. Reprint, Menston, Eng.: Scolar Press, 1968.

Quintilian. *Institutionis oratoriae*. Ed. M. Winterbottom. 2 vols. Oxford: Oxford University Press, 1970.

Rabelais, François. *La vie tres horrificque de grand Gargantua*. Ed. V.L. Saulnier and Jean-Yves Pouilloux. Paris: Garnier-Flammarion, 1968.

Raby, F.J.E. *A History of Christian Latin Poetry from the Beginnings to the Close of the Middle Ages*. 2d ed. Oxford: Oxford University Press, 1953.

———. *A History of Secular Latin Poetry in the Middle Ages*. 2 vols. Oxford: Oxford University Press, 1957.

Rand, E.K. *Ovid and His Influence*. Boston: Longmans, 1925.

Reiss, Edmund. *"Fin' Amors:* Its History and Meaning in Medieval Literature." *Medieval and Renaissance Studies* 8 (1979): 71–99.

Reynolds, L.D., ed. *Texts and Transmissions: A Survey of the Latin Classics*. Oxford: Clarendon Press, 1983.

Reynolds, L.D., and N.G. Wilson. *Scribes and Scholars: A Guide to the Transmission of Greek and Latin Literature*. 3d ed. Oxford: Clarendon Press, 1992.

Rico, Francisco. *Vida u obra de Petrarca*. North Carolina Studies in Romance Literature and Language 33. Chapel Hill: University of North Carolina Press, 1974.

Riddell, James A. "Ben Jonson and 'Marlowe's Mighty Line.'" In *A Poet and Filthy Play-Maker: New Essays on Christopher Marlowe*, ed. Kenneth Friedenreich, Roma Gill, and Constance Kuriyama, 37–49. New York: AMS Press, 1988.

Robathan, Dorothy M. "An Introduction to the Pseudo-Ovidian *de Vetula*." *TAPA* 87 (1957): 197–207.

———. "Ovid in the Middle Ages." In *Ovid*, ed. J.W. Binns, 191–209. London: Routledge, 1973.

Robertson, D.W. *A Preface to Chaucer: Studies in Medieval Perspectives*. Princeton: Princeton University Press, 1962.

———. "The Concept of Courtly Love as an Impediment to the Understanding of Medieval Texts." In *The Meaning of Courtly Love*, ed. F.X. Newman, 1–18. Albany: State University of New York Press, 1968.

———. *Essays in Medieval Culture*. Princeton: Princeton University Press, 1980.

Rose, Mary Beth. *The Expense of Spirit: Love and Sexuality in Renaissance Drama*. Ithaca: Cornell University Press, 1988.

Rudd, Niall. *Lines of Enquiry: Studies in Latin Poetry*. Cambridge: Cambridge University Press, 1976.

Salverda de Grave, J.J., ed. *Eneas: Roman du XIIe siècle*. 2 vols. Paris: Champion, 1964.

Scheludko, Dmitri. "Ovid und die Trobadors." *Zeitschrift für romanische Philologie* 54 (1934): 128–74.

Schmidt, Paul Gerhard. "The Quotation in Goliardic Poetry: The Feast of Fools and the Goliardic Strophe *cum auctoritate*." In *Latin Poetry in the Classical Tradition: Essays in Medieval and Renaissance Literature*, ed. Peter Godman and Oswyn Murray, 49–65. Oxford: Clarendon Press, 1990.

Schrötter, Wilibald. *Ovid und die Troubadours.* Halle: Niemeyer, 1908.

Scott, John. "Dante's Francesca and the Poet's Attitude towards Courtly Literature." *Reading Medieval Studies* 5 (1979): 4–20.

Shakespeare, William. *A New Variorum Edition of Shakespeare: The Sonnets.* Ed. Hyder Rollins. 2 vols. Philadephia: Lippincott, 1944.

———. *Mr. William Shakespeares Comedies, Histories, and Tragedies.* London: n.p., 1623. Reprint, ed. Helge Kökeritz, New Haven: Yale University Press, 1954.

———. *Shakespeare's Sonnets.* Ed. Stephen Booth, New Haven: Yale University Press, 1977.

Shapiro, Norman, trans., and James B. Wadworth, ed. *The Comedy of Eros: Medieval French Guides to the Art of Love.* Urbana: University of Illinois Press, 1970.

Singleton, Charles. *An Essay on the "Vita nuova."* Cambridge: Harvard University Press, 1949.

———. "Dante: Within Courtly Love and Beyond." In *The Meaning of Courtly Love*, ed. F.X. Newman, 43–54. Albany: State University of New York Press, 1968.

Smarr, Janet Marie. "Poets of Love and Exile." In *Dante and Ovid: Essays in Intertextuality*, ed. Madison U. Sowell, 139–51. Binghamton: State University of New York Press, 1991.

Smith, Bruce R. *Homosexual Desire in Shakespeare's England: A Cultural Poetics.* Chicago: University of Chicago Press, 1994.

Solodow, Joseph B. "Ovid's *Ars Amatoria*: The Lover as Cultural Ideal." *Wiener Studien* 11 (1977): 115–16.

Southern, R.W. *The Making of the Middle Ages.* New Haven: Yale University Press, 1953.

Sowell, Madison U., ed. *Dante and Ovid: Essays in Intertextuality.* Binghamton: State University of New York Press, 1991.

Spallone, Maddalena. "Il Par. Lat. 10318 (Salmasiano): Dal Manuscritto Altomedievale ad una raccolta enciclopedica tardo-antica." *Italia medievale e umanistica* 25 (1982): 1–71.

Stapleton, M.L. "Nashe and the Poetics of Obscenity: *The Choise of Valentines*." *Classical and Modern Literature* 12 (1991): 29–48.

Steane, J.B. *Marlowe: A Critical Study.* Cambridge: Cambridge University Press, 1964.

Stevens, John. *Medieval Romance.* London: Hutchinson, 1973.

Stevens, Martin. "The Performing Self in Twelfth-Century Culture." *Viator* 9 (1978): 193–212.

Sturm-Maddox, Sara. *Petrarch's Metamorphoses: Text and Subtext in the "Rime Sparse."* Columbia: University of Missouri Press, 1985.

———. *Petrarch's Laurels.* University Park, Pa.: Penn State University Press, 1992.

Tafel, Sigmund. *Die Ueberlieferungsgeschichte Ovids Carmina amatoria verfolgt bis zum 11. Jahrhundert.* Tübingen: Heckenhauer, 1910.

Terence. *P. Terenti Afri comoediae.* Ed. Robert Kauer and Wallace Lindsay. Oxford: Clarendon Press, 1958.

Thibault, John C. *The Mystery of Ovid's Exile.* Berkeley: University of California Press, 1964.

Thomas d'Angleterre. *Les fragments du Roman de Tristan: Poème du XIIe siècle.* Ed. Bartina H. Wind. Geneva: Droz, 1960.

Thurlow, Peter A. "Ovid's *Amores* III.iv: Its Reception in William of Aquitaine, Sebastian Brant, and Middle High German Literature." *Reading Medieval Studies* 10 (1984): 109–34.

Tibullus. *Tibullus: A Commentary.* Ed. Michael C.J. Putnam, Norman: University of Oklahoma Press, 1979.

Traube, Ludwig. *Vorlesungen und Abhandlungen.* Vol. 2, *Einleitung in die lateinische Philologie des Mittelalters.* 1911. Reprint, Munich: Beck, 1965.

Utley, Francis L. "Must We Abandon the Concept of Courtly Love?" *Medievalia et Humanistica*, n.s., 3 (1972): 299–324.

Vanossi, Luigi. *Dante e il "Roman de la Rose" saggio sul "Fiore."* Firenze: Olschki, 1979.

Verducci, Florence. "The Contest of Rational Libertinism and Imaginative License in Ovid's *Ars amatoria.*" *Pacific Coast Philology* 15 (1980): 29–39.

———. *Ovid's Toyshop of the Heart: "Epistulae Heroidum."* Princeton: Princeton University Press, 1985.

Veyne, Paul. *Roman Erotic Elegy: Love, Poetry, and the West.* Trans. D. Pellauer. Chicago: University of Chicago Press, 1988.

———, ed. *A History of Private Life.* Trans. Arthur Goldhammer. 4 vols. Cambridge: Harvard University Press, 1987.

Vinaver, Eugene. *The Rise of Romance.* Oxford: Oxford University Press, 1971.

Viscardi, Antonio. "Scoperta dei rapporti fra la tradizione letteraria latina e medio-latina e le nuove letteratura volgari." *Storia letteraria d'Italia: Le origini.* Milan, 1934. 3d ed. Milan: Vallardi, 1973.

———. "Le origini della letteratura cortese." *Zeitschrift für romanische Philologie* 78 (1962): 269–91.

Waller, Marguerite R. *Petrarch's Poetics and Literary History.* Amherst: University of Massachusetts Press, 1980.

Wheeler, A.L. "Propertius as *Praeceptor Amoris.*" *Classical Philology* 5 (1910): 28–40.

Whitbread, George Leslie. *Fulgentius the Mythographer.* Columbus: Ohio State University Press, 1971.

Wilkinson, L.P. *Ovid Surveyed: An Abridgement of "Ovid Recalled."* Cambridge: Cambridge University Press, 1962.

Index